PRIVATE LABEL

PRIVATE LABEL

Turning the retail brand threat into
your biggest opportunity

Keith Lincoln and Lars Thomassen

**KOGAN
PAGE**

London and Philadelphia

Publisher's note

Every possible effort has been made to ensure that the information contained in this book is accurate at the time of going to press, and the publishers and author cannot accept responsibility for any errors or omissions, however caused. No responsibility for loss or damage occasioned to any person acting, or refraining from action, as a result of the material in this publication can be accepted by the editor, the publisher or the author.

First published in Great Britain and the United States in 2008 by Kogan Page Limited
First published in paperback in 2009

120 Pentonville Road   525 South 4th Street, #241
London N1 9JN   Philadelphia PA 19147
United Kingdom   USA
www.koganpage.com

© Keith Lincoln, 2008, 2009

ISBN   978 0 7494 5593 4

British Library Cataloguing-in-Publication Data

A CIP record for this book is available from the British Library.

Library of Congress Cataloging-in-Publication Data

Lincoln, Keith.
   Private label : turning the retail brand threat into your biggest opportunity / Keith Lincoln and Lars Thomassen.
      p. cm
   ISBN 978-0-7494-5593-4
   1. Retail trade. 2. Branding (Marketing) --Management. 3. Brand name products--Management. I. Thomassen, Lars. II. Title.
   HF5429.L52275 2009
   658.8'27--dc22

                              2008049606

Typeset by Saxon Graphics Ltd, Derby

Contents

Acknowledgements   *xiii*

Introduction: the new privatization   **1**

Part 1   Understanding the opportunity   **11**

1   Private facts   **13**
         The nature of the beast   13
         The global facts   13
         The local facts   14
         The brand facts   17
         The people facts   19
         The dependence facts   19
         The category facts   21

2   Private myths   **23**
         Myth 1: Private Labels are for people who
         buy Private Label   23
         Myth 2: We buy Private Label now and then   24
         Myth 3: Private Labels are for people with no money   25
         Myth 4: It can't grow any bigger   25
         Myth 5: Private Labels are not business builders   26
         Myth 6: People don't like Private Label   27
         Myth 7: Let's call it anything except a brand   28
         Myth 8: It's not profitable anyway   28

3	**Private past**	**30**
	We've seen it all before!	30
	But a funny thing happened 'on the way to the forum'!	31
	The new old thing	32
	Freedom brands – blame the French	33
4	**Private present**	**36**
	The trends show the way	36
	It's a brand, stupid!	39
	The US experience	41
	The UK experience	42
	A closer look at some key brands	45
	And the trend continues…	48
5	**Private future**	**49**
	How big can it get? As big as you want it to get!	49
	The volume versus value distortion	51
	Heaven or hell, opportunity or threat	53
	Will it continue to grow?	54
	What determines the future?	55
	Private Label drivers	56
	The online driver	57
	The Tesco effect	58
	Part 1 summary and implications	58
Part 2	**Identifying the opportunity**	**61**
6	**The S&S X Global Research Report**	**63**
	An 'all parties' perspective	63
7	**The shopper perspective**	**65**
	Let's start with the shopper	65
	Achieving product parity	68
	Category differentiation	70
	The shopper's Private future	74
8	**The brand perspective**	**79**
	The silent wall	79
	The other side of the coin	82

9   **The retailer perspective**   **86**
        Finally the retailers!   86

10   **The overall perspective**   **90**
        We agree to disagree   90
        Part 2 research summary: key points   90

Part 3 **Retailizing the brand opportunity**   **95**

11   **For every threat there's an opportunity**   **97**
        Back to spiffing!   97
        Redefining the brand   98
        Better understanding the threat   100

12   **The Private principles**   **104**
        The Private Label Way   104
        The 10 principles   106

13   **Private principle 1: Running the risk and
        living the reality**   **107**
        Headlines   107
        Reorganize to reflect the future, not the past   108
        Begin by asking three questions   110
        Become PRIVATE CENTRIC   110
        Why the conventional simply isn't good enough   111
        Summary and opportunities   112
        Actions to consider   114

14   **Private principle 2: Retailize and be radical**   **115**
        Headlines   116
        Avoiding the conventional   116
        Question the status quo   117
        Make sure you're not a commodity   118
        Love me do, love me not   119
        To supply or not?   120
        Cut the tail   123
        Develop a brand price architecture   124
        Decide if you are 'in' or 'out'   125
        Prove you still have a role   125
        Summary and opportunities   126
        Actions to consider   127

15   **Private principle 3: Tomorrow's global, social and**
          environmental issues are your opportunities today   **128**
          Headlines   128
          Trusting in the future   129
          Greenwashing versus realizing the big issues   131
          The big issues defined   134
          Big global issue 1: health issues   135
          And it's not just the small brands   142
          Big global issue 2: participation issues   143
          Big global issue 3: lifestyle issues   145
          One for all and all for one   146
          Summary and opportunities   147
          Actions to consider   147

16   **Private principle 4: Educate, navigate and inspire**   **148**
          Headlines   149
          Become the educators   149
          Ensure you have the armour to compete   150
          How to build tomorrow's loyalty?   152
          Get real!   155
          Summary and opportunities   158
          Actions to consider   159

17   **Private principle 5: Winning 'mind shelf' is the**
          name of the game   **161**
          Headlines   162
          The fight for space   162
          A very new shelf of the future starts to emerge   163
          Consistent, consistency   166
          Category disruptors   166
          Summary and opportunities   168
          Actions to consider   168

18   **Private principle 6: Innovate, imagineer and involve**   **169**
          Headlines   170
          i, i and i   170
          i number one… innovation   171
          i number two… imagineer   177
          i number three… involvement   180
          Summary and opportunities   183
          Actions to consider   183

19	**Private principle 7: Restore and reinvent the store**	**184**
	Headlines	185
	The retail store of the future and how it would look	185
	Fresh every day	190
	Really, really understand the shopper	191
	Involvement retailing	195
	Summary and opportunities	197
	Actions to consider	198
20	**Private principle 8: Catalyse your communications and brand from till to TV**	**199**
	Headlines	200
	Creativity is all – but where should it be?	200
	Build yourself a private room	204
	Private creation	204
	Customize the creative reaction	206
	Keep them creatively surprised	207
	Strive to improve your retail positioning	209
	Get closer	210
	Creatively extend in-store	211
	Getting them to love you	211
	Summary and opportunities	214
	Actions to consider	215
21	**Private principle 9: Collaborate and cooperate through co-opetition**	**216**
	Headlines	217
	Co-opeteting	217
	Brand co-opetition	217
	Retail co-opetition	221
	Summary and opportunities	222
	Actions to consider	223
22	**Private principle 10: Shopper solutions steal share of wallet**	**224**
	Headlines	225
	Money, money, money	225
	Ideas, ideas, ideas	227
	Summary and opportunities	230
	Actions to consider	232

Part 4   Retailizing the retailer opportunity   233

**23   For every opportunity there's an even bigger
            opportunity**   235
            The rise of the responsible retailer brand   235
            What's new and what's next ?   237
            WFM – a way forward   238
            Traffic lights for health   239
            What's the real benefit?   242
            Summary   242

24   Retailer Private principles 1 to 5   243
            Accept too   244
            Changing the mentality   244
            Embracing the big issues   246
            Multi-tier Private Label strategy   248
            Crowd clout   250
            Summary and opportunities   252
            Actions to consider   253

25   Retailer Private principles 6 to 10   255
            The intention economy   256
            Learning how to innovate   258
            Learning to involve   262
            Learning how to imagineer   264
            Relationship marketing   265
            Keep it simple   266
            Learning how to brand   267
            Dealing with change   268
            Dealing with reality   268
            Summary and opportunities   269
            Actions to consider   270

Part 5   Conclusions   271

26   Realizing the opportunity together   273
            Brand opportunity summary   275
            Retailer opportunity summary   278

Postscript: Privatizing the brand   **281**

Appendix 1   *Saatchi & Saatchi X Research Questionnaire*   *288*
Appendix 2   *Key references*   *291*

Index   *293*

Dedicated to PRIVATE and BRAND buccaneers everywhere.

Acknowledgements

Many people have contributed to this book, and we would like to thank them all. But in particular we would like to thank the following people for their thoughts, direct help and guidance throughout. In no particular order:

C Migeul Brendl, PhD, Associate Professor of Marketing, INSEAD
Martin West, CEO, Ashdown Group
Bruce Vierck, Strategy Director, RTC Worldwide, Chicago
Martin Lindstrom, Brand Futurist and author of *BRANDsense and BRANDchild*
Roy Webster, Group brand Manager, ASSA ABLOY Worldwide
Magnus Von Reymond, Yale Retail Manager, ASSA ABLOY Worldwide
Ulf Erlander, CEO, SWE, Stockholm
Olle Hard, Partner, SWERETAIL, Stockholm
Lew Pringle, Former Worldwide Board Director, BBDO Worldwide
Xavier Oliver, Chairman, BBDO, Spain
Tom Watson, Worldwide Board Director, BBDO Worldwide
Susan Froggatt, Sue Froggatt Training and Consulting
Paul Freeman of s4p.com
Michael Coyle, Former EVP, Cordiant Europe
Paul Lincoln, Chief Executive, National Heart Forum
Chloe Lincoln, daughter, researcher and proofreader
Kristina Eklund, Jens Lanvin and Mia Wahlstrom of Opinion Bengal, Stockholm
Mathias Dittrich of DLF, Sweden
Egil Brathe of Movement.nu

Mathias Segelman of RTV
Helen Kogan, Jon Finch and everyone else at Kogan Page
POPAI
BrainJuicer internet research company

And finally a particular thanks to Saatchi & Saatchi X for their creative, strategic and intellectual input throughout, especially Phil White, Planning Director, and Simon Hathaway, Managing Director.

Thank you all

Keith Lincoln
Lars Thomassen

Introduction: the new privatization

> The reverse side also has a reverse side.
>
> Japanese proverb

Finding the reverse side

Private Label has been growing at least at twice the rate of famous household brands over the past 10 years. In fact, there is much talk these days about the growth of Private Label or 'retail brands' around the world. Or maybe we should say PRIVATE BRANDS. Because brands indeed they are at the end of the day. And brands we shall treat them as throughout this book. That talk centres around many issues. But the one that stands out is **survival**.

Survival for today's brands against the inexorable growth of Private Label everywhere you look, and increasingly in every category. Survival for retailers if they don't have the best Private Label brand offerings for their shoppers to keep them locked in and loyal to their banner. Survival for manufacturers if they don't have enough capacity utilization to justify their investments. Survival for agencies as Private Label communications lead to a significantly reduced overall expenditure and perhaps more tactically driven shopper marketing activity. Survival for marketers as they increasingly feel the squeeze and query their role in a world where consumer packaged-goods brands seem to be losing their salience and appeal.

But let's forget talk of survival. Let's turn this issue on its head and seize the **opportunity** that it represents. Opportunity for brands to reinvent themselves through dramatic innovation. Opportunities for retailers to truly innovate their offerings. Opportunities for manufacturers to optimize their production capacity. Opportunities for agencies to reinvent communications. Opportunities for all of us as shoppers to get ever-better-value offerings. Opportunities for everyone to drive the key forces shaping today's and tomorrow's society.

Yes, Private Label isn't a curse. In fact it may well be a gift. A gift that forces all of us to re-examine the status quo. A gift that forces us to move positively with some of the key major forces shaping today's society and work more effectively and collaboratively together.

Our reverse side from survival is simply opportunity.

SEIZE THE OPPORTUNITY BEFORE IT SEIZES YOU

A gift that is increasingly relevant to us all whether we be in the UK, USA, China or Scandinavia. Whether we like it or not, every major fast goods category in the world will soon have Private Label. Private Label has been growing at least at twice the rate of famous CPG (consumer packaged goods) brands over the last 10 years. How has Private Label grown at such phenomenal speed indicated above, and what lessons does it offer players in the more broadly defined FMCG (fast-moving consumer goods) markets? We tend to think of it as a food experience – but increasingly it's a total consumption experience. Globalization of taste, retailers and people has made Private Label a global reality. The face of today's retailer is increasingly Private Label. Understand it. It's not about to go away. Deal with it.

Maybe from now on we should call them PRIVATE BRANDS. Maybe if we started calling them brands instead of labels we would build very different strategies to compete. Brands are obsessed with fighting their nearest branded competitor. Do they act as if Private Label is their nearest branded competitor? Maybe they should and maybe they'd act very differently in practice if they did.

The brand has moved on. In essence it's become **privatized** as Private Label has become a branded force in its own right. It can no longer be dismissed as a mere label. It's much, much more.

Why the conventional simply isn't good enough

> I don't like talking in terms of market share. I don't want to share my market with anyone.
>
> Larry Light, CEO, McDonald's

Although taken out of context, for this reason, perhaps more than any other, Private Label is proving divisive, putting brand owners on the back foot and retailers on the offensive. Neither party seems particularly willing to discuss it openly or to collaborate on anything beyond production. Brands have taken retailers to court for copycatting and retailers have de-listed household brands from their shelves. There's little room for concession. With Wal-Mart's overall Private Label share of sales at 40 per cent, Tesco's at 50 per cent (with ambition to increase it to 70 per cent) and Aldi's at 95 per cent (interestingly down from 100 per cent, as some well-known brands have been recognized as indispensable, eg Haribo), all eyes are on the future. In fact on both sides of the fence, for one reason or another, the words 'survival' and 'Private Label' are often to be found in the same sentence.

As we will go on to show, Private Label is one of the biggest challenges branded manufacturers face. It not only represents your biggest single branded competitor, but it is controlled by the thing that makes your business possible in the first place – a selling distribution channel. To compound issues further, it increasingly distorts accepted shopping behaviour and consumption patterns. It is a brand that can sometimes account for two out of three of your customer's physical purchases. A brand that is increasingly seen as a parity (at least) quality and value alternative. A brand that can outweigh and out-image any conventional brand through leveraging the corporate power and spend of the retailer. A brand that can lead manufacturers into a vicious spiral of business decline. A **trillion dollar** industry which must be the least analysed and least understood industry around, when you consider its sheer size and potential impact. An industry that is going to grow a lot bigger in the years to come. Hundreds of billions of dollars of revenue will be potentially diverted from brand owners to this force. Are you sure you have your plans ready? Your solutions?

So what do people recommend as the solution? Lower price, improve quality and be more innovative. **Come on!** Not only is this a solution that you should be undertaking as a normal part of your business development, it simply isn't good enough. This is a challenge that demands the unconventional and exceptional. Rise to that challenge, or else.

Private Label is a brand owner's **wake-up call**. Wake up to business reality. Wake up to the shopper. Wake up to what your company can potentially do. Wake up to real proactivity. Wake up to an opportunity to put your company back in touch with the rest of the world. Private label has risen out of the conventionally held belief that companies can win and beat the competition by creating either greater value for their customers (or shoppers) at a higher cost (manufacturer brands) or reasonable value at a lower cost (retailer brands). In other words, it's a choice between differentiation (or innovation) and low cost, and it is fair to say that retailers have slipstreamed in the former only then to deliver the latter consistently in spades to the shopper. As Coke (and Tesco) will also tell you, having your brand on every street corner pays dividends. As some of our research highlights will show, however, there is still a large quality/value perception gap between Private Label and established manufacturer brands, with only 4 per cent, 8 per cent and 10 per cent (respectively in Sweden, the UK and the United States) believing that Private Label could be more expensive than a manufacturer's own brand, despite the fact that in some cases (eg Tesco Finest) it already is. As far as the shopper is concerned at least, one can't survive without the other, and generally speaking, manufacturer brands are best placed to deliver on 'innovation' and retailers on 'value'. Only 16 per cent of shoppers across all markets genuinely believe that, in the future, it is possible to imagine a store with retailer own-branded products only. So we believe that the opportunity is there for brands to reinvent themselves continually through shopper insight, deeper brand involvement and innovation. The opportunity is there for retailers to add value continually. The opportunity is there for manufacturers to optimize their production capacity and for agencies to reinvent communications. But most importantly of all, the opportunity is there to surprise and delight the shopper continually and far exceed all their expectations.

The other solution often proffered is to get into producing Private Label for yourself. However, Private Label should be forcing you to examine the very basic nature of the business you're in and question whether it's good enough to take you forward. Question your products. Question the way you sell and to whom. Question whether you're really tapping into the agents of change. Question your corporate mission. Question whether you have the right people and structures to deal with this fundamental challenge.

Finally, Private Label is equally a challenge for retailers. Knowing how to control it profitably without damaging the very nature of the business you're in. And the suppliers you're dealing with. Yes, you may think you can live without them. **But we say, be very, very cautious.** You need each other if you are to be a truly efficient selling machine in terms of selling to the shopper. Additionally, we live in an era where the big multinational retail chains are being set up by the media as the new corporations to hate. How do you avoid this? You use Private Label as your messenger, a messenger that not only shows that you offer outstanding value and prices, but that shows you actually care about your shopper and his or her long-term social needs. And you're genuinely doing everything you can to help them. More about this later – a lot more.

Very finally, Private Label is a hidden force to a large extent. The conservative nature of the literature on the subject tends to downplay its real role in the world – a role which is far from conservative in practice, and a role where arguably Private Label is the single biggest influence on our businesses and brands today. It has been systematically underestimated and under-researched by brands, marketing consultants and academics. This needs to change.

We will not treat the subject as conservative. We will treat it as radical – radical in every sense, from impact today to impact tomorrow. And like all radical issues it needs radical solutions. Those strategic solutions will range from accepting Private Label for what it is and where it's going to using Private Label to ensure that organizations embrace the big issues we face today. Creative communications both within and outside the store and the product will be critical, as will a genuine desire to 'co-opetete' (a blend of cooperate and compete), rather than compete.

Very, very finally, we like to think of ourselves as missionaries when it comes to this subject – missionaries who will help convert a threat into an opportunity. We are as much a do-tank as a think-tank when it comes to this mission. Use our words both ways.

THERE WILL BE A LOT OF ANALYSIS, FACTS AND RESEARCH IN THIS BOOK. **BUT ABOVE ALL** THERE WILL BE ACTIONS. OPPORTUNISTIC ACTIONS FOR BRANDS. OPPORTUNISTIC ACTIONS FOR RETAILERS. OPPORTUNISTIC ACTIONS FOR EVERYONE WORKING TOGETHER

> It is not necessarily a threat. It's a challenge and an opportunity.
>
> Swedish Marketing Director, Saatchi & Saatchi X survey

How do we define Private Label?

We define Private Label as retailer brands: brands owned and sold by the retailer and distributed by the retailer. That can include, of course, the Private Label brands we normally refer to as the mass FMCG distributors' labels, ie the likes of Wal-Mart, Tesco and Carrefour. However, it also includes the single-brand retailers that pervade the world, from Gap to IKEA to H&M. We will talk about all of them, but concentrate our discussions on the role of Private Label in the mass retailers. Private Label covers all products that are produced by, or on behalf of, a specific retailer for sale in their stores. Other commonly used terms include 'store brand' and 'own label'. If you want a simple definition, it is that Private Labels are RETAILER BRANDS. That retailer brand can be a major part of a mass FMCG retailer or it can be a standalone specialist retailer like H&M.

What this book covers

We have developed a programme specifically to help you identify those opportunities for yourself and allow you to turn the Private Label problem into a genuine business opportunity. The approach is for senior management in any company that wants to deal with this growing issue more effectively. Our experience to date has shown us that senior management has enormous interest in this area as it represents their most critical strategic issue, one that continues to grow in importance, one that needs a guide. Senior management, from brand manufacturers and retailers alike, need to better understand the implications of their Private Label developments. Let us also not forget the communications industry, which has increasingly to take the lead in this area.

The programme flows into five parts:

1. **Understanding the opportunity**. Here we examine the facts and myths that surround Private Label in order to establish where it's heading and the likely impact it will have on your future business.
2. **Identifying the opportunity**. By using the Saatchi & Saatchi X research report we will focus on the issues that are directly relevant to your business. We will also help you fully understand the situation from a shopper, brand and retailer perspective.
3. **Retailizing the brand opportunity**. We have developed a wheel of opportunity based on **10 principles** around which the programme takes you in order for you to find the actionable opportunities for your brands and your retail efforts and realize your full brand potential. We believe the **10 principles** – 10 commitments in essence – can guide thinking and actions when it comes to the subject of Private Label. They're summarized below. We're not pretending these principles are a Pandora's box to guaranteed success. In fact it will probably come as no surprise that there is no silver-bullet formula. We do, however, believe that by looking at the 10 principles we can all get that little bit nearer. And that little bit more successful. And that little bit more obsessed.
4. **Retailizing the retailer opportunity**. Here we apply our 10 principles via our wheel of opportunity to specifically examine the further opportunities open to the retailers – opportunities to build further on the success they have achieved to date.
5. **Conclusions and implications**. A final look at what this shows us. And how we can all win, win and win by truly working together.

The 10 principles

1. *Running the risk and living the reality*. Here we look at the need for organizations to truly come to grips with the Private Label phenomenon and stop hiding their heads in the sand. Only then will they develop the proactive steps needed, in some cases, to guarantee their survival. The world is becoming essentially a private one... not a branded one. Private is the natural state and if you can't beat it, join it.

2. *Retailize and be radical*. Here we ask companies to use the power of their brands to fully realize their retail potential – to 'retailize' themselves. That power will only be realized by being radical. We need radical thinking, radical solutions and radical implementation for tomorrow.

3. *Tomorrow's global, social and environmental issues are your opportunities today.* Here we look to the future – there are clearly a number of key global issues radically shaping our society today. They will equally radically shape the role of the retailer, resulting in new ways to communicate, present and sell products. Brands and retailers must embrace these changes TOTALLY to avoid stagnation. These changes are permanent, very influential and equally they're counter to a lot of today's accepted practices. Failure to change will lead to change being thrust upon you.

4. *Educate, navigate and inspire*. Here we look at the new role of branding. The role of branding is changing. It's increasingly a role of education to help develop societal needs. Brands and retailers have a new macro responsibility which they must embrace. Educating the shopper responsibly is a prime business prerequisite. You must meet your social needs in a socially responsible way.

5. *Winning 'mind shelf' is the name of the game*. Here we look at the evolving shelf. It's not about mind space. It's not about shelf space. It's about mind shelf space. The brand has gone from a creator of mind space to a creator of mental images disproportionate to its shelf space. Make sure you have your share.

6. *Innovate, imagineer and involve*. Here we look at how you can use the three i's to their fullest. Innovate like you've never innovated before. Innovate for a purpose. Always provide far more for more. Bring back the power of brand imagery. Involve the shopper. Ideally do all three and combine their power.

7. *Restore and reinvent the store*. Here we look at the store revolution. Today's store concepts are mostly designed for the passive consumer of yesterday. They need to be redesigned for the active, informed shopper of tomorrow. They need to be redesigned for the 'lean' revolution in manufacturing that is descending upon us. They need to be redesigned for the changing, increasingly localized nature of distribution.

8. *Catalyse your communications and brand from till to TV*. Here we look at how you can redirect and re-catalyse the power of your communications. It's not about mass communications. It's about catalytic

communications. It is about making things happen at the point of action. It is about making things happen to drive shoppers to the point of action.

9. *Collaborate and cooperate through co-opetition.* Here we look at more ways to collaborate in the future. Let's face it, most Private Label brand strategies and executions are here to stay. Brands must cooperate either with each other or with retailers or both. Co-opetete with your competitors. Co-opetete with your suppliers. Co-opetete or die.

10. *Shopper solutions steal share of wallet.* Here we come back to money. Yes, we all want to make a profit – get an even greater share of the wallet. Providing shopper solutions will help us steal that share of wallet. Our ultimate objective is win–win–win. Win the retailer, win the shopper, win the brand owner. Win, win, win. But be careful of the downside.

When you understand these principles, and hopefully this book helps, you will start to see Private Label for what it really is. Not a threat, **but an opportunity**. This is a challenge that demands the unconventional and exceptional. We will use the retail wheel of opportunity as a systematic way of bringing up the points where we can encourage proactive actions and the realization of opportunities. We must literally make the growth of Private Label one of the single biggest issues in your business. We must be radical and creative in our approach. The approaches recommended so far, essentially by the academic and research community, are frankly in our view not anywhere near progressive enough. Changing pricing strategy, doing a few more innovations and promotions is not going to change the picture. Reinventing the way we approach Private Label, the way the organization sees it and the way we deal with it are the dynamic keys we need to move you forward. Let's turn this issue on its head and seize the opportunity that it represents. Then we will all **win–win–win**.

How to use this book

This book has been put together from a wide variety of sources: academic, commercial, original research, left-brain thinking. We're not pretending that what we say is a path to guaranteed success. In fact it will probably come as no surprise that there is no guaranteed formula.

However, the book will help you in the search for one. If you find it, please tell us. Other people will want to know. Lots of them!

Figure 0.1   The private wheel of opportunity

Part 1

Understanding the opportunity

Here we examine the facts and myths that surround Private Label in order for us to establish where it's been, where it's at and where it's heading, and the likely impact it will have on your future business.

Private Label worldwide is estimated to be a business with a revenue exceeding one trillion US dollars.

That's some label!

1 Private facts

> The Chinese use two brush strokes to write the word 'crisis'. One brush stroke stands for danger; the other for opportunity. In a crisis, be aware of the danger – but recognize the opportunity.
>
> John F Kennedy (1917–63), Speech in Indianapolis, 12 April 1959

The nature of the beast

Just to make sure we truly understand the nature of the beast, let's look at some prescient facts. These facts are taken from three prime published sources (Nielsen, IGD, Datamonitor). The real and most visible battlefield of the Private Label war is being fought in the mass retail grocery brands where the extent and influence of Private Label brands have not been yet determined. Retailer brand success is **not a law of nature**. It varies significantly by country, category customers and consumers. Let's look at some of the facts that define the nature of this phenomenon.

The global facts

Globally it is clear that Private Label is in danger of taking over our world. And particularly our CPG world:

- When you look at CPG categories, Private Labels have virtually an annual penetration of 100 per cent of households in all key European countries, and in all developed economies in general. In short, in essence nearly **everybody** now buys Private Labels.
- Retail store brands are now present in over **95 per cent** of consumer packaged goods categories.
- **Seventeen dollars out of every 100 dollar**s are being spent on Private Label products across the world, encompassing Europe, North America, Asia Pacific, the Emerging Markets and Latin America. In other words, nearly one in five of our hard-earned pounds, euros or dollars.
- CPG is only part of the game, however. Private Label is **everywhere you look**, with some estimates indicating almost every country worldwide and 2,600 categories now being involved with Private Label. In other words, if Private Label hasn't touched your category to date… it will soon enough.
- Private Label is particularly concentrated in the mass CPG retailers. Private Label often accounts for more than half of all CPG purchases as measured by **value**. In other words, **one out of two products we often buy** is a Private Label. In some countries they represent more than one-third of the CPG market. But in volume, and hence usage, it is even higher. Taking average retailer brand prices of 33 per cent below manufacturer brands, usage share in some retailers is well above 50 per cent and often approaches two out of every three physical purchases.

The local facts

Clearly this impact is very variable, with the Private Label phenomenon impacting different countries in very different ways:

- Overall, Europe leads the world in Private Label sales with a 23 per cent share, followed by North America at 17 per cent. European countries top the list with shares of 25 per cent or more (Switzerland, Germany, Great Britain, Spain and Belgium).
- Sweden and Italy are the countries with the lowest penetration. In Italy no retailer has significant national reach because of the significant differences between the different geographical regions, so there is little scope to build a large nationwide brand that benefits

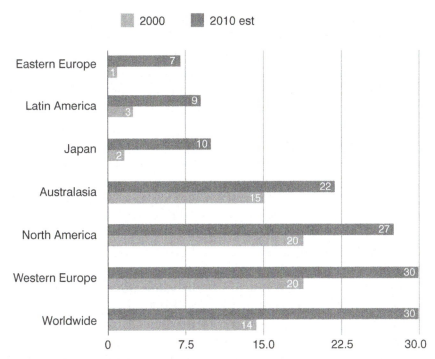

Figure 1.1 Private Label CPG regional share of sales (per cent)
Source: M+M planet retail 2005

from economies of scale. Sweden is both a small country where economies of scale are again a problem and one where consumers apparently have significant trust in the functionality and quality of brands. Spain and Germany showed double-digit growth between 2001 and 2006, while Italy showed only moderate growth of less than 2 per cent. The rest of Europe has seen sound growth rates of around 5 per cent a year.

● Private Label growth is **continuing to outpace** that of manufacturer brands. The only exception to this is in Latin America, where despite Private Label sales growing by a healthy 5 per cent, manufacturer brands outpaced them, growing by 7 per cent. Interestingly, Latin America experienced the largest growth of manufacturer brands worldwide in 2005. In general, Latin America continues to be a far less developed Private Label market than the rest of the world.

- Although starting from a smaller base, Private Label in the Emerging Markets saw the fastest growth over 2005, up 11 per cent. Private Label now holds a 6 per cent share of sales in the Emerging Markets. This growth was primarily driven by the increasing strength of the modern trade (where Private Label goods are more prevalent), as well as the entry of Private Label products into new categories.
- **Interestingly, the region with the most developed Private Label market saw the greatest gain in share points.** Private Label sales grew by 4 per cent in Europe in 2005, while aggregated sales of manufacturer brands remained flat. The big can get bigger. The result was a gain of 0.7 share points for Private Label. This growth is illustrative of the fact that sales of Private Label have not peaked... even within the largest Private Label markets.
- Private Label is most prevalent in Switzerland where its share is nearly half of total CPG retail sales **by value alone**. Not exactly the country you would expect to be the world leader in Private Label.
- Private Label share has increased from 12 to 34 per cent in Germany alone over the past 30 years. **Private Labels have outgrown brands in the United States in 9 out of the past 10 years**. And there's no end to it. Coles, the Australian mass retailer, has publicly stated that it wants to increase its Private Label share from

	2001 % penetration	2006 % penetration	2011 % penetration	2001 sales value $bn	2006 sales value $bn	2011 sales value $bn
France	18	21	22	30	38	45
Germany	17	26	31	38	62	79
Italy	14	14	14	16	17	19
Holland	18	21	22	6	8	9
Spain	15	22	25	13	23	31
Sweden	12	14	15	4	5	6
UK	30	37	40	54	77	95
Europe	19	24	18	186	263	324

Figure 1.2 Private Label CPG European country data (per cent)
Source: CPG PL adapted from Datamonitor

13 to 30 per cent in the near future. Heavily Private Label dependent chains are beginning to emerge from hard discounters, such as Aldi and Lidl in Europe and Whole Foods and Trader Joe's in the United States.

The brand facts

From being perceived as a 'non-brand', Private Label has come a long way:

- Private Label as a whole is the **biggest brand in the world** and bigger than any single retailer (including Wal-Mart). It is, of course, the single biggest brand of any individual retailer. Wal-Mart Private Label is 50 per cent bigger than any single manufacturer's company's total brand portfolio. Aldi and Tesco Private Label are the sixth and seventh biggest CPG brands in the world. Tesco alone is arguably, as a brand, 50 per cent bigger than Coca-Cola. And we insist on calling it a 'label'! Talk about self-denial!

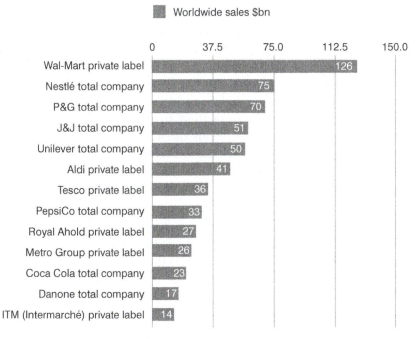

Figure 1.3   Worldwide brand and Private Label sales (per cent)
Source: Fortune Global 500/M+M planet retail 2005

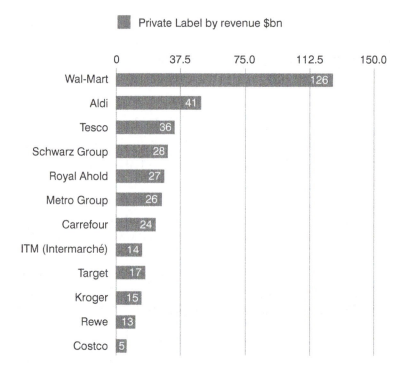

Figure 1.4   Worldwide Private Label sales by mass retailer
Source: Fortune Global 500/M+M planet retail 2005

- Private Label has become an increasingly critical brand for retailers, accounting for large shares of their turnover. Wal-Mart leads the way in overall size. But Aldi leads the way in dependence, with 95 per cent+ of its turnover now being Private Label attributable.
- Private Label sales continue to grow and in fact **grew globally by 5** per cent in 2005, while their manufacturer counterparts grew by only 2 per cent. In other words, 150 per cent more. The result was a global gain of 0.4 share points for Private Label. The growth of Private Label is either new growth or at the expense of brands. The growth of brands (when it occurs) is at the expense of other brands.
- In 60 out of the top 80 CPG categories (**three out of four**), Private Label brands have outpaced the growth of manufacturer brands, resulting in share gains.

The people facts

But, of course, Private Label isn't just about size. It's about whether people actually want it. And what they want it for:

- Private Label literally **appeals to everyone** from the young to the old, from the rich to the poor and from singles to large families. **No single conventional brand can claim such a democratic acceptance.**
- Retailers increasingly create powerful brands that increasingly meet consumer needs. There is **growing consumer acceptance that Private Label is as good as a brand**.
- Private Labels generally remain a very high value offering, with **Private Label brands priced a third lower than manufacturer brands** on average worldwide.
- On a category basis, the average FMCG price differential ranges from Private Label being priced 46 per cent lower in Personal Care products to just 16 per cent lower for Refrigerated Food. At the individual country/category level, however, there are a number of examples where Private Label products have an average price that is **more expensive** than the manufacturer brands. One reason for this is the small but rapidly increasing presence of 'premium' Private Label products.
- Intense promotional price 'wars' among manufacturers have been a contributing factor to lower manufacturer price points. **Private Label has lowered prices and continues to do so.**
- It is interesting to note that **there is not a direct correlation between lower price and largest share.** Of the five FMCG product areas with the smallest price differential in comparison to manufacturer brands, three have the largest share of Private Label and two have the smallest.
- It's a **major part of the shopping experience** with, for example, 82 per cent of British shopping trips including Private Label products. Most people buy Private Label at least once when they shop.

The dependence facts

While the world gravitates towards Private Label, it's clearly upsetting the traditional power balance between retailers and brand owners:

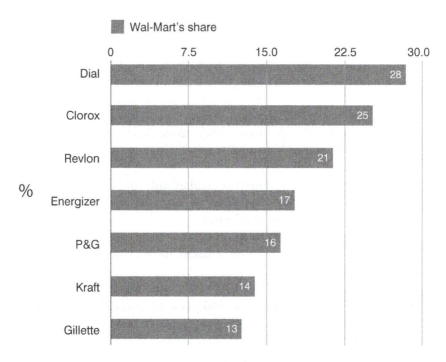

Figure 1.5   The Wal-Mart revenue dependence
Source: company account estimates

- While Private Label is important to the retailer, it's worth noting that **retailers are becoming very important to the manufacturers**. As Figure 1.5 shows, a single retailer like Wal-Mart now accounts for approximately 20 per cent on average of the global revenue of the giant CPG companies. The top 10 retailers typically account for 30 to 45 per cent of a CPG's company's worldwide sales.
- This degree of dependence has never happened before to this extent. Of course, on a country-by-country basis that dependence becomes extreme. Finland, for example, where four mass retailers account for 92 per cent of the CPG market. **This essentially means that most manufacturer's brands have four customers!** In Sweden, where ICA accounts for 50 per cent+ of the mass grocery market, most manufacturers depend on one distributor for half their volume! Not somebody you'd want to offend too often. Now Swedes are an extremely civilized people... but it's somewhat hard to believe that discussions are open-ended and equal. It's like playing

a football game where you have one player and the opposition has eleven. Guess who's going to score the most goals?!

- **Retailer concentration is a key factor in Private Label development**, albeit with some noticeable exceptions such as the Nordic regions where Private Label development to date has lagged.
- **Discounters continue to play a significant role.** This is mainly the hard discounters of Germany whose influence continues to grow across Europe. The one notable failure has been ASDA in the UK, which recently retreated from its experimentation in the area. Aldi, with a 95 per cent share of Private Label, is the second biggest Private Label brand in the world and arguably the sixth biggest CPG brand.

The category facts

Private Label affects almost every category in one way or another. There seems to be no such thing as category immunity:

- **The fastest growing categories are not always the smallest categories.** Refrigerated food has the highest CPG share of Private Label, worldwide, across product areas. Paper Products, Plastic Bags & Wraps has traditionally been the strongest product area for Private Label sales. Although Private Label shares in this product area are still strong and continue to experience growth, Private Label Refrigerated Food now tops the list, with an aggregated share of value sales of 32 per cent. The most significant share of Private Label sales within this area is the Refrigerated Complete Ready Meals category (Private Label had a 2005 value share of 47 per cent). Retailer development of Private Label brands to meet the needs of their shoppers for convenient meal alternatives has resulted in the growth of this category. Private Label shares within the areas of Personal Care, Cosmetics and Baby Food are the smallest at less than 5 per cent.
- The drive for value is seen in many non-CPG categories, notably clothes. Private Label or store brands in 2006 account for 45 per cent of total US apparel sales, up from 35 per cent two years ago. In children's clothing the share is in excess of 65 per cent. Clearly the rise of retailers like Gap, H&M and Zara has contributed to this exceptional penetration. In the UK, ASDA has increased its per cent of customers who want to buy clothes from 8 to 33 per cent in five years.

- **No categories seem to be invulnerable.** Barnes and Noble has said that 10 to 12 per cent of its books will be Private Label by 2008, and even financial services, through the use of store credit cards, are part of this phenomenon. Or finally look at Decathalon, a French sports retailer with well over 300 stores, which has sales of $3.5 billion plus. It has increased its Private Label share to 50 per cent and has even developed what it calls passionate brands (only in France) for customers who are passionate about sports.

In other words, Private Label is everywhere, everyone buys it, almost everyone loves it and it's continuing to grow.

DOES THIS SOUND LIKE A DYING FORCE????

2 Private myths

> The great enemy of the truth is very often not the lie – deliberate, contrived and dishonest – but the myth, persistent, persuasive, and unrealistic. Belief in myths allows the comfort of opinion without the discomfort of thought.
>
> John F Kennedy, 35th president of United States, 1961–63

Many myths that have helped create an illusion of ignorance have been told about Private Label over the years. These myths have caused some to fear, some to ignore and some to embrace. Let's cut through some of those myths. And find the reality.

Myth 1: Private Labels are for people who buy Private Label

There's a generally held belief that the only people who are into Private Label buy Private Label. However, data (ACNielsen | Homescan) clearly shows that Private Labels have an annual penetration of 100 per cent of households in all key European countries, and in all developed economies in general. In short: everybody now buys Private Labels. **So people who buy Private Labels ARE all of us!** There was a time when buying Private Label was a down-class and a 'naff' thing to do. These days are gone for ever. It's now a ubiquitous part of our lives.

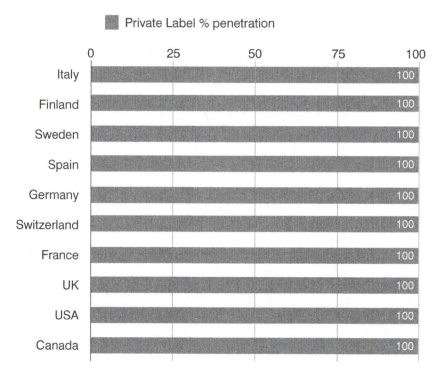

Figure 2.1   Private Label household penetration (per cent)
Source: ACNielsen

Myth 2: We buy Private Label now and then

There is also an assumption that the buying of Private Label occurs infrequently and is not deeply embedded in our purchase habits. The truth couldn't be more opposite. Once again, a fact-based assessment indicates the contrary. Taking France (an average sort of European Private Label market) as an example, the percentage penetration of Private Labels is high or very high for almost 50 per cent of the CPG categories – suggesting that they no longer comprise a niche market. As Private Label pervades more and more categories, Private Label becomes our prima facie purchasing habit.

Myth 3: Private Labels are for people with no money

There is yet again a general assumption that Private Labels are for 'low-income' households or those that need to economize by buying bigger sizes. While it is true that Private Labels were originally more popular among lower-income households as well as larger families owing to the need to economize, this was a very long time ago. This notion no longer holds true. A look at household data indicates that a greater proportion of lower-income households do indeed purchase Private Labels, but higher-income households aren't far behind either. In Europe, the market share of Private Labels across revenue levels indicates that they possess a near equal share of purchases for lower-income households (32per cent) and higher-income households (28per cent). **In other words, the rich like it as much as the poor.** Private Label literally appeals to everyone from the young to the old, from the rich to the poor and from singles to large families.

Interestingly, this is true globally as well. Looking at the percentage share of Private Labels across household sizes indicates that, as is usually assumed, Private Labels do own a greater market share (33 per cent) of purchases within larger households. However, Private Labels have a very similar share of expenditure (30 per cent) among smaller households too, demonstrating that the base of Private Label households is expanding.

Myth 4: It can't grow any bigger

Or it's getting so big that it has to get smaller. There is little evidence of a peaking of the Private Label phenomenon. In fact in its so-called mature markets it is often growing faster than ever. And new categories are exposed to the phenomenon every year. Our proprietary S&S X research later shows that from a shopper perspective the attraction of Private Label continues to grow unabated, whether you're in the UK or the United States.

Myth 5: Private Labels are not business builders

Another generally held assumption is that Private Labels do not really build traffic in stores as they're only for the poorest of us and restricted to commodities. Actual purchase behaviour data from ACNielsen | Homescan offers a more nuanced assessment: Private Labels have found their way into 82 per cent of shopping baskets in Great Britain, 73 per cent of shopping baskets in France, 70 per cent of shopping baskets in Switzerland – in these countries, Private Labels managed to be relevant for all households, for all demographics and for all shopping trips. In contrast, Finnish and Italian shopping baskets showed a significantly lower presence of Private Labels (34 per cent and 26 per cent respectively). This is an effect of a lower overall market share but is also due to different shopping habits, with a predominance of traditional shops (Italy) or an emphasis on more frequent shopping trips and smaller basket sizes (Finland). This also conclusively proves that Private Label development is not solely influenced by factors such as quality, price, positioning etc, but is also a function of retail structure and rooted shopping habits in a given country.

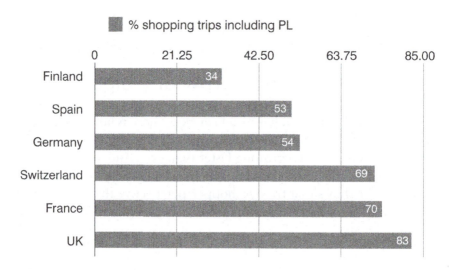

Figure 2.2   Private Label shopping trip penetration (per cent)
Source: ACNielsen

Understanding how people shop is therefore an even greater prerequisite to determining their preference for Private Labels. These facts are a clear signal that brand owners will need, now more than ever before, a better understanding of household purchase patterns and motivations to cultivate an enduring loyalty that will prevent the threat of Private Labels. In this context, going beyond traditional marketing approaches and preconceived ideas, to understand both consumers' and 'shoppers', will be the key to success.

Myth 6: People don't like Private Label

This may be the biggest myth of all. Our own retailization study conducted in conjunction with ACNielsen in late 2005 clearly showed that people increasingly do like Private Label. A fact that's not going away. Unlike the myth.

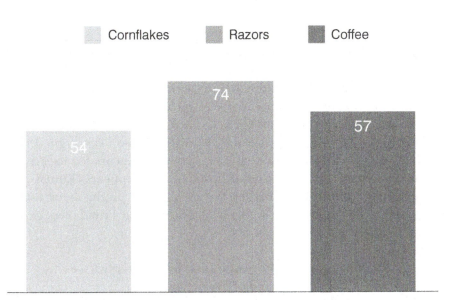

% people who think Private Label is at least as good as a brand – UK

Figure 2.3   Private Label/Brand comparison
Source: International Nielsen Retailization Survey

Myth 7: Let's call it anything except a brand

Private Label, own label, retailer labels etc. The word 'label' is a misconception... not one enjoyed by the shopper, who sees them as 'real' brands in their own right. Brands that mirror the retailers that own them. And as we mentioned earlier, the major Private Label brands are in fact some of the biggest brands in the world... not labels. It's not a label liked by few that fails to grow your business. But some people will continue to believe what they want.

Myth 8: It's not profitable anyway

It sure is. The Boston Consulting Group showed that it is indeed profitable (BCG, 2003). Between 1996 and 2003, US retailers gained more than 50 per cent of the total growth in profits that occurred between retailers and brands. Not everyone agrees. A McKinsey study (McKinsey, 1995), which reviewed 60 food categories, claimed that half of the Private Label products produced less profit per cubic metre than their brand-leader counterparts. However, it should be noted that this study was commissioned by Coca-Cola and Pepsi. Who might be a little biased!

In the UK it has been estimated that retailers' share of profits went from 18 to 38 per cent between 1982 and 2000, with a corresponding drop of 20 percentage points for manufacturers' profits. Tesco's profits don't keep growing for no reason. However, it has been argued that when you add all the costs that a retailer really incurs for its Private Label products, it may not be as profitable as it appears (Kumar and Steenkamp, 2007). But whether Private Label is profitable or not, it certainly is affecting the potential profitability of the brand owners.

So our new privatized brand is:

a mainstream consumption brand everywhere
and of every type
genuinely liked by people for the value and quality offered
growing bigger and bigger
growing more profitable (maybe)

He transfers goods from manufacturers to consumers. HE IS A SPECIALIST IN PHYSICAL DISTRIBUTION. He simply provides warehouses where consumers can buy their products with the help of lists.

Pellegrini, 1996

3 Private past

We've seen it all before!

Once upon a time we lived in a very private world... a simple world... a physical communications and distribution world. That time was a long time ago in a distant world where people had just started learning to sell things. A world where stores were beginning to display their wares. A world where the physical presence of the product was used to attract the attention of new customers. A world where brands didn't exist... just products sold by a retailer. Sound familiar? Sound like a retail brand? Sound like Private Label?

This was a world that lasted a very long time, from the Greeks through the American War of Independence to Queen Victoria and beyond. The world and the age of retail brand power. The world of retailers that sold their own brands. A world where the only connection to the customer was the retailer. The start and the end point.

Life was so simple in those days of limited choice and easy propositions. Product messages were so simple and so rational. That's all anyone wanted to hear... what is it and what does it do? To see a product you simply looked and touched and experienced. Private Label at its most basic.

Brands as we know them today really only started appearing 100 or so years ago when manufacturers realized that by having a brand they could supply many retailers at once while controlling the image themselves. Slowly, very slowly their presence grew. Slowly, very slowly they became the connector to the customer, rather than the retailer. Slowly they became the power in the market.

Then the revolution came... the TV and the days of mass communication arrived. This era has lasted well over 50 years and has had a profound effect on the world of communications. And the world of brands. TV literally built the brand of today through its unrivalled power as a mass communicator. Brands, rather than retailers, became the force that drove markets and the age of brand power emerged. Retailers simply became distributors for the ever more powerful and ever more global brands.

These were the days when the brand ruled and everyone listened. The shop was merely a channel for consumption. Brands could be more imaginative and far more emotional than a mere retailer could ever be. The emotion and the mass media took over as promoting products moved farther and farther away from the shelves they started on.

Surely consumers would no longer be swayed by the rational when the rational was so easily copied from day to day. Surely our mass communication messages were so powerful that once mass awareness had been registered on our mass audiences, then choice would be obvious and stores an easy way to access that choice. The age of push was here.

But a funny thing happened 'on the way to the forum'!

In this world of emotional mass imagery, mass became niche. TV became TiVo as consumers selected to do without the messages. Mass became very expensive and targeted. Niche became relatively cheap. The media channels themselves became more and more diluted and more and more different as more and more channels became available. With over one billion people online and more than two billion using mobile phones, the era of instant mass communication of knowledge had arrived. The era of reaching very discrete audiences very effectively had arrived. In this new world we don't attempt to persuade on a mass scale – we select our key audiences and inform them. We particularly inform about the rational – supply the product information our discerning shoppers increasingly demand. We merely present our brand credentials and hope people are interested enough to discover. Maybe we need more. The power of mass communications has ceased to be.

To make matters more confusing, the era of the shopper arrived. The thing is, we love shopping. We worship it. It has become the very essence of modern society. The ever-continuous shopping addiction has become one of the major trends of today's society. Welcome to the age of pull, the age of the shopper. Consumers are increasingly researching and setting the price for their consumption. They are challenging traditional push-thinking retailers and brands. In a world where brands cannot convince as they once could and the shop has become a focus for our lifestyles, a new era of even greater retailer power was bound to emerge.

This doesn't mean that brands are void and irrelevant, but it does mean that the future is not brand-driven in the way we thought it was. It's shopping-driven... and that has huge implications for the way we create new products and new brands.

Communication has changed... it's gone back to terra firma... it's rediscovered the physical. It's returned to the shelf. It's returned to a new PRIVATE world. We have a new PRIVATE revolution... but one with a difference... it's also emotional through the power of experience. We've returned to those early days when people stopped, looked and listened. But they also need a new positive world of experience. And now we have unprecedented abilities to re-create that atmosphere and experience with the power of today's communication and design tools. And today's private brands.

END OF FAIRY STORY

The new old thing

As we have said, it's worth remembering that Private Labels or retail brands are not a new thing and in fact have been around for a very long time. They are far from being a new phenomenon. Retailers like Sainsbury's in the UK had started retail labels in 1869, as had the Co-op in France in 1929. A&P in the United States with it's Eight O'clock breakfast coffee and Marks & Spencer in the UK with its St Michael brand have been selling Private Label for well over a century. However, the changes were few (Kapfererr, 1998). The real rise of them in modern times started in the 1920s when retailers noticed a shrinking profit margin for branded goods. According to Strasser (1989), until the mid-1920s they thought they also paid for the advertising costs of national brands. Wholesalers were even more reluctant, since they were losing their power over branding. In the United States they sometimes had their own unadvertised labels and, therefore, they disliked the changing rules of the game in favour of manufacturer brands. For most of the 20th century, retailers were relatively small when compared with brands. However, the real revolution started in the 1970s when retailers started to develop national chains.

Freedom brands – blame the French

During the 1970s, retail brands or actually labels attracted more attention, but they were often regarded as cheap and low-quality products. Until the 1970s, labels were mainly used to communicate a

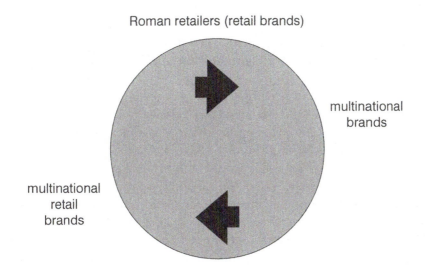

Figure 3.1 The world has gone full circle and some more

low-price profile for stores. The French retailer Carrefour, however, was a pioneer in Europe and introduced *produits libres* (free products) in 1976. These brands were known as banner brands – umbrella brands, and they were a new type of brand. Carrefour wanted to show that their products could be as good as a manufacturer's strong brand but without a brand name and with lower prices.

These banner brands represented the first really offensive strategy against manufacturer brands and were positioned as the new consumers' champions. Carrefour even used the term 'freedom' to name the new product line. The retailers were seen as the liberators of consumers and communicated a new identity. Only in France would we start with freedom!

Several retailers then experimented with low-price no-name products, or generics. Competition increased and consumers became somewhat confused by these products. The retailers themselves had begun to move away from just price and begun to emphasize quality and service to a greater extent. Generics were seen as extensions of their labels and competed with them and not with the manufacturer brands. Generics weakened profitability and were at odds with the quality image that the retailers were seeking. As a result Carrefour launched a policy of corporate branding and stopped selling the freedom line. It was not until the middle of the 1990s that generics were introduced again, for example in the UK. Because of this development, retailers have learnt how important it is to build brands successively and in line with their identity. They realized that there was no point in having a Private Label unless it was synonymous with their corporate offering. As a result the Private Label brand of today has become a brand in its own right, and not merely a way of supplying cheap goods.

In addition, the increasing scale and internationalization of the retailers has significantly changed their relative power with respect to the manufacturers. At the beginning of the new millennium, we can see that retailers are following the manufacturers and becoming international and multinational retail chains. And in some cases, beginning to exceed considerably the scope and flexibility of today's multinational brands. This development means stronger and larger retailers with more resources that can be used for new retail brands and new store concepts. The brand battle for strategic position in markets has begun and is a reality in the 21st century. If you want to read about more Private Label facts we recommend the book *Private Label Strategy* by

Nirmalya Kumar and Jan-Benedict E M Steenkamp (2007). This has by far the most comprehensive analysis of retail brands today. However, we want to get beyond the analysis to the solutions, which now form the bulk of this book.

4 Private present

The lure of the distant and the difficult is deceptive. The great opportunity is where you are.

John Burroughs (1837–1921)

The trends show the way

The late 1990s onwards has seen the real developmental explosion of Private Label and brought us to where we are today. Private Label is growing across the world and particularly in Europe and the United States because it taps into several prevailing consumer trends. By better understanding those trends we can better understand the rise of Private Label:

- **Status reduction**. Frankly we are not as snobby as we were in the 80s and 90s and it has become much more acceptable to buy a Private Label without losing status. Even the rich do it. We remember in the 70s when even as a student you wouldn't be seen dead with a bright yellow Private Label pack or even more dreadfully one with blue stripes. TODAY'S PACKAGING AT LEAST MATCHES AND OFTEN IN OUR VIEW EXCEEDS BRAND PACKAGING. This situation is exacerbated by the retailer stranglehold on distribution and shelf display, which means they can select the best shelves for their shiny new packs.

- **Brand loyalty reduction**. Brands have lost some of their aura and consumers are far more likely to switch between brands, supermarkets and Private Labels. Our International Retailization survey in 2005 clearly showed this to be so, when shoppers indicated low levels of desire to maintain brand choice when their products weren't available.
- **Convenience is the name of the game**. Brands are still important to consumers, but convenience rules all. Our own international Nielsen Retailization study clearly showed this, as indicated in Figure 4.1, when shoppers, if presented with the dilemma of moving store or essentially switching brands, in most cases prefer to stay where they are. The king of convenience nearly always rules over brand power.
- **We all love a bargain**. Shoppers are becoming more obsessed about buying value-for-money wherever they can. This phenomenon is visible everywhere, from the internet to our search for cheap clothes. Private Label is an important way of achieving this. That probably explains why over 2,600 categories worldwide now have Private Label products. What isn't clear, however, is the fact that the progress of Private Label is a rather variable phenomenon and

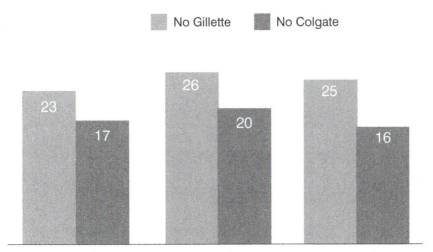

Figure 4.1 Convenience vs loyalty – would you change store if your brand was not available?

Source: International Nielsen Retailization Survey

tends to be a clear function of what retailers have done to stimulate the growth of Private Label. So while everyone searches for value... they don't always get it.

● In the United States, Private Label food on average costs around 28 per cent less than the branded equivalent. In Europe the discount is larger – at 36 per cent on average. Any worries that consumers have about the economy will only strengthen Private Label. And thanks to politicians, we are always worrying about the economy. And it's certainly not just food alone. As we mentioned earlier, Private Label or retail brand clothes now account for 45 per cent of total US apparel sales, up from 35 per cent two years ago. Value retailers in the UK have fundamentally changed the way people shop for clothes, with nearly one in four pounds spent on clothing now being spent with a value retailer (Verdict research). The market is now worth nearly £8 billion ($16bn) and accounts for most, if not all, the growth in the clothing market. The value model relies on scale, cost efficiencies and high footfall to support its low prices and high-volume sales. Smaller operators have little opportunity to match them.

● **Trading up**. Shoppers increasingly like luxury products. While on the surface this would seem to be incompatible with buying Private Label, things are a-changing. Premium Private Label lines are now

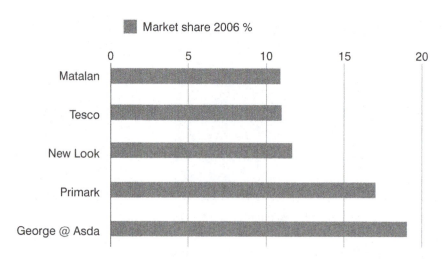

Figure 4.2   Top 5 value UK retailers
Source: Verdict

being extensively developed to capture this expenditure. And as the stores' image continue to increase, it is more and more acceptable for them to fill this position. It is just as possible for that luxury offering to be available in so-called obviously luxury products as it is for it to be available in fruit juice commodity products. Tesco, for instance, offers the least expensive orange juice in its store and also the most expensive!

- **Involvement**. Shoppers are into shopping in a big way. It's often the leading social event of their lives, however sad that may be. Boring old shelves have had their day. And supermarkets have increasingly to lead the way in adding excitement and entertainment in people's lives. And when it is newly introduced (as it has been in many US chains recently), Private Label offers something out of the ordinary. In fact, it is Private Labels that are increasingly developing innovative new products rather than merely copying branded products. As our own research will later show, Private Label is looking more and more innovative these days. Furthermore, in a well-run Private Label programme excitement can be maintained very successfully with new product variants – particularly new flavours and fragrances. Consumers are looking for more interest in their lives, including when shopping in the supermarket.
- **Freshness**. Growing consumer interest in fresh food and drinks benefits Private Label because it is strongest in the very markets that consumers perceive to be freshest, namely chilled and minimally prepared products – an area the retailer controls.
- **Health**. The significant linkage in consumers' minds between 'fresh' and 'healthy' provides another potential platform for the future growth of Private Label. We will talk about this later, because the health issues represent a fundamental shift in today's society, a shift of such magnitude as has not been seen for many a year. It provides significant opportunities for brands and retailers, particularly when they work together.

It's a brand, stupid!

Figure 4.3 shows the brand/Private Label battlefield of the future – and of today. Clearly there's not much to choose between a brand and a Private Label these days. Maybe that's because a Private Label is increasingly a brand. Or to paraphrase Bill Clinton: **'It's a brand,**

TREND	BRANDS HAVE IT	PL HAS IT
status	+	+
loyalty	+	+
bargain	+	+
premium	+	+
involvement	+	+
freshness	+	+
health	+	+
innovation	+	+
convenience	+	+

Figure 4.3   The future battlefield

stupid'. Maybe from now on we should call them **PRIVATE BRANDS**. Maybe if we started calling them brands instead of labels we would build very different strategies to compete.

The increasing propensity of Private Label to match brands' power and offerings has resulted in increasing mass consumer acceptance. Private Label enjoyed a 24 per cent share of the European CPG market in 2006, and 16 per cent in the United States – despite a commonly held belief in the United States that they have the most Private Labels in the world. Not only is Private Label penetration higher in Europe, but it has also been growing faster than in the United States. The future may well see the reverse. Growth of the Private Label market in food, drinks, personal care and home hygiene in the United States and Europe has been driven by a growth in quality and an increasing desire among consumers to maximize their household budgets. Although the drivers and core trends vary on a national basis, the overwhelming trend across nearly all countries and categories is for Private Label to increase as a proportion of consumer spending. Americans are no different from the French in this respect. They want good-quality products they can afford. And one of the richest countries in the world has led that trend... Switzerland. If the Swiss can make half their value purchases in the private arena, so can we all.

Let's pause for a moment to consider two very different markets, the United States and the UK.

The US experience

Private Label sales have grown at more than twice the rate of branded food sales over the past 10 years. In the United States the Private Label CPG industry is worth less than half of that in Europe, with a sales value of US $114bn. Private Label accounted for 23 per cent of food sales and 7 per cent of drinks sales in 2006. The proportion for personal care was 10 per cent and for home hygiene 5.5 per cent.

Private Label now accounts for 16 per cent of all US CPG sales value. However, growth in the most recent years has been distinctly slower and the average for the period 2006–11 is expected to be considerably less than that achieved in 2001–06 (Nielsen). Nevertheless, average growth of nearly 4 per cent per annum is predicted.

This rapid growth is basically due to the key consumer trends we cited earlier. But there are also a number of specific competitive factors that are very specific to the United States that will mean the continuing growth of Private Label there:

- the growth of specialty chains with higher than average Private Label sales;
- the development of value chain Private Labels will continue;
- the arrival of the UK's Tesco, with its heavy focus on Private Label, in the convenience store channel. The US retailers shouldn't under-estimate Tesco – it may well be the Wal-Mart of the future. Internationally Tesco has proved very adept at localizing and adapting to new markets (unlike Wal-Mart).

Despite the current lower levels of Private Label penetration, more affluent households are increasing the volume of Private Label that they buy. In the United States one of the reasons why it is increasing among these households is because they are more likely to shop at the new breed of Private Label-focused specialty supermarkets such as Trader Joe's.

The UK experience

The UK provides a good example of where this trend could ultimately lead. There, Private Label is already well established among more affluent households. In fact, higher-income households actually allocate a greater proportion of their consumer packaged goods (CPG) spending to Private Labels. This is due to the presence of:

- grocery stores with affluent customer profiles and exclusive Private Label programmes (eg Marks & Spencer and Waitrose);
- premium Private Labels in all of the major supermarkets (eg Tesco, ASDA, Sainsbury's);
- strong Private Labels in the drugstore channel (eg Boots, Superdrug).

The UK is arguably the most sophisticated Private Label market in the world. Lessons for the future can be learnt here, which is why we refer to the UK so much in this book. Private Label has been moving away from a generic-only offering to a hybrid approach over many years. The UK Private Label food and drink market now includes three distinct strata that aim to catch a wide range of consumer spending. Such a strategy dovetails well with the trend for sacrificial spending, where consumers more frequently modify their spending preferences to suit circumstances and priorities across diverse product categories. The diversification of Private Label ranges in the UK has improved the image of Private Label as a whole, as consumers of all income groups are able to make savings or opt for indulgence. Private Label has become more 'democratic', which has removed some of the social stigma attached to generic offerings.

The rest of Europe lags behind the UK in penetration terms for several reasons, many of which reflect the unique structure of UK retailing:

- Retailer concentration in the UK grocery market is particularly high, with the top five supermarkets dominating to an extent generally not seen in the rest of Europe (except Scandinavia).
- The UK's retailers have been quicker than those elsewhere to respond to consumer demand and fill unmet market needs. Tesco has an underlying pledge to provide 'everything' you need in life,

from nappies to coffins. Hence the launch of Tesco's funeral services. We'll be getting married there soon. It's hardly surprising that some Brits call the UK TESCOLAND these days. What else is there?

- UK grocery retailers have expanded beyond groceries into a great many other categories. They have even launched very successful clothes ranges, George at ASDA arguably leading the way.
- The UK's personal care market is dominated by chains such as Boots and Superdrug, which also have successful Private Label brands – high-quality, high-value Private Label brands.
- The UK has Marks & Spencer – a dominant high-street retailer which has had one brand, St Michael, as its only brand. St Michael has always been perceived as a high-quality affordable brand and has led the way in innovating many categories, most noticeably food. They alone with their brand account for 4 per cent of UK food.

In addition to this we have the British shopper, a creature who is obsessed with value. Look at the exponential rise in internet retailing in the UK to see this in action. Look at the number of cheap package holidays the British take. At the same time, cultural factors also make a difference. Together, these points suggest that the UK will remain ahead of mainland Europe in terms of Private Label penetration and sophistication for some time, and also that there are valuable lessons for non-UK retailers and famous brands to learn from the example of the UK market.

The factors that influence the UK apply at different levels in different countries in Europe, and indeed help to explain the differences in penetration. But there are anomalies as we mentioned before like Italy and Sweden.

As we have seen, the British retailing scene is one of the world's more developed Private Label markets – but as elsewhere, Private Label's share varies greatly by category and by retailer (Banks, 2006). In recent years brands have been fighting back and it looked as though Private Label market share was declining in Britain, albeit slowly.

In more recent times, however, re-launches of retailers' sub-brands, and more remarkably, the growth of Premium Private Labels such as Sainsbury's 'Taste the Difference' and 'Tesco Finest' have seen a resurgence in the overall performance of Private Labels.

No longer is Private Label about being cheap copies, 'ripping off' brands with inferior packaging and specifications. Consumer

	quality	price	kids	organic	healthy	other
TESCO	finest bistro eat me freeze me	value mega value	kids	organic	healthy living free from meals for one doctor carb control	Italiano simple fair trade grab and go easy steam
ASDA	extra special	smart price	great stuff	organic	good for you	George
Sainsbury	taste the difference	low price basics	blue parrot kids cafe	So organic	be good to yourself free way to 5	Italian, Indian, Oriental, easy steam, American fair trade
M&S	gastropub		loved by kids		count on us	

Figure 4.4   The UK sub-brands

acceptance of Private Label grows as premium quality, higher pricing, and innovation-based category leadership increase within the Private Label ranks. Increasingly, Private Label sub-brands are being professionally marketed – and of course, retailers have the advantage that they can launch multi-category sub-brands into a far greater number of categories than a single manufacturer can hope to do.

Tesco alone accounted for half the increase in UK retail space in 2006. It can basically do what it wants. This drive is likely to continue as retailers seek to increase their competitive position while simultaneously seeking to boost their profitability. All this adds to even higher levels of commoditization within categories – by forcing brand leaders to reduce prices in order to remain competitive.

And things don't get any better. A report in 2006 across 50 categories studied in the UK showed that the average retail selling price realization per unit of volume/weight basis was down by 2 per cent. Only 14 categories managed to garner a higher current yield versus two years ago – all the rest were down. This indicates interesting times ahead for the UK's consumer product market; the beginning of a new era of even more fierce competition from both ends of the market, with players struggling to edge the competition out even as they redefine the market's structure itself.

A closer look at some key brands

> The hunters are becoming the hunted.
>
> Kotler, 2001

Tesco

The Tesco brand, launched in Great Britain in 1924, was one of the earliest Private Label brands sold. Today, Tesco sells 12,000 Private Label lines which have gone from a quarter of its revenue 10 years ago to half today. Eleven billion dollars (£5.5bn) of its turnover is non-food and it's into everything from financial services to books to phones. With over $70 billion total turnover, that's a lot of Private Label. Today, alongside the Tesco Value brand (usually depicted by blue and white stripes), Tesco has a premium-quality brand, Tesco Finest, which also spans most product areas in the store. Overall, Tesco has been responsive to consumers and cultivated its store brands to respond to a variety of consumer needs and beliefs.

Tesco operates a multi-format operation designed to tune into the customers' requirements wherever they may be:

Tesco Direct – internet orders delivered direct
Tesco Express – local convenience stores
Tesco Metro – city centre convenience stores
Tesco Superstores – for weekly shopping
Tesco Extra – giant out of town hypermarkets with considerable non-food.

In broad terms they have the quality–price spectrum covered, as we can see in Figure 4.5. All sorts of sub-brands exist in these four areas. Tesco Organics was launched over a decade ago to provide consumers with a variety of organic foods, from cookies to sausages. In response to the growing share of the population with allergies or intolerances, Tesco Free From includes over 150 products which are gluten, wheat or milk

Tesco PL variants	sub brands	% portfolio estimate
premium	finest	10
sub premium	special	10
commodity	standard	50
generic	value	30

Figure 4.5   Tesco variants

free. The Tesco Healthy Living range includes over 500 products which have reduced fat, sugar and sodium for consumers who prefer a healthier alternative.

Similarly, Tesco Carb Control was specifically developed to make it easier and more convenient for consumers to follow a low-carb eating programme. On a more ethical note, Tesco Fair Trade products are Fair Trade certified, which means producers and small suppliers in the developing world are guaranteed in theory to receive a fair price for their produce contained in these products.

In clothes they have sub-brands like Cherokee, Back to School, Florence and Fred and F&F. Finally, Tesco Kids includes products from toothbrushes to fun-size apples designed to cater specifically to the next generation.

Furthermore, Tesco has also used its brand equity to expand into personal finance, insurance and the telecommunication industry.

Tesco literally gives you everything from birth to the grave. Why go anywhere else to shop? Just look at how Tesco puts insights at the centre of its activities (Figure 4.6). This a key truth about Tesco – they clearly go out of their way to understand their shoppers. As brands, we have to be careful they don't understand them more than we do!

Figure 4.6 Tesco insights

President's Choice

With the launch of the first President's Choice (PC) products in Loblaws in 1984, the aim was to offer better value to Canadian consumers. Today, the brand has expanded beyond a price-point focus to offer quality, health-focused alternatives to consumers in Canada as well as the United States, the Caribbean, Hong Kong and Israel. PC Blue Menu is aimed at the growing demands of health-conscious consumers. Focusing on nutrition, PC Blue Menu provides healthier options, including low-fat, low-calorie and high-fibre products.

Similarly, as a result of consumer demand for organic foods, PC Organics offers a range of organic foods including organic juices, cereals, produce and baby food. PC Mini Chefs extends the range of

President's Choice products to provide parents with a healthy option for their children as well.

President's Choice has now expanded its product offerings from food products to non-food items, including household and beauty products, pet food, lawn and garden and general merchandise and more recently financial services and telecommunications.

And the trend continues...

On a similar, more news-breaking note, 7-Eleven has just responded to a growing consumer need for healthy foods by introducing a line of Private Label functional foods and beverages under its Formula 7 name. IRMA, a well-known Danish retailer, continues to launch variants priced well above brands. And so on...

Finally, it's interesting to note that all these Private Label brands have frankly often been more innovative than their conventional branded counterparts. Brands should learn from this trend before it's too late.

5 Private future

How big can it get?
As big as you want it to get!

The best way to predict the future is to invent it. And then manage it. The limits of Private Label are currently undetermined but it seems almost certain that they have not been reached.

Figure 5.1 shows we've got a long way to go. By 2010 Private Label will over a 10-year period have increased by more than 50 per cent worldwide, 50 per cent in Western Europe, 40 per cent in North America, 300 per cent in Latin America and 500 per cent in Japan. Clearly not a declining phenomenon.

In a number of countries, category penetration of Private Label is still significantly underdeveloped. As Private Label offerings are expanding into new markets and categories, global share will, of course, grow. For example, in Switzerland, where 97 per cent of all the FMCG categories have Private Label entries, the total Private Label share is high at 45 per cent. In the Philippines, however, where only 26 per cent of the FMCG categories have a Private Label presence, the share for Private Label is less than a percentage point.

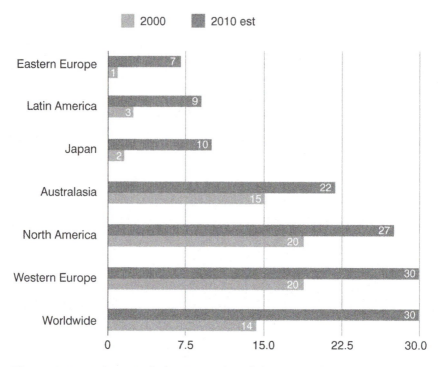

Figure 5.1   Private Label CPG regional share of sales
Source: M+M planet retail 2005

How big will it grow? Today, Private Label has a 17 per cent share of market globally and it is still growing. Even in the most developed market of Switzerland, Private Label continues to extend its reach. In 2006, Private Label in Switzerland gained yet another share point. The differential between the 17 per cent global share and Switzerland's high of 45 per cent is a good place to begin our predictions for the future. Somewhere in between these two percentages may be the answer, but it is important to note that as the share in Switzerland grows so does the upper boundary of this range. And who knows where Switzerland will end up.

As retailers with strong Private Label offerings expand their reach across categories and countries, Private Label will continue to challenge the position of branded products in the minds of consumers. How high they will grow is yet to be determined. The lowest level of CPG Private Label development is seen primarily in three product areas: personal care, cosmetics and baby food. Interestingly, personal care Private Label products are available in most countries, but the Private Label

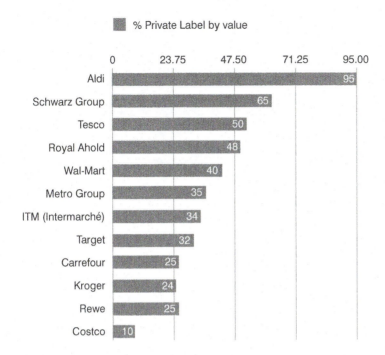

Figure 5.2   Private Label by value
Source: Fortune Global 500/M+M planet retail 2005

share is still only at 5 per cent of value sales. For example, shampoo Private Label products are available in most countries, but Private Label market share in this category is limited to 3 per cent. For cosmetics, however, availability of Private Label products does limit the value share. Lipstick/gloss and eyeshadow Private Label brands are only available in some countries.

The volume versus value distortion

Finally, we have to note that all our share measurements are value-based and this in itself distorts the true picture. If we look at share for Private Label among the major retailers by value, we get some pretty impressive figures, from Aldi standing out with most of its shopping baskets containing only Private Label to Tesco with half its basket by value being its own Private Label brands to Carrefour with almost a third of its baskets being Private Label.

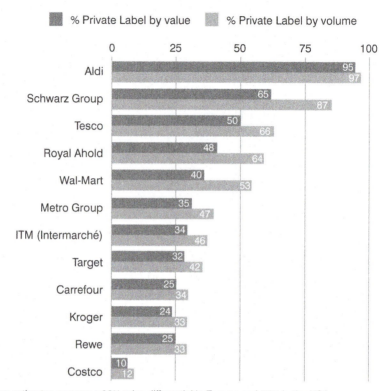

% Private Label by value   % Private Label by volume

0	25	50	75	100

Aldi — 95 / 97
Schwarz Group — 65 / 87
Tesco — 50 / 66
Royal Ahold — 48 / 64
Wal-Mart — 40 / 53
Metro Group — 35 / 47
ITM (Intermarché) — 34 / 46
Target — 32 / 42
Carrefour — 25 / 34
Kroger — 24 / 33
Rewe — 25 / 33
Costco — 10 / 12

volume estimates assume a 36% price differential in Europe and 27% in the USA on average

Figure 5.3   Private Label value and volume
Source: Fortune Global 500/M+M planet retail 2005

However, the true picture should be based on a volume calculation. According to our estimates and assuming a 36 per cent price differential in Europe and 27 per cent in the United States, on average the picture looks significantly more alarming. Now we can see that two out of three physical purchases at Tesco, one out of two at Wal-Mart and one out of three at Carrefour are Private Label. It's the physical measure that matters because this is more a reflection of the shoppers' need and actual behaviour. And by selecting as much Private Label as shoppers clearly do, they limit their real choice when it comes to brand choice. Clearly brands are fighting for a smaller and smaller share of the shopping trolley. And a smaller and smaller share of physical consumption.

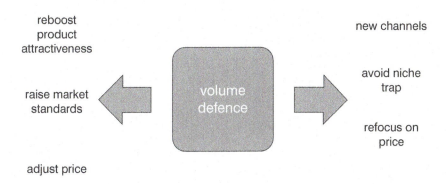

reboost product attractiveness

new channels

raise market standards

volume defence

avoid niche trap

refocus on price

adjust price

Figure 5.4   The volume defence

This is a particularly worrying trend for brands because VOLUME is the main driver of a brand's profitability. The big risk for CPG brands is becoming more and more marginalized, turning into products that are low-frequency exceptional purchases. In CPG it is volume that creates the margin. That means the defence of volume must stay at the core of their business strategy:

$$\text{Total margin} = \text{Unit margin} \times \text{Volume}$$

If the volume falls, the real profitability of the brand falls and it becomes marginalized as a consumer purchase – a very dangerous position to be in. Brands cannot afford to trade up too much. They need to fight the battles where real volume is obtainable and that is the price battle area.

Heaven or hell, opportunity or threat

An excellent paper published at the 2005 ESOMAR conference had this illuminating title: **heaven or hell, opportunity or threat**. This really spells out the future of the Private Label world very clearly and the choices we face as brands or retailers (Figure 5.5). It doesn't take a rocket scientist to see that there are two basic scenarios that emerge. The rest of this book will be about choosing which scenario you want. We believe there's been way too much talk about the threat scenario. It's time to explore the realistic and obtainable opportunity scenario.

Going forward from 2006 until 2011 it is forecast that the annual growth rate in Private Label spending across Europe will be lower than experienced in 2001 to 2006. The already sizeable Private Label

THREAT AND HELL	OPPORTUNITY AND HEAVEN
Brandless world	Balanced world
Limited consumer choice	Real consumer choice
Commodity for everything	Segmentation continues
Cheap, cheap, cheap	Price segmentation
TESCOLAND	**SHOPPERLAND**

heaven or hell!

Figure 5.5   Heaven or hell!

market in Europe maybe reaching maturity. This does not mean that the threat posed to famous brands will subside and evaporate entirely, but that the basis of competition will change. And there are some markets that have a long way to go to reach maturity. And new categories. Private Label offerings will need to become more focused on quality and to raise the stakes in terms of innovation to compete with famous brands.

Will it continue to grow?

The question outstanding is whether Private Label sales will continue to grow. The answer is most certainly yes. Illustrative of this is what is happening in Western Europe. Despite the fact that it is Private Label's largest, most developed market, Private Label brands gained nearly a share point in 2005, growing in sales by 4 per cent while sales of manufacturer brands in over 80 CPG categories measured remained flat.

Although the growth of Private Label ultimately rests with the consumer, a critical key is the expansion and concentration of retailers. Those markets with the highest share of Private Label, not surprisingly, also have some of the highest levels of retailer concentration. As retailers enter new markets, they bring their Private Label brands with them.

It is almost impossible to generalize the development of retail brands. An international survey in 1999 of 37 leading companies and 8 international retailers, conducted by McKinsey, concluded that 47 per cent of the decisions concerning retail brands were central decisions. An effective relationship with these retailers from the manufacturer's point of view was therefore deemed essential.

When asked: 'If you do not have business with the top five global retailers today you will not be in business in five years time':

- 35 per cent saw this development as an opportunity;
- 30 per cent saw a threat in the short term, but an opportunity in the long term;
- 35 per cent saw this a threat only.

We wonder what they'd say today?!

What determines the future?

The size of the markets and the retail concentration of the market seem to be of importance. These two aspects, according to Laaksonen and Reynolds (1994), either create a prosperous environment for retail brands to grow, or hinder the development of retail brands. However, the interdependence of these two aspects is not clear cut in all countries. Sweden and the other Nordic countries have the highest concentration rates in Europe. On the other hand, retail brand penetration has been comparatively low. Furthermore, there is talk about polarization between the leading manufacturers' brands and the retail brand in certain product categories. This is evident in a sophisticated market as the UK, but also in France and Germany.

Private Label drivers

However, there are many drivers of Private Label growth in Europe, most of which will continue unabated. In particular:

- The long-term depressed economic environment in Western Europe vis-à-vis the United States drives consumers towards Private Label, especially in the hard discount stores.
- Less negative stigma as quality and packaging improve.
- Increasing retailer concentration across Europe. There is little sign of this decreasing, despite various calls for monopoly investigations from Sweden to the UK.
- Retailers' desire to drive margins, benefit from scale and improved negotiating power with brands is unlikely to go away.
- Retailers' increasing focus on 'differentiation' vis-à-vis their retailer competition drives them to use Private Label as their main differentiator.
- Competitive pricing and cost efficiency remain top of the agenda at retailers.
- Private Label will become generally more sophisticated.
- Retailers will require tailored solutions as they increase their sales by seeking new formats from garage stores to ever-bigger hypermarkets.
- No curbing of retailers' buying power.
- Further manufacturer consolidation as the weaker brands find it harder and harder to survive.
- International retailer influence will accelerate.
- The role of regional buying alliances will increase to generate scale.
- It becomes more a 'brand' than ever.

Private Labels started as a strategy to provide consumers with low-priced alternatives to branded products. Their distinguishing features were a low price and matching product quality. They did not use many of the brand-building techniques traditionally used by manufacturers. Aspects such as product innovation, packaging development and the creation of 'brand personalities' and positioning were conspicuously absent. This has now changed dramatically. Today, retailers use Private Labels to build and sustain the image of their entire franchise. 'Premium priced' Private Labels are now common. So are Private Label ranges with specific consumer promises such as 'environmentally friendly' and 'good and healthy life'.

The implications of this will be felt widely. As Private Labels broaden their appeal through the addition of new consumer values beyond price, manufacturers will need to pay even greater attention to differentiating and developing their brands. Experience suggests that there is no single 'silver-bullet' response strategy in such a scenario; what works for one brand may not work for another. Instead, it requires a careful examination of brand architecture, consumer choice criteria, category dynamics and competitive strategy in the context of global, regional and local trends.

The online driver

We will briefly touch on the future impact of the internet here as this is a standalone factor in its own right and one we will come back to later. It's clear that the internet will have a profound effect on Private Label growth. Recently we heard that even Apple Inc was worried about Private Label on the internet – a brand you would expect to be insulated from such matters. However, in the UK the major online retailer Dixons, which until recently had been the largest high-street retailer until it switched overnight to the web, launched its own Private Label MP3 player. Rumours abound that at one stage it was outselling Apple's iPod – a previously undentable market leader. If these rumours are true, nobody and no product are sacrosanct from the Private Label invasion. The internet has made Private Label a reality for retail brands and maybe nowhere is this clearer than at Tesco, which has one of the UK's most visited websites.

It is essential for famous brand manufacturers to work with supermarkets, and it can be beneficial to leverage supermarkets' loyalty databases. However, it would be unwise to rely on the retailers' ownership of consumers for direct marketing and consumer insight – particularly in cases where brand objectives clash with the retailers' own Private Label programmes. In this context it makes sense for companies to build their own consumer databases, both for direct marketing purposes and in order to gain unique insights into consumer behaviour. The internet offers an excellent way of achieving this goal, allowing brand owners to communicate directly with consumers without the intervention of retailers and other intermediaries, particularly as consumer trust in traditional advertising is eroded. Building a compelling web presence can be an excellent way not only of raising consumer awareness of a given product but also of building consumer databases.

The Tesco effect

We'll leave this section with one final thought. The world, as we know, has become a very small place. The world of increasingly large, increasingly international retailers has noticed the incredible success of Tesco with its increasingly premium Private Label variants. They are starting to imitate that success. If you can copycat brand success, why not copycat retail success? If only a small number of them succeeded a new wave of Private Label growth would be unleashed worldwide.

Pam Boynton, director of marketing at Daymon Worldwide, said: 'In the 1980s and 1990s, Private Label began to follow the brands. In the 21st century, what we're seeing is that Private Label is starting to lead the brands and that's an exciting place to be at this point.'

Part 1 summary and implications

We can clearly see that the Private Label phenomenon has arrived and is unlikely to disappear any time soon. With the increasing globalization of retailers and the new opportunities of the internet, an ever more dominant Private Label presence seems highly probable and inevitable. And that presence will be everywhere... in every country... and in every category.

Brands

Implication 1: It's here to stay, make the most of it. It's increasingly clear that Private Label is maturing to near-brand, if not total brand, status. It can't be ignored or pigeonholed into a strategically irrelevant status. It's very relevant and potentially a brand's biggest nightmare.

Implication 2: Turn a threat into an opportunity. There's always a positive side to the negative side. Here, that positive is your wake-up call to readdress most of what you do and move your strategy onwards.

Retailers

Implication 1: Use for positive change. The very nature of your Private Label offerings is undergoing profound change. Use that change as a catalyst to move forwards, preferably with your brand suppliers.

Implication 2: Turn an opportunity into an even bigger opportunity. The very success of your Private Label offering should be telling you a lot about your destiny and real future. Use that success and knowledge to better position your self for an even more competitive future.

Part 2

Identifying the opportunity

By using the Saatchi & Saatchi X research report we will focus on the issues that are directly relevant to your business. We will also uniquely help you fully understand the situation from a shopper, brand and retailer perspective.

**In many markets one out of two physical products we buy
is a Private Label.**

Which brand can claim that?

6 The S&S X Global Research Report

An 'all parties' perspective

As we described in our Introduction, we have extensively explored published research data worldwide on the subject of Private Label, from Nielsen Worldwide to Datamonitor to IGD. This data has been very useful and helped us set out the major trends to date. However, we thought it was essential to go deeper and explore the motivations of all three Private Label participants: the retailers that develop and sell them, the brands that compete and often manufacture them, and of course the shopper who ultimately buys them and determines their ongoing future. So our study was born.

This study is **unique** in that it is the only study to our knowledge to look at all three major participants in the Private Label arena simultaneously on a global basis. By understanding all the parties better we hope we can realize an opportunity – to reverse the threatening nature of Private Label.

Together with Saatchi & Saatchi's global retail and shopper marketing agency, Saatchi & Saatchi X, the authors conducted a major online internet quali-quantitative study in three major regions of the world. Using a fast, efficient quali-quant online research tool provided by BrainJuicer we were able to get real-time responses from a panel of over 1,000 shoppers. Thanks to the Saatchi & Saatchi network and the global membership base of POPAI (Point of Purchase Advertising International), we were also able to survey and speak to over 50 brand owners and retailers, from FMCG companies through to fashion, DIY, health and beauty, and electronics, focusing our efforts on four countries that represent the diversity of private label positions today:

- **The United States**: a relatively developed Private Label market to date that is rapidly showing signs of more change.
- **The UK**: arguably, as we have already suggested, the most sophisticated Private Label market in the world, one you need to know in order to know the future.
- **China**: a development market where Private Label, from a very low base, could become a major force in years to come.
- **Sweden**: one of the most concentrated retail markets in the world where, paradoxically, Private Label until recently has been at relatively low levels, but may be changing. A market that appears to contradict the conventions that high retail concentration leads to high Private Label share... to date!

We decided to focus on only four countries to ensure we had data clarity. That way we believe we can get to the issues that really matter.

We would also like to extend our thanks to **POPAI** (the world's leading representative of in-store practitioners) who helped Saatchi & Saatchi X, with their global membership, get nearer to the retailers and manufacturers that matter. Their help, support and input have proved invaluable.

Our aim is not to confuse you with numbers, but to open your minds through showing you where the world is going and what the participants are saying (or sometimes not saying). In essence we provide a very up-to-date snapshot of what's really going on. Then we show you the strategies and actions which lead to opportunities in Parts 3 and 4. As we said up front, these strategies will not be conservative in nature, which they have been to date. To beat a revolution, you need a revolution.

7 The shopper perspective

Let's start with the shopper

The first thing we noted was the overwhelming tendency to buy Private Label products, with the vast majority of respondents saying they currently do (Figure 7.1). The United States somewhat surprisingly leads the way with 93 per cent of shoppers claiming that they currently buy Private Label. China comes last with a still high 69 per cent of shoppers claiming purchase.

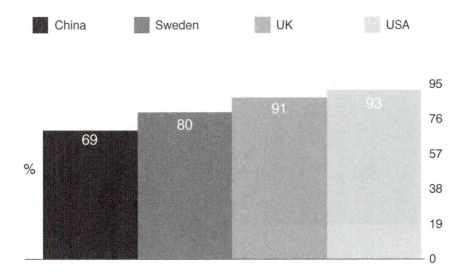

Figure 7.1   Private Label purchases
Source: S&S X report

Clearly the world likes Private Label everywhere we look, developed market or not. This becomes even more apparent when we look at the number of shoppers who currently claim to buy a mixture of Private Label and brands, with Sweden, the UK and the United States at nearly 100 per cent, with China not far behind. Private Label affects us all, wherever we may be (Figure 7.2). When you look at the reasons they buy, it clearly divides into three camps (Figure 7.3). Their rationales are diverse, but purchase is clearly linked to conventional strong brand characteristics, ie quality, value and trust. Reasons for rejection are indifference and faith in brands.

> The quality is guaranteed, the brand is really up to the mark, worth trusting, unique, cheap in price.
>
> Chinese shopper

The ones who currently buy clearly have strong positive opinions ranging from a perspective of good value for money to a guarantee of quality. Even the likely-to-buy camp is positive, with comments of more restrained praise.

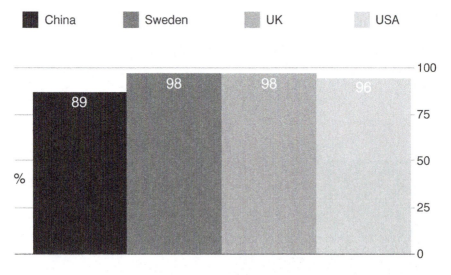

Figure 7.2   Private label purchase mix
Source: S&S X report

currently buy	likely to buy	unlikely to buy
The quality is guaranteed the brand is really up to the mark, worth trusting, unique, cheap in price	Those branded ones are all expensive, those non-branded ones are also not that bad	Feel that it is not professional
There are similar products that are cheap in price, in comparison the quality of these products is assured	Following the approval of the retailer, it is possible to accept its brand of products	I really don't care for retailer own branded products
Value for money, the quality is guaranteed	Because after a period of testing, the product quality is the basis for its survival, moderate price	Prefer to buy a brand that I recognize
As long as one thinks it is good, and the price is suitable, it doesn't matter if it is a domestic brand	Moderate pricing, variety of products, the quality is also not bad	Because I want to buy the RIGHT brand, so that I know what I'm getting!

Figure 7.3   Private label purchase behaviour
Source: S&S X report

The price is low and the quality is generally as good as the more expensive products.

Swedish shopper

The unlikely to buy are more outrightly dismissive. But they are a minority, as we have clearly seen, and an increasingly small minority at that. So why is this desire to buy Private Label so high? And so positive? Clearly one of the key reasons is the vast overall perception that Private Label is at least as good as a brand. The days of cheap and nasty Private Label have gone forever, with 9 out of 10 shoppers on average worldwide seeing Private Label as good or fairly good value compared to brands (Figure 7.4). Clearly not much convincing is needed to put the Private Label brand into the conventional branded space.

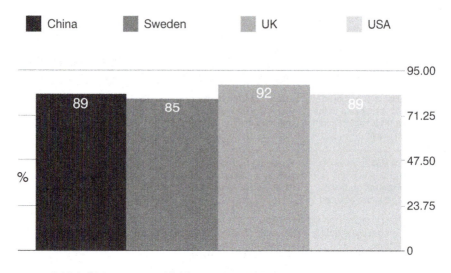

I think PL is very good/fairly good VALUE compared to a brand

Figure 7.4 Private Label value
Source: S&S X report

Achieving product parity

However, when it comes to quality (Figure 7.5), the brand stacks up well also, with 7 out of 10 shoppers on average saying that Private Label is at least as good as a brand. The brands out there should take some reassurance from this. But equally they should be worried that two-thirds of the population SEE NO DIFFERENCE. In other words, Private Label is nearing product value parity with brands and not far behind in product quality parity – hardly a good starting point for the future. The positive side of this is further borne out when we look at the general perception of a brand's quality, with 9 out of 10 shoppers seeing brands as generally good quality (Figure 7.6). Quality, yes. Value, no. Just think of your recognized competitors. If they were achieving product parity with you, you'd be seriously worried and doing something about it. Do you have the same response to Private Label?

The UK difference comes out strongly when we look at the quality issue, as the UK consumer clearly sees Private Label and brands in the same quality camp (Figure 7.7). When comparing respondents who see Private Label as fairly/very good quality, Figure 7.7 shows this more

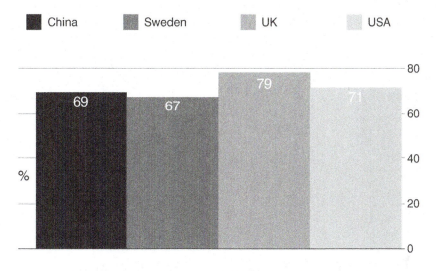

I think PL is very good/fairly good QUALITY compared to a brand

Figure 7.5 Private Label quality
Source: S&S X report

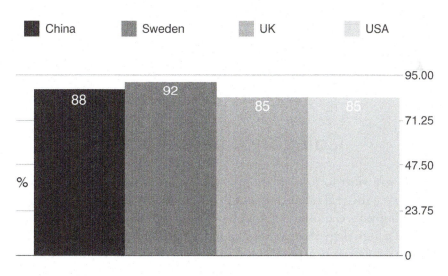

I think BRANDS are generally above average QUALITY

Figure 7.6 Brand quality
Source: S&S X report

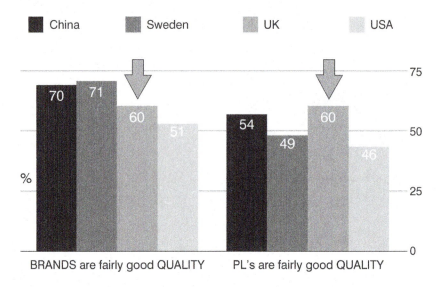

Figure 7.7   Brands vs Private Label
Source: S&S X report

clearly, with 60 per cent of respondents seeing brands and Private Labels on the same quality level. In other words, product parity has been achieved.

> There is not always a branded alternative.
>
> UK shopper

Category differentiation

When you start to look at shoppers' behaviour across categories you start to see the real penetration of Private Label. While some categories have shoppers claiming low regular buying behaviour, ALL categories exhibit a high degree of occasional purchase. This is particularly critical for the categories that exist at low levels of Private Label development, because it clearly points the way to the future. If the occasional buyer can be converted into a regular buyer, Private Label will take off in that category in the short, medium and long term. Clearly Private Label DIY, electronics, cosmetics and alcohol have the potential to become as Private Label saturated as food.

Occasional PL Purchase Today = Regular PL Purchase Tomorrow

Equally, within food, sectors as yet undeveloped, such as health foods and organic, are wide open. To date, these new health sectors represent growth categories, but their development is relatively minor when compared to the mainstream – somewhat surprising, when the reality of our new world is staring us in the face. When every other news headline is about health issues related to food and when the world's most successful retailer these days seems to be Whole Foods Markets, it doesn't take a rocket scientist to see where we're going. It does, however, take a desire and some fuel. That desire has been arguably lacking to date, as retailers and brands, despite their rhetoric, fail to fully embrace the new directions and do what they can to protect the past. Figures 7.8 to 7.11 show these changes in more detail, country by country.

CHINA	regularly buy	occasionally buy
fresh food	75	22
ready meals	57	36
cereals	54	35
dairy	52	29
snacks	52	42
personal care	38	50
health foods	49	38
DIY	49	43
clothes	48	38
confectionery	25	62
cosmetics	30	41
beer, wine and spirits	22	31
medicines	19	46
razors & blades	17	46
electronics	15	55

Figure 7.8 Private Label categories in China
Source: S&S X report

SWEDEN	regularly buy	occasionally buy
fresh food	38	53
ready meals	11	63
cereals	11	64
dairy	33	28
snacks	13	68
personal care	37	43
health foods	9	37
DIY	18	53
clothes	11	64
confectionery	13	68
cosmetics	12	35
beer, wine and spirits	8	37
medicines	8	43
razors & blades	34	14
electronics	6	59

Figure 7.9   Private Label categories in Sweden
Source: S&S X report

UK	regularly buy	occasionally buy
fresh food	69	26
ready meals	30	52
organic	21	36
dairy	60	29
snacks	–	–
personal care	29	50
health foods	15	38
DIY	–	–
clothes	25	64
confectionery	20	60
cosmetics	7	37
beer, wine and spirits	15	45
medicines	28	56
razors & blades	13	43
electronics	10	58

Figure 7.10   Private Label categories in the UK
Source: S&S X report

USA	regularly buy	occasionally buy
fresh food	42	37
ready meals	16	56
cereals	34	44
organic	11	33
dairy	52	36
snacks	34	58
personal care	36	39
health foods	9	46
DIY	4	40
clothes	17	68
confectionery	22	51
cosmetics	9	32
beer, wine and spirits	9	21
medicines	36	53
razors & blades	18	46
electronics	7	53

Figure 7.11   Private Label categories in the United States
Source: S&S X report

> Some of them are cheaper, with better nutritional profiles than the name brands.
>
> US shopper

Also of particular note is electronics, a sector often thought to be immune to Private Label because of technological insulation. Despite relatively few shoppers claiming to buy Private Label electronics regularly, more than half our sample claim to buy occasionally. In other words, there is a perception that it exists and if it's supplied the right way the conversion from occasional to regular purchase could be significant. Our previous reference to Dixon's and Apple's iPod shows this all too clearly.

> With large items, I prefer a name I know I can trust but I might consider buying Private Label.
>
> UK electronics shopper

Finally, clothes, with four out of five shoppers claiming to buy Private Label regularly/occasionally – astonishingly high figures from a fashion-conscious, brand-conscious sector. In theory at least!

Figure 7.12 is a summary of the non-food sectors, clearly showing the overall direction. UP!

The shopper's Private future

From here we went on to evaluate shoppers' perspective on the future. And yes, they do think Private Label has a future! When asked whether they strongly or slightly agreed that there were no brands that couldn't

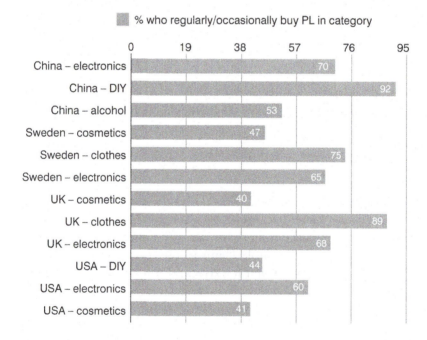

Figure 7.12   Private Label category summary
Source: S&S X report

become Private Label categories, up to 87 per cent in the UK agreed, 73 per cent in the United States, 65 per cent in Sweden and 57 per cent in China (Figure 7.13). Hardly a forecast of decline for the future. And maybe it's our shoppers who really know best! They certainly seem to think so.

Shoppers clearly think that Private Label is here to stay and they want it to stay (Figure 7.14). When asked whether they were likely to buy in the future if they didn't buy now, we got some striking figures for China: 29 per cent of Chinese non-buyers thought they would buy in the future. That's nearly a third of your market! Remember, in the developed countries most of them buy both anyway.

Clearly China may not be the brand market of the future if this is to be believed. When asked further whether they saw the future of Private Label becoming premium, 8 out of 10 on average agreed, with China recording 9 out of 10 (Figure 7.15). The western nations were clearly very consistent in this perspective. There is evidently a strong directional drive to a better-quality future for these products as they increasingly reach brand parity. It's maybe worth remembering that an estimated one-fifth of Chinese brands are actually or at least believed to be counterfeit, which is hardly a good starting point for brand credibility.

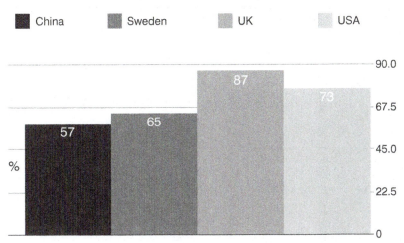

% who strongly/slightly agree that THERE ARE NO LIMITS TO WHICH BRANDS CAN BECOME PL

Figure 7.13   Private Label limits
Source: S&S X report

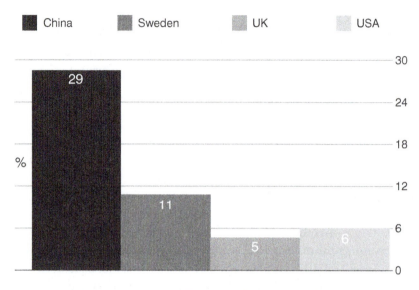

I do not currently buy PL, but am likely to in the future

Figure 7.14 Private Label future purchase intentions
Source: S&S X report

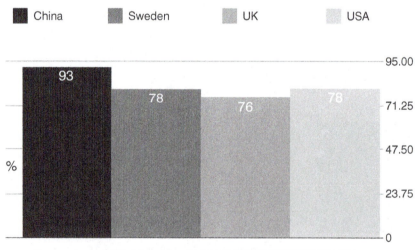

% who strongly/slightly agree that IN THE FUTURE THERE WILL
BE MORE PREMIUM PL

Figure 7.15 PremiumPrivate Label future expectations
Source: S&S X report

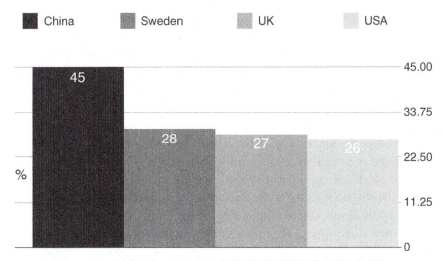

Figure 7.16   Private Label future price
Source: S&S X report

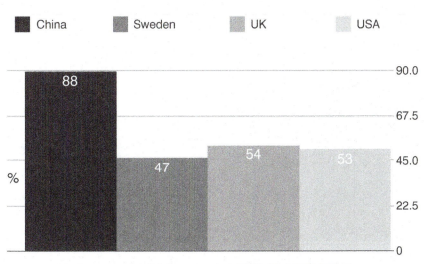

Figure 7.17   Private Label innovation
Source: S&S X report

On further examination and probing, more than 25 per cent of shoppers on average in the developed countries even saw Private Label as being more expensive than brands (Figure 7.16) – a frankly amazing figure. In China, nearly one out of two felt this to be true. Somebody must be doing something right. Or the brand Private Label differential is eroding.

This was partly explained by the fact that almost half of shoppers in the developed countries saw Private Label as innovative as a brand – an even more remarkable performance (Figure 7.17). And in China it was 9 out of 10. Who's really understanding the trends best?

Finally, we thought we'd see if shoppers envisaged a future of Private Label stores alone. On average, more than 4 out of 10 shoppers across all countries strongly or slightly agreed that they saw a future where the store would be Private Label only (Figure 7.18). So do we! Fortunately for brands, however, only 16 per cent of shoppers across all markets genuinely believed (ie strongly agreed) that in the future, it is possible to imagine a store with retailer own-branded products only.

On balance, guess who's winning the battle for shoppers?

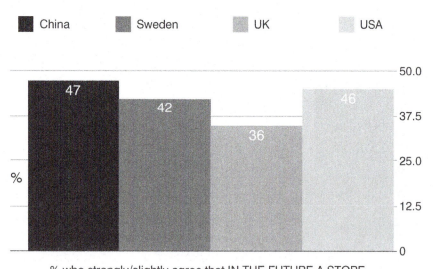

Figure 7.18   Private Label future penetration
Source: S&S X report

8 The brand perspective

The silent wall

Here the silent wall starts to emerge... the subject you shouldn't speak of. We were delighted to get responses from a significant number of brand owners in our four countries. But it's interesting to note how many of those companies requested to be anonymous. One hundred per cent of respondents in China, the UK and the United States asked for anonymity, and nearly 70 per cent in Sweden. We interviewed over 50 different brand owners from a wide range of categories across all four markets and in fact beyond, as many of our respondents had broader experience and responsibilities. It was also important to maintain anonymity where requested and, interestingly, 100 per cent of respondents in the UK asked for their names and companies to remain anonymous, with those in Sweden being the least concerned. For the sake of consistency and brevity in this book, all shall remain so, although where permission is given details of our respondents can be found in the original research debrief. The same applies for retailers.

> A large number of Private Label products have entered the market over the last few years and they have drastically increased their market share.
>
> US brand owner

Approximately a third of our respondents produced Private Label as well as competing against it. Out of the 30 per cent or so of brand owners that also produce Private Label products, the top reason was for the sake of 'partnership and profitability'. For the 70 per cent that didn't, the chief reason given was that their company had based itself around 'strong brands and innovation'. If we look at this through the lens of joint value creation, then of course the two needn't be exclusive. Strong brands can work together.

There was clear differentiation between producers and non-producers when it came to their rationale. The main reason for producing across all countries was profitability and the need for partnership. The main reason for not producing Private Label was a belief that their companies should be about strong brands and innovation. Private Label couldn't be part of that picture.

> Our company bases itself around strong brands and innovation.
>
> US manufacturer

When it comes to determining the degree of the Private Label threat to brands, the UK stands out as the clear leader, with 100 per cent of respondents arguing that Private Label was an increasing threat to their business. Given that the UK is by far the most sophisticated Private Label market in the world, this is somewhat worrying. In the UK, for instance, there is a Tesco store in pretty much every UK postcode. The average store has over 12,000 Private Label lines.

The degree of sophistication is the source of that threat. Remembering that our sample was across a range of categories from electronics to food, the UK clearly stands out (Figure 8.1).

The United States feels it's under control. But there again Tesco has only just arrived! It will be very interesting to see what impact it makes in the years to come. While Tesco is very adaptable internationally (unlike Wal-Mart), it normally chooses to make Private Label a key force in its competitive arsenal. The other countries are lower, with the UK and United States scoring less than 50 per cent. Maybe they should worry a bit more. The simple fact is that the channel and not the brand manager controls the brand. The annual IGD trade briefing for Tesco

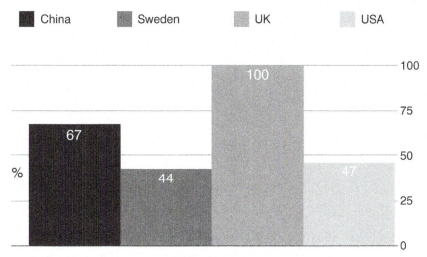

% brand owners who believe PL is an increasing threat to their business

Figure 8.1   Private Label threat to brand owners
Source: S&S X report

in the UK in 2007 brought this home very clearly, when over 1,500 of Tesco's key suppliers sat quietly and diligently in a conference theatre in central London to be told how they could help Tesco meet their commercial objectives and give their shoppers something more than just price and promotion.

Lost business. Lost customers. Less bargaining power. Lower margins.

Swedish brand owner

Some of our products have almost no barriers to entry.

US brand owner

Retailers are stretching their premium credentials into branded territory.

UK brand owner

Retailers have increasingly added a 'DI' metric. Despite the positive performance of our branded product in our category, retailers are still looking to source product. At the same time, they're looking to build their store image with house brands rather than nationally branded products.

US brand owner

We fight for shelf space with it every day.

US brand owner

As you can see above, a lot of reasons for worrying about Private Label were cited. One respondent said very precisely: 'What is really threatening is that we do not know where their limit is.'

The other side of the coin

On the other side of the coin, brand owners also see the opportunity.

Huge opportunity for better partnerships and growth with strategic retailers.

US brand owner

What is perhaps even more illuminating are some of the reasons cited for not viewing Private Label as a threat.

It is not a threat as it is today and I do not believe it will be in the future.

Swedish non-food brand owner

I assume Private Labelling can be a costly endeavour for the party creating it and I would assume the cost would be carried over to the consumer purchasing the product.

US electronics brand owner

China	Sweden	UK	USA
strong emotional brand	cooperation	brand building investment	brand building investment
differentiate and innovate	differentiate and innovate	differentiate and innovate	differentiate and innovate
in-store support	category management	differentiate in some way	widen the trust gap

Figure 8.2   Brand owner strategies to help them against Private Label
Source: S&S X report

Clearly some brand owners still see Private Label as less of a problem, despite the earlier results we showed from shoppers who increasingly see Private Label as a force applicable to any category. This in itself does not surprise us. As we have stated in our earlier books, it is clear that most brand owners do not understand their shoppers very well. There is a clear gap between the perception of the shopper buying the brand and the brand owners themselves. It will be interesting to see who is right in the long run. We're pretty sure we know.

One of the most interesting things to emerge is the difference between shoppers and brand owners when asked the reasons why they buy Private Label. Shoppers cite mainly value for money and price. Brand owners cite availability, store presence and retail equity. They even mention lack of product availability and better products. Seems we have very different perspectives on reality.

There is even more illuminating data (Figure 8.2) when we ask brand owners which strategies might help them against Private Label. Clearly

	China	Sweden	UK	USA
PL is growing	100	100	100	81
in the future there will be more premium PL	67	88	100	85
PL is damaging our profitability	67	78	50	52
there are no limits to what PL can become	33	55	75	29
in the future PL could be more expensive than a brand	–	66	75	48
there are no limitations as to what product can become PL	33	55	75	29
PL is as innovative as a brand	67	33	25	29

% brand owners who agree/slightly agree

Figure 8.3   Brand owners opinions
Source: S&S X report

there is a degree of consistency about this across the world, with imagery and innovation clearly standing out.

> Lost business and customers. Less bargaining power. Lower margins.
>
> Swedish brand owner

Probably the most revealing output comes back when we ask brand owners about the future of Private Label. One respondent summarized this as *'Private Label will increasingly go from poor quality for poor households to a great deal for smart households.'* As Figure 8.3 shows, the future for brands competitively looks difficult. This is particularly so in the UK, which records some of the more extreme numbers. The UK brand owners see no limits to Private Label (75 per cent), more damage to their future profits (50 per cent) and more expensive Private Label (75 per cent). Twenty-five per cent even think Private Label is innovative as a brand!

In the United States the comments are equally revealing.

> Private Labels will work hard to out-innovate brands.
>
> Swedish brand owner
>
> Private Labels increasingly look like a branded item.
>
> US brand owner
>
> Some products require expensive capital, deliver an experience, or require expertise that requires investment that might take away from retailers' core competencies.
>
> US brand owner

The last comment is perhaps wishful thinking – in an increasingly difficult world.

9 The retailer perspective

Finally the retailers!

The view from the retailer's side of the fence is a lot more difficult to fathom. In fact, out of the hundreds of invitations we sent out to retailers to participate in the research across the world, only six actually agreed and participated. Now the wall of silence seriously starts to descend. And in fact in Sweden it's complete. Despite repeated attempts, no Swedish retailer wanted to offer an opinion of any sort. This either means they have no thoughts or that their thoughts are not ones they want to repeat, at least publicly. We suspect the latter. The market for Sweden looks set for a rough ride in future years if this silence is any indication. We start with the fact that the two largest developed countries that we surveyed, the UK and the United States, clearly do not see Private Label becoming less important in the future. In fact, clearly the opposite – 100 per cent of respondents in the United States clearly thought so.

> My business is understanding how in-store communications affect shopper behaviour. As shoppers move through different categories in-store, the information that is relevant, useful or interesting to them changes. The dynamism in Private Label products (eg Tesco Finest), especially in categories like chilled and frozen, is changing shoppers' expectations of the category, and therefore the type of information that will influence their purchasing behaviour.
>
> UK retailer

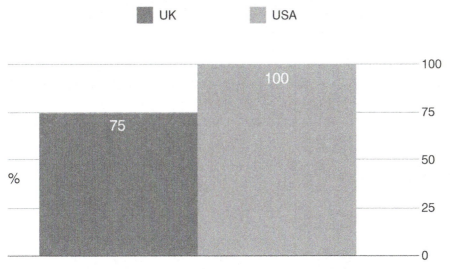

% retailers who think PL will become more important to their business

Figure 9.1 Private Label importance
Source: S&S X report

When you ask retailers why people choose Private Label, apart from price and quality, they tend to focus on packaging and trust. The trust reference is particularly interesting as this is the very essence of a brand – and the very territory they can least afford to lose ground in. If brand owners want to get really alarmed, Figure 9.2 should do a good job! It's admittedly from a small sample size. But the results are somewhat consistent... to put it mildly. Clearly the Private Label phenomenon, from a retailer perspective, isn't about to go away any time soon. If brands want to hide their head in the sand... so be it. The UK in particular is very specific, with 100 per cent of respondents generally agreeing with our statements of future expectations. One hundred per cent of UK retailers say it's growing, profitable, has no limits and could potentially fill our stores. The United States isn't far behind. These results agree with our own unpublishable (ie they wouldn't give permission) conversations from many retailers in these parts of the world.

	UK	USA
PL is growing	100	100
in the future there will be more premium PL	100	100
PL is an important source of profitability to our business	100	75
in the future PL could be more expensive than a brand	100	100
there are no limitations as to what product can become PL	100	50
PL is as innovative as a brand in terms of its shopper offer	100	100
in the future you can imagine your store as PL only	100	–
we will promote more PL in the future	75	75

% retailers who agree/slightly agree

Figure 9.2 Retailers opinions
Source: S&S X report

Private Label initiatives such as Tesco Finest and Sainsbury's Taste the Difference, built on the growing bond between the retailer brand and their customers, is the key driver of this change.

UK retailer

Trust, packaging, quality, taste and price.

UK retailer

'Trust', of course, is the very essence of a brand and with obsessive commitment towards customer service, convenience and increasingly community and sustainability issues, the trust gap between Private Label and manufacturer brands is getting smaller and smaller. ASDA in the UK, for instance, has just announced its new range of organic ready meals for kids in the UK and Ireland. But fundamentally, one of the key differences between the way brands and retailers view Private Label, and perhaps why Private Label is proving so successful, is that retailers understand what their shoppers actually want and how they behave. Tesco has built its business from the bottom up on Club card data.

As traditional brand loyalty swings increasingly over to the retailer and the role of the manufacturer brand in the category mix is beginning to change, brand owners are only just beginning to realize what retailers have known for years: that supermarket shoppers don't buy brands so much anymore. They buy solutions.

> The dynamism in private label products (eg Tesco Finest), especially in categories like chilled and frozen, is changing shoppers' expectations of the category, and therefore the type of information that will influence their purchasing behaviour.
>
> UK retailer

Retailers envisage greater innovation and more premium Private Label that responds to an ever-wider range of shopper needs, from organic to healthy, locally grown to ethically responsible. Absolute commitment to authenticity, convenience and accountability is now very much top of the corporate agenda.

10 The overall perspective

We agree to disagree

Our snapshot has clearly shown that Private Label dominates our lives (Figure 10.1), whether we be a shopper, manufacturer or retailer. However, while shoppers and retailers see a brighter Private Label future, brand owners are increasingly failing to meet the challenges this phenomenon represents. We need to turn this dominance into a realizable business opportunity – for all parties concerned. It seems that in some ways shoppers understand the Private Label phenomenon best, brands the least, and retailers often don't want to talk about it anyway! The Private Label phenomenon is here and thriving, and not going away. And the opportunity cost is getting larger.

Part 2 research summary: key points

Shoppers

- There's an overwhelming and increasing preference to buy Private Label products. The buying of Private Label increasingly dictates consumer choice, with many mass retailers now selling half the value of their products as Private Label to today's shoppers, with ambitions to sell even more. In volume terms that can mean two out of three purchases.
- People buy for all sorts of reasons as well as price.

	UK retailer	UK brand owner	UK shopper	US retailer	US brand owner	US shopper
in the future there will be more premium PL	100	100	76	100	85	78
there are no limits to what PL can become	100	75	87	50	29	73
in the future PL could be more expensive than a brand	100	75	27	100	100	26
PL is as innovative as a brand in terms of its shopper offer	100	25	54	100	29	53

% who agree/slightly agree

Figure 10.1   All three party views
Source: S&S X report

- Private Label/brand parity is almost here. Nine out of 10 shoppers worldwide see Private Label as good or fairly good value compared to brands. In fact, in the UK parity has arrived, with shoppers claiming they see equal quality across multiple categories. That inevitably means that Private Label is already a well-established and trusted consumer choice.
- Private Label is becoming a universal phenomenon across all categories, from FMCG to consumer electronics. Shoppers see no limits to this phenomenon.

> With large items, I prefer a name I know I can trust but I might consider buying Private Label.
>
> UK electronics shopper

- The future looks very bright, with shoppers seeing Private Label with more innovation, more premium products, higher prices and growing penetration from a shopper's perspective. Shoppers also believe that:
  - In the future there are seen to be few limits as to which products can become Private Label.
  - In the future there will be more premium-type Private Label products that could be more expensive than a brand.
  - In the future Private Label will be as innovative as brands and may be sold exclusively.

Brand owners

- They're happy to talk about it... confidentially!
- All markets feel under pressure from Private Label. The UK is the market where brands feel most under pressure. In fact 100 per cent of respondents see it as threat to their business.

> A large number of Private Label products have entered the market over the last few years and they have drastically increased their market share.
>
> US brand owner

- There is a clear difference in the perception of why shoppers buy Private Label. It seems brand owners have a different perspective on reality.
- Imagery and innovation are seen as the way to compete. But shouldn't they be doing that anyway!
- The future looks bleak, from increasing Private Label penetration to expanding category penetration.
- The future for brands competitively looks difficult. This is particularly so in the UK, which records some of the more extreme numbers. The UK brand owners see no limits to Private Label (75 per cent), more damage to their future profits (50 per cent) and more expensive Private Label (75 per cent); 25 per cent have even come to think that Private Label is as innovative as a brand!
- As traditional brand loyalty swings increasingly over to the retailer, the role of the manufacturer brand in the category mix is beginning

to change and brand owners are only just beginning to realize what retailers have known for years: that supermarket shoppers don't buy brands so much anymore. They buy solutions.

Retailers

- Not everyone was forthcoming, especially in the UK and Sweden!
- When you ask retailers why people choose Private Label, apart from price and quality, they tend to focus on packaging and trust. The trust reference is particularly interesting as this is the very essence of a brand. It is no longer guaranteed.
- Retailers see an increasingly dominated Private Label world, with 100 per cent of UK retailers saying it's growing, profitable, has no limits and could potentially fill our stores. The United States isn't far behind.
- The dynamism in Private Label products (eg Tesco Finest), especially in categories like chilled and frozen, is changing shoppers' expectations of the category, and therefore the type of information that will influence their purchasing behaviour.
- They envisage greater innovation and more premium Private Label that responds to an ever-wider range of shopper needs, from organic to healthy, locally grown to ethically responsible. Absolute commitment to authenticity, convenience and accountability is now very much top of the corporate agenda.

> Welcome every problem as an opportunity. Each moment is the great challenge, the best thing that ever happened to you. The more difficult the problem, the greater the challenge in working it out.
>
> Grace Speare

The full Saatchi & Saatchi X Private Label research report is also available to purchase direct. For more information about the research and/or the Joint Value Innovation workshops to help you deal with Private Label, contact Keith Lincoln, co-author of the book *Private Label*, or Phil White, Planning Director, Saatchi & Saatchi X (klincoln.retailization@gmail.com; phil.white@saatchix.co.uk).

Part 3

Retailizing the brand opportunity

Here we show brand owners how to fully realize the brand opportunity that the growing Private Label threat has given you. In essence, retailizing your brand. We have developed a wheel of opportunity based on the 10 principles which we take you around in order for you to find the actionable opportunities for your brands and your retail efforts.

Private Label sales grew globally by 150 per cent more than brands in 2005.

11 For every threat there's an opportunity

Back to spiffing!

We're repeating this quote from our first book as we believe it to be more relevant than ever and particularly so when we discuss the subject of Private Label. Brands and retailers should embrace the opportunity that Private Label represents and stop getting obsessed about theoretical threats and destructive wars which serve no one, least of all the customer. Private Label is here to stay. Make the most of it.

FOR EVERY THREAT THERE'S AN OPPORTUNITY

We'd like to quote from Lew Pringle, one of the architects of modern-day advertising, now retired, who was responsible in his days at BBDO Worldwide for developing a large number of the proprietary research methodologies that have helped explain the effect of advertising over the years:

> Ceding control to the retailer has gone on far longer than 20 years. It was evident in the 60s and we all railed against it. It started the first day the first brand manager spiffed his way onto his first shelf – rather than FORCING his way on with consumer muscle. Even the P&G's bought sales at the end of the year with spiff money. Each of

the dollars was better spent on behalf of the brand – in a long term calculus. It nevertheless was SPENT – for less return – on short term performance. This increased the power of the retailer over the brand.

And a cumulation of short terms has become the long term. In my opinion it's INATTENTION to these basics on the part of brand managers and brands that have thrown the game to the retailers. The retailers, on the other hand, DID their homework. They knew what they were selling and who they were selling it to.

Let's go back to some of those basics now and start paying more attention. Let's avoid the INATTENTIONS of the past. Let's be truly attentive as we tune into the future.

Redefining the brand

> A product is something that is made in a factory; a brand is something that is bought by a customer. The products can be copied by a competitor; the brand is unique. A brand can be quickly outdated; a successful brand is timeless.
>
> King in 1990

The first of those basics we need to return to is the brand. Maybe we need to review the classic definition to take account of the private brands of today. When you think about it, retail brands are now nearer to this definition than manufacturer brands, which have become further and further away from the real customer – the shopper. If retail brands become increasingly unique they have a real chance to become the champions of brands: the new brand leaders – the new timeless winners.

Our attention should start by re-examining the basic nature of a brand. If we look at a classic definition of brands classified on a strategic basis, we come up with an interesting grid (De Chertanoy and Macdonald, 1998). In this grid (Figure 11.1) the power brand is seen as the ultimate goal when creating a brand. This is where most of the 'old and famous' brands of today believe they are. High cost, high price, high value... brands you can trust.

	low relative cost	high relative cost
high value added advantage	benefits brand	power brand
low value added advantage	commodity	productivity

Figure 11.1   Brand advantage vs brand cost

The problem for most of the old and famous brands today is that they have lost some of their trustworthiness – customers do not feel they are given enough value for their money and new actors such as retailers increasingly offer brands that do. Brands will either regain some of that trust or cease to be. It was the core of their souls and the fact that it is eroding in today's society is of extreme worry for manufacturers. As our research just showed, parity has gone or is going. We suspect trust is not too far behind. Brand trust is simply eroding away:

- eroding because it's so difficult to get your message across;
- eroding because the 'shopper' is back in charge;
- eroding because choice avalanches have often led to market blandness and increasingly ignorable brands;
- eroding because retailers increasingly believe they can do their own thing, in their own way;
- eroding because the brand has lost some of its emotional appeal.

There is a strong argument that the power brand of tomorrow will be a Private Label one. Private Labels are increasingly premium and increasingly offer value added at least on parity with today's 'power' brands. Consistency is one of the cornerstones of successful branding. This has been understood by the retail chains in the UK in particular.

Loyalty from the brand consumer cannot be bought, it must be earned. There is increasing evidence that the retailers are earning that trust and eroding the traditional brand core. Once it's gone it will be very hard to win back.

Even today you see brands unthinkingly adding to this position. Mars in May 2007 in the UK decided to change the vegetable extract ingredients in their chocolate bars to animal ones. We don't know who let this happen. But clearly they weren't concerned about brand trust. Not surprisingly, the vegetarians of the UK became very upset, and very vocal. Hundreds of complaints were received and the press had a field day, noting that Mars had decided to feed vegetarians animal ingredients. To their credit Mars did a complete volte face, apologized unreservedly for their mistake and reversed it.

So what does the future hold for your brands? And how do they compete? BUT before you compete you need to know your competition better.

Better understanding the threat

There's a multitude of analyses of the various forms of Private Label which somewhat overcomplicate the obvious. It's an area we could well accuse of academic over-segmentation. When you boil it down, however, it comes down to three forms of Private Label out there. By clearly knowing those forms we can more clearly develop strategies against them. Those three forms are:

* retailer commodity brands;
* retailer copy brands;
* retailer premium brands.

Let's take them one by one.

Retailer commodity brands are the cheap generic variants of brands with which retailers started the Private Label revolution and which almost died away to re-emerge again today. They are high-volume, low-margin, low-profit brands for retailers. Even retailers question their value. Why does a brand even bother to worry about them? If they think they are their competition, maybe they should be reassessing the business they're really in. Arguably it isn't the branded one!

Retailer copy brands are the copycat brands that mimic your brands to death at a lower cost. Copycat brands are all about transferring profit and revenue from the brands to the retailers. They account for one out of two Private Label brands. These are the brands that understand there is no such thing as a product lead and less and less of an image lead. These are brands that range from Tesco's value offerings to high-street retailers offering their own unique value propositions, like Zara and H&M. Zara in particular is a brand that through its 'fast fashion strategy' is literally copying ideas wherever it can find them, as fast as it can. We explained this in detail in our case study in our last book, *How to Succeed at Retail*. Zara is known as the master of spotting new fashion trends and being able to translate them into products that are affordable phenomenally fast and place them into an environment that's conducive to selling fashionable products at a price that is very mass market. It has established extremely efficient internal systems for bringing products to market at speeds the competition can only dream of. Zara has made a virtue of short response times. Zara's speed from idea to store is extremely impressive, the objective being to ensure that the stores carry the clothes the shoppers want at the exact time they want them. Zara prides itself on the fact that, within 30 days from iden-tifying a trend, it can have the clothes on the racks, leaving the competitors confused and playing catch-up. Zara excels at an impressive game of being at the forefront of fashion trends, a game that secures better margins and continuous sale(s). Zara's large design teams are constantly busy playing the trend-spotting game, churning out more than 1,000 new styles every month. Luckily they are not working entirely on their own. Zara has an insane drive for involving everyone in the trend game, with the goal of staying ahead.

Zara and retail brands like H&M also show us a very important point when it comes to how you spend your communications money. Neither brand spends much above the line on mass communications. Instead, they prefer to showcase their products at their retailers, particularly through expensive window displays. Sometimes the simplest approach can be the best. Conventional brands lack this showcasing capability. Maybe they need to find ways to achieve such an objective.

Retailer copy brands are one of the main threats to brands today, as the retailers increasingly derive their profitability from such offerings. It is estimated that almost half of Private Label revenue comes from this area.

Retailer premium brands are the threat of the future. Although there has been a significant expansion in the number of value Private Label lines over recent years, the average price discount to branded goods has remained relatively static in both Europe and the United States. This is because of the parallel development of premium Private Labels. The first example was the UK's Tesco chain with its Finest range, launched in 1998 and now extending to more than 2,000 lines. Sainsbury's followed with its Taste the Difference range in 2000.

Sainsbury's is now the retailer's single largest Private Label sub-brand with annual sales of around £450m across almost 1,000 product lines. In the United States new standards of premium Private Label have been achieved by the rise of specialty supermarket chains such as Trader Joe's, Wegmans, Whole Foods Market and Wild Oats. These have invested heavily in their Private Label offerings in both packaged and fresh foods. The growth of this segment has in turn prompted many traditional supermarkets such as Albertson's to launch their own premium ranges.

The development of tiers of Private Label builds on one of the advantages of Private Label – namely the efficient use of the retailer's brand name in marketing. Investment in retailer brand-building can be leveraged by all the sub-brands in the Private Label range.

	competitive base	% of retail turnover estimates	should brands have a competitive strategy?	traditional competition factors
commodity	price	30	no	nothing
copy	value for money	50	maybe	the best value at the best price
premium	the best in class	20	yes	innovation and class

Figure 11.2   Private label variants

A recent study (McKinsey, 2000) showed that developing a strong brand in the retail industry results in real financial benefits. Why shouldn't it? This is after all the formula that's been applied to brand success for 50 years. Why should a retailer be any different? These are new brands that are aiming to beat the old brands and become brand leaders in their own right. These are the brands that are increasingly priced at a premium position to brands, and these are the brands that effectively differentiate retailers from their retailer competitors – something they're far more interested in than differentiating themselves from brands. This is fast becoming one of the major trends in retailing. They're literally everywhere, from Loblaw's Decadent chocolate chip cookies, which quickly became market leader in Canada after its regional launch, to Wal-Mart's version of the same product called Sam's Choice.

It is clear from the grid shown in Figure 11.2 that the brand needs to compete against two variants in particular: the copy and the premium retailer's. Copy, because this is causing huge margin pressure now. Premium, because this is the future of your brand. If it disappears, long live retail brands. Long live brands.

Traditionally we would compete on value, innovation and image. But we need more.

WE NEED TO REGAIN BRAND TRUST

We will now go on to show you how to regain that trust for yourselves. We will start by identifying the principles we believe are necessary for you to adopt before you can progress.

12 The Private principles

The Private Label Way

One thing in life and business is certain. We are all travelling towards the future at 60 minutes per hour, no matter what we do or who we are. We are all going to arrive there, no matter what. How can we best prepare for it?

> If the future teaches us anything, it's that it hasn't happened yet.
>
> *Fortune*, 'What's next' article, 5 February 2007

The above has held true over the years and helps explain why visions of the future look so futuristic, and often unbelievable. Ours hopefully will look real. Whether you're a conventional brand or a traditional retailer, the one thing we all can and need to prepare for is the increasing role Private Label will play in our business lives. This is not a phenomenon that's going to go away – in fact the complete opposite. It will grow and grow, and particularly at the premium end where real margins can be achieved. Our first book, *Retailization*, talked at length about the difficulty companies face in achieving sales today. Achieving sales has become an ever more difficult task in today's world as brands are increasingly squeezed by retailer power, Private Label growth, media fragmentation and shoppers' demands. The second of these squeezes, Private Label, is, however, a squeeze that never seems to become any less tight. Brands can only really fight that squeeze by reconnecting to their shoppers with relevant new, actionable insights that constantly change their shoppers into buyers; that turn a threat into an opportunity; that allow you to **retailize** your brand, ie connect shoppers to your brands through the power of retail thinking.

Brands and retailers need to use these squeezes to maximize their strategic advantages. They don't want or need to fight wars that neither side will win. They need to fight battles that they can influence and potentially win. The war will be won or, as we prefer to say, the armistice will be signed when four specific battles are played out:

- retailer power into cooperative power;
- media fragmentation into directed, targeted communications;
- consumer atrophy into shopper power;
- Private Label threat into Private Label opportunity.

To help you (retailers and brands) we have identified 10 principles – 10 commitments in essence – which we believe can guide your thinking and actions when it comes to the subject of Private Label. We call this The Private Label Way. We're not pretending these principles are a Pandora's box to guaranteed success. In fact there is no silver-bullet formula. We do, however, believe that by looking at the 10 principles that make up The Private Label Way you can get that little bit nearer. And that little bit more successful. And that little bit more obsessed.

As we said in the Introduction, you must literally make the growth of Private Label one of the single biggest issues in your business. You need to be radical and very creative in your approach. The conventional approaches recommended so far, essentially by the academic and research community, are frankly in our view not anywhere near progressive enough. Changing your pricing strategy, doing a few more innovations and promotions is not going to change your business to the significant degree you need to. Reinventing the way you approach Private Label, the way your organization sees it and the way you deal with it, are the important first steps you will need to move you forward. Private Label is often treated as an academic subject. Academic this subject can be, but maybe it shouldn't be.

Organizations around the world are increasingly aware of the power of Private Label. But, simply put, they do not know how to deal with it. One of us remembers when he was a brand manger for Maxwell House nearly 25 years ago. At the time he had the biggest advertising and below the line budget in the UK and was about to meet the chief buyer at ASDA, the third biggest UK retailer. The meeting was in his view a farce and extremely demeaning. He was told what was going to happen as far as sales of his brand were concerned and he wasn't even allowed a point of view. ASDA wanted to encourage sales of their Private Label as their first priority. He left the marketing industry soon after, deciding there were better ways to lead a life.

We have to move beyond the theory to the practice. Find practically and creatively inspired new directions. Your reward for dealing with the issue is the ultimate reward for any brand... customer loyalty. Loyalty means sustained sales. Loyalty means growth. Loyalty means a future. We are living in a world where everyone searches for the next sale. Make sure that next sale is yours. And the next one. Let us help you through The Private Label Way... to realize the full retail potential of your brands, people, company and suppliers.

We hope these principles become more and more apparent the more you read, whether you're a brand or a retailer.

The 10 principles

1. Running the risk and living the reality.
2. Retailize and be radical.
3. Tomorrow's global, social and environmental issues are your opportunities today.
4. Educate, navigate and inspire.
5. Winning 'mind shelf' is the name of the game.
6. Innovate, imagineer and involve.
7. Restore and reinvent the store.
8. Catalyse your communications and brand from till to TV.
9. Collaborate and cooperate through co-opetition.
10. Shopper solutions steal share of wallet.

13 Private principle 1: Running the risk and living the reality

Here we look at the need for organizations to truly come to grips with the Private Label phenomenon and stop hiding their heads in the sand. Only then will they develop the proactive steps needed to, in some cases, guarantee their survival. The world is becoming essentially a private one... not a branded one. Private is the natural state and if you can't beat it, join it.

> In the middle of difficulty lies opportunity.
>
> Albert Einstein (1879–1955)

Headlines

- The increasing search for convenience and economy by today's knowledgeable shopper is the real reason for the explosive growth of Private Label.
- Retailers are merely supplying that need for their customers as they see best.
- With the increasing relevance of the retailer as a brand, the label has become a brand in its own right.
- This trend is fast becoming a global norm for most categories wherever they are sold.

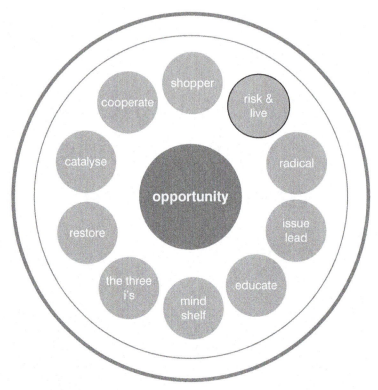

Figure 13.1 Risk and live

- The world is essentially a private one... not a branded one. Private is the natural state. If you can't beat it, join it.

Reorganize to reflect the future, not the past

Given these big issues and the increasing privatization of brands, is there anything positive a brand can do to influence its future directly? To realize the opportunity? **There sure is!**

We will use the retail wheel of opportunity as a systematic way of bringing up the points where we can encourage proactive actions and the realization of opportunities. Starting with **acceptance. Accepting the risk and living the reality.**

We have been so focused on the consumers that we have forgotten our other customer – the retail chains. I think this is typical for most multinational manufacturers of groceries with old strong brands. We work in a traditional way, trying to make the best TV commercials, advertisements etc, but we have realized that retailers are becoming more powerful than ever before. We need to change our focus! We need to change the mentality of the entire organization. This is hard – especially for the older managers. They are not open minded and they are still working in the 60s. The speed is essential and the plans we made three months ago are already too old. Retail chains merge change so fast – and this means multinational strong retail chains. Still, we do not want to become a private-label supplier. So, if we should be able to keep up with another important customer – the retailers – we need to change the way we regard retailers in total. But as long as new marketing managers just learn mass marketing management and traditional brand management – we cannot expect to change this as quickly as we need to.

(Quote from a brand manufacturer in Brussels in the autumn of
1998 (Ossiansson, 2004))

This is a more than 10-year-old quote. But he pretty well hit the nail on the head. We have been so focused on the consumer that sometimes we miss the reality.

It's still amazing to us how little the reality of Private Label is accepted by most brand organizations. As our S&S X research showed, brands seem to be denying the state of Private Label to a large extent. Half of our respondents in the United States and the UK claimed that Private Label wasn't damaging their profitability. We find this somewhat difficult to believe given the pressure on the brands' share positions, yet alone the price pressure. All the evidence to date certainly indicates the opposite. The rise of the premium Private Label is clearly here to stay. It's interesting to note that in the United States, although 85 per cent of respondents felt there would be more premium Private Label in the future, only 48 per cent felt they would be more expensive. Sounds like a contradiction to us.

It should be numero uno on your strategic priorities list. To make it a priority you need to fully understand the nature of the beast and make sure everyone else does too – especially the CEO. Private Label isn't a nuisance you have to deal with occasionally. It isn't a label. It's your number one brand competitor. It's not a threat, unless you become obsessed about thinking like that.

Begin by asking three questions

1. Are top executives focused on this issue?
2. Are they preparing action plans to deal with this increasing threat to their businesses viability?
3. Are they actually doing anything?

If the answer is 'no' to these questions your company is heading for trouble. Fast.

Become PRIVATE CENTRIC

It's time to get serious and consider ways forward – constructive, proactive ways forward. You should start by considering getting rid of some of the archaic structures with which we surround ourselves – structures like sales forces and marketing departments. Reorganize along private lines. Appoint a Private Label director who drives your private strategy, determining how best to compete, determining whether to manufacture and supply. The Private director becomes your most critical communications director internally and externally. Reorganize along issue lines. Have directors of the big issues (more about the big issues in principle 3) who are responsible and accountable for making these things happen.

BEFORE BRANDS CAN BEAT PRIVATE LABELS THEY MUST
RADICALLY CHANGE THEIR MINDSET.
ACCEPT THE NEW REALITY
ACCEPT THEY'RE NOT INFERIOR BRANDS
ACCEPT THEY'RE BRANDS IN THEIR OWN RIGHT
ACCEPT THEY'RE GOOD QUALITY
ACT AS IF THEY'RE YOUR NO 1 COMPETITOR

Some companies are already doing just this. Arla, a major Scandinavian dairy company, to date have enjoyed low levels of Private Label activity in their business sectors. This is a situation unique to Scandinavia as Private Label dairy is the dominant market player in most markets of the world. However, they see the writing on the wall and have decided to appoint senior managers to be responsible for controlling and managing their future Private Label activities, whether it be fighting Private Label or producing it. Private Label has become a number one priority for them, one that increasingly dominates their commercial agenda.

Why the conventional simply isn't good enough

Private Label is one of (if not the) biggest challenges you face and will remain so in the foreseeable future. It is often your biggest single branded competitor and it is controlled by the thing that makes your business possible in the first place – a retail channel. It also increasingly affects accepted shopping behaviour and consumption patterns. The increasing search for convenience and economy by today's knowledgeable shopper is the real reason for the explosive growth of Private Label.

Retailers merely supply their customers as they see best. With the increasing relevance of the retailer as a brand, the label is now very much a brand in its own right. This new powerful brand can account for the majority of your shoppers' purchases in some retailers and is increasingly seen as a near parity quality and value alternative. With retailers increasing communication spend they can potentially outweigh and out-image any conventional brand, leading manufacturers into a vicious spiral of decline.

Unfortunately the normal recommended solutions are not enough. Lower price, improve quality and be more innovative. **It is simply not enough!** This is a challenge that demands the unconventional and exceptional. Rise to that challenge, or else.

Private Label forces you to go back to basics. Forces you to examine the very basic nature of the business you're in and question whether it's good enough to take you forward. Forces you to question your products and the way you sell and to whom. Forces you to question whether you're really tapping into the agents of change. Forces you to question your corporate mission. Finally, question whether you have the right people and structures to deal with this fundamental and growing challenge. Ensure that Private Label is taken into account in all your key decision-meeting forums. Very few of your key company's operational decisions are Private Label independent these days. It should be up there with the financial criteria and other organizational parameters that dictate your operating efficiency. It should become as standard that everyone questions the relevance of their decisions to your ability to deal with Private Label. Yes, you are now running the risk of dealing with this issue head on. But that is the reality of the world today. Failing to deal with it could be disastrous for your long-term future.

Accept doesn't means surrender. It means dealing with reality in a creative, proactive way. There are a multitude of actions you could consider. They start with the CEO, who has a key responsibility to motivate his or her employees and stretch them to achieve their personal best. The CEO must make sure people know that dealing with Private Label is a very key priority. He or she must make them enthusiastic about the task ahead. He or she must make them accept the reality. He or she must set and change the mindset.

Summary and opportunities

It all starts with accepting the situation and the reality. Then you will start to make the right decisions, however radical and risky they are. The world is essentially a private one... not a branded one. Private is the natural state. If you can't beat it, join it:

- Opportunity 1: Become PRIVATE CENTRIC. Significantly change your organizational structure to reflect today's private world. The Private director becomes your most critical communications director internally and externally.
- Opportunity 2: Become PRIVATE ACTIVE. Make all your resolutions for dealing with Private Label proactive ones. The days of being reactive have gone. You need to take the initiative in everything you do.
- Opportunity 3: Make the shopper seek the BRAND PRIVATE OPTION, not a private brand/label option. Make the shopper realize again and again why brands are different and special – and very private to them.

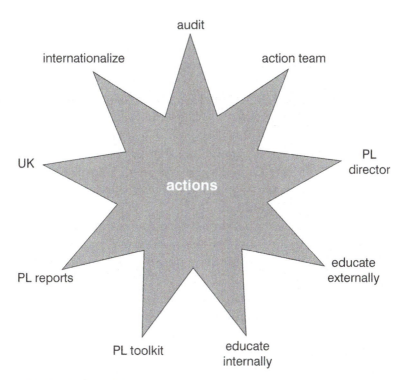

Figure 13.2 Risk and live actions

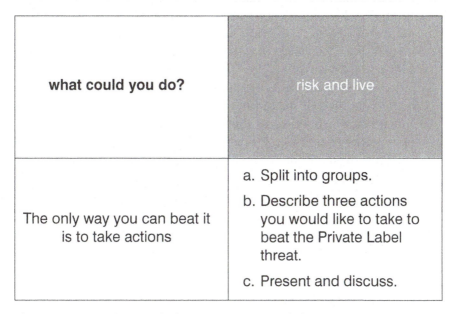

what could you do?	risk and live
The only way you can beat it is to take actions	a. Split into groups. b. Describe three actions you would like to take to beat the Private Label threat. c. Present and discuss.

Figure 13.3 Private Label management workshop exercise

Actions to consider

Here are just a few of the actions that could help:

1. Start by doing a Private Label audit to fully evaluate how well you stack up against your key Private Label competition. What initiatives do you currently take? What initiatives could you take?

2. Form a Private Label action team that has direct responsibility for developing Private Label response strategies. Form action teams to cover individual key accounts and the Private Label strategies you need to succeed with them.

3. Appoint a Private Label director, equivalent in rank to your sales and marketing director, who has operational managerial responsibility for producing proactive opportunities arising from Private Label.

4. Think about the impact of Private Label from an international perspective. It is increasingly a multi-border operation. What you see in one country will soon be in another. Monitor the situation and anticipate it.

5. Go and look closely at the UK market. The future may well be here. Ignore your local excuses and realize that behaviour increasingly travels. Make sure you're ready.

6. Produce a Private Label tool kit which not only explains the true nature of Private Label to your organization (the facts and the myths), but also clearly lays out principles and rules for dealing with it. Make sure that the tool kit is available on the corporate intranet and is used in key training sessions. By knowing the threat better you can only deal with it better.

7. Initiate quarterly Private Label reports to track your organization's operational response to Private Label and the effect it is having on your business. You do it for competitive brands. Why not do it for your biggest competitor?

8. Get employee involvement by asking everyone for ideas that improve your Private Label competitiveness.

9. Set up industry bodies to ensure consumers realize that the brand needs their support more than ever and that brands are simply the best.

10. Above all, accept that Private Label is here today and here to stay.

14 Private principle 2: Retailize and be radical

Here we ask companies to use the power of their brands to fully realize their retail potential – to 'retailize' themselves. That power will only be realized by being radical.

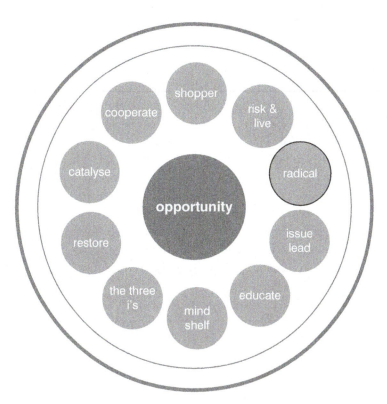

Figure 14.1 Be radical!

Headlines

- We live in radical times where fundamental societal changes are afoot.
- The solutions of today are not the solutions of tomorrow.
- We need radical thinking, radical solutions and radical implementation for tomorrow.
- Radical can be good.
- Radical can be right.
- If you want to be sure of the future, create it yourself.

Avoiding the conventional

You read all the Private Label analysis reports around and what do they do, apart from sending you asleep? Frankly, nothing. A radical revolution has happened. Radical solutions are needed. Solutions along the lines of 'we must improve the quality of our offering' are all very nice. But do they change anything? Not really, if you are honest. Assess your real brand position with respect to Private Label and then take the steps you must take before those steps take you away. Always, always seek radical solutions. You'll need them.

We're very tired of seeing the same old boring solutions proposed again and again... lower price, innovate some more, be nice to them and improve quality. These sorts of solutions are going to take you as far as they have so far. NOWHERE. Simply put, it's a brave new world and it needs brave new solutions, not conventional ones. The chart shown in Figure 14.2 says it all. Look at brand and Private Label behaviour in Germany over the past five years. Guess who's winning? And winning by a mile? Private Label is up 50 per cent and number one brands down 8 per cent. If you're a number two brand, you're down 15 per cent and three or below you're down 30 per cent! There's clearly only one winner here.

It's time to stop. It's time to stop the conventional. It's time to get radical. Or else you simply won't have a business to run.

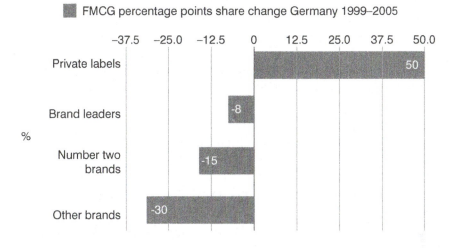

Figure 14.2 The German revolution
Source: GFK

Question the status quo

Always, always turn your thinking on its head. Question the status quo. Let's look at coffee, for example, in a new hypothetical world. If you were thinking and being radical, things could change:

- **Make their Private Label your brand**. Coffee from Nescafé and Tesco. Why is it only coffee from Nescafé or Tesco? What's wrong with Tesco's Nescafé range?
- **Make their best your cheap**. Why can't you produce a very cheap range of the 'finest coffees' from the world and call them yours and compete directly with the likes of Tesco, on price and quality? Make their label yours. This, after all, is exactly what they're seeking to do.
- **Withdraw your range**. When life has become unbearable and non-profitable, make the right decision… retreat. Which brand last had the guts to do that?
- **Distribute everywhere you can**. Get involved in concept stores. Get involved in local markets. Get involved in web selling. Why isn't there a site out there selling just great brands only direct?
- **Sell the right to sell your brand**. Who knows if your brand power is as big as Tesco or Carrefour or Wal-Mart. Maybe you ask the retailers for a fee to sell your brand. That would be a novel concept!

You could even ask them to go back to the good old days when retailers funded the brands' advertising budgets. Get advertising income from retailers and localize it. Sounds like a dream. Maybe or maybe not?

- **Buy a big retailer**. Buy one of the big retailers and make it a value brand retailer. Or even take a stake and a place on their board.

Now you're really beginning to treat Private Label as a brand and react like a brand. Competition is good! It's about time they had some.

Make sure you're not a commodity

You could argue that from a retailer's perspective, manufacturer brands are commodities available at many competing retail chains. By introducing Private Label the retailer differentiates itself from other chains. When you think about this, it is a somewhat ludicrous situation to be in and one that is extremely avoidable. WHY DOESN'T A BRAND PRODUCE RETAILER VARIANTS THAT ENHANCE THE RETAILER AS WELL AS THE BRAND? What's wrong with Tesco Nescafé with that Tesco point of difference? And is it really that difficult to do? With three chains increasingly capturing most retail markets, in Europe at least all you need is three variants – or four because you keep the original. Those three variants should have subtle perceived differences that relate to individual retailers' positionings, but still maintain the overall brand integrity. Maybe the advertising should also reflect the changed strategy.

Imagine an advertising campaign that really hammers out the point of difference. If you're afraid to do it yourself alone, get the other brands to join up with you and do a generic anti-Private Label campaign. Show the shoppers there is a difference when they buy a brand. But make sure you have a real difference first. Advertising puffery has had its day.

Remember the classic Pepsi Coke challenge test of the 1980s? A campaign that asked consumers to choose the best brand in a filmed blind-tasting session? A very successful campaign for Pepsi, as they dared to do it. Actually, at the time they felt they had little choice as Coke was making significant inroads to their business. They needed to be brave. Be radical. Apply that thinking to a Private Label shopper challenge.

Love me do, love me not

You need to learn to potentially love Private Label. Not an easy task for some. Brands traditionally dislike Private Label for some very clear reasons. They are regarded as detrimental to brand strategy; they reduce brand equity and your ability to charge a premium; they can cause conflict with a retailer, as the retailer is both a customer and a competitor. Additionally, they actively encourage retailers to question why such a brand premium exists and they lower retailers' reliance on a particular manufacturer, allowing tougher price negotiations.

While the above is a very good rationale for not loving Private Label, it is clearly going to get worse before it gets better. But this position is now being challenged even more so. Premium segmentation Private Label is offering retailers higher margins and overall Private Label is acting as a powerful catalyst to the lowering of category pricing and setting a ceiling on brand prices. The pace of Private Label growth is attractive and exceeding brand growth by a significant margin. Just look at the history in the UK since 1975 (Figure 14.3).

In turn, this is inducing brand loyalty falls in a price-driven market. Even additional growth from discounters is restricted as they launch more variants of their own.

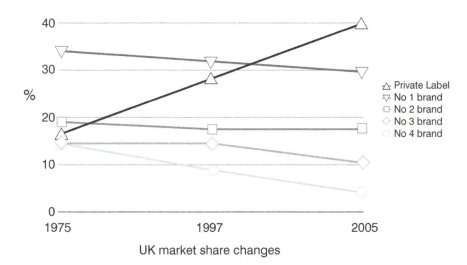

Figure 14.3 UK market history
Source: market share structure/Taylor Nelson Sofres/IGD

These factors are here to stay and you need to view the enemy in a new way, with a new, more balanced perspective. Slowing growth means that all avenues must be explored. Private Label is forcing you to consider new possibilities and opportunities, and particularly the possibility of supplying Private Label direct. At the very least you need to evaluate those possibilities:

- Is this an opportunity to work in close partnership with retailers?
- Could it increase your ability to shape and mould future category development?
- Could it be an effective use of your spare production capacity?
- Could it lead to looking beyond your local focus for regional deals that provide volume?

However, as we indicated earlier, you need to address some key basic questions first. Always ask some basic questions. Will you need dedicated manufacturing facilities? What is your supply guarantee? You MUST be the lowest-cost provider. Are you?

To supply or not?

Of course, you always have the option to join the success and become a supplier. But that success may not be as gainable as it might first appear. The reasons to supply are fourfold. Here are some reasons they don't make sense:

1. **Utilizes spare capacity.** One of the most often cited reasons is the need to mop up capacity. However, if you were honest, is the utilization of this spare capacity profitable or not? There is considerable evidence that producing Private Label lowers your overall margins – hardly good business sense or maximizing shareholder value. If your competitive brands want to lower their margins, let them. Don't commit business suicide first.

    A recent study on a US company proved that it would have to sell four units of Private Label to make as much money as selling one unit of a branded product (Kumar and Steenkamp, 2007). Apart from not making much sense, it's a good way to commit economic suicide. Now this isn't clearly the case all the time and there may be cases where it makes sense. But be very careful before you venture too far.

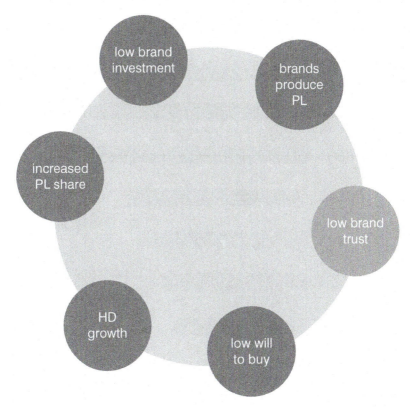

Figure 14.4   The vicious circle

2. **Strengthens relationships with key distributors.** What a load of
   baloney! There is absolutely no evidence that by supplying a retail
   brand you will be treated better. In reality the opposite is probably
   true. You lose respect and negotiating power, let alone your technology, formulations and innovations. If you're the best, why on
   earth would you want to give it away?
3. **Stops key competitors doing it**. Frankly, given what we just said,
   you should be encouraging them!
4. **Greater purchasing power vis-à-vis its suppliers**. Enough said
   already. The reality is you are more likely to enter a vicious cycle of
   manufacturing decline. See Figure 14.4 for the extent of that
   decline.

Never forget...

Brand power = Market power

Market power today = Retailer power = Retail brands

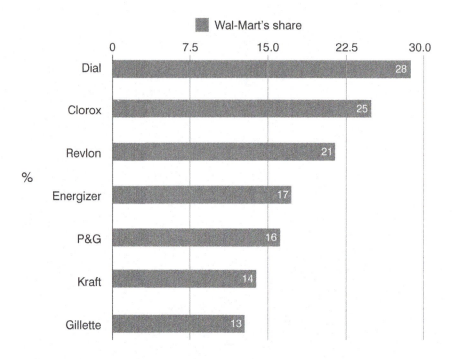

Figure 14.5   The Wal-Mart revenue dependence
Source: company account estimates

The equation has changed; brand power has been replaced by retailer power. The top 10 retailers typically account for 30 to 45 per cent of an FMCG company's worldwide sales. And in the case of Dial, the top 10 retail customers account for 57 per cent of its sales (Figure 14.5). This, however, does not show the real extent of the problem. When it gets down to local level it can be a nightmare, particularly so in Europe where retailers are so concentrated. Take Sweden, where one retailer has a 50+ per cent share (ICA). How do you negotiate when half the market is one player? Frankly you don't, as a recent article published in the *Daagens Industrial* made clear, when the CEO of ICA said it was the brands' job to become more and more efficient and they should stop complaining so much! A recent UK Monopolies Commission highlight report suggested that squeezing retailers isn't such a bad thing if consumers get a good deal. And you think you can be conservative?

So where does that leave us? We can determine a few basic rules to guide us and that we should check ourselves against:

1. Private Label is not for followers who are stuck in the middle. If you are a company with a weak brand, make a choice: be a committed Private Label producer or really grow your brand.
2. Private Label production is to be avoided in commodity markets, unless you seriously want to lose money.
3. If you're going to produce Private Label, ensure you differentiate your brands and Private Label... differently.
4. Select the right retail partners – ones who respect you.

Also ask yourself some basic questions before moving to Private Label production:

- Do you want to work with the trade?
- Does it match your company vision?
- What areas do you want to produce in?
- Can you select the right trade partners?

Two possible routes will emerge from this self-questioning:

1. **Not at all.** You have unique products with defendable innovations.
2. **Go all the way** and make a committed strategic choice.

Cut the tail

The impact of Private Label is clear. Review the efficiency of your product portfolio – cut 'the tail' before the retailer does. Stop being obsessed with adding shelf space. Make sure the shelf space you've got delivers that maximum profit for you and the retailer. If it doesn't, find a different shelf. Work out the shelf space required to really sell your brand. The branded assortment may reduce. Your effectiveness won't. Make sure you have a clear rationale for each product. If you don't find one, discontinue. Change the pricing architecture of the category to reflect your new more effective brand. Category management skills become essential and key to demonstrating your rationale.

Develop a brand price architecture

For mass market supermarkets the obvious strategy for competing with value-focused retailers and, in the case of the United States, premium specialty chains is to adopt a series of Private Labels at different price points. The option of developing a brand architecture around price is equally open to brands. In particular, value brands are an underexploited area. Introducing such a brand into a portfolio helps to capture a wider range of consumer spending.

Rolling out a value brand has another important benefit: it ensures that the existing premium brands within a portfolio are further distanced from the low-price end, serving to protect their premium image. Producers who have such diversified portfolios are better insulated against the long-term changes in a market and can protect their premium products with the use of more selective distribution.

In the United States, the Proctor & Gamble brand has launched Charmin – a basic sub-brand which will appeal to Private Label and value retail shoppers alike. Such value lines should be designed and marketed to appeal to the heaviest consumers of Private Label (lower-income households and families, particularly new and larger ones). This might mean larger pack sizes and marketing copy that talks about

brand	strategy
brand 1	Retain brand leadership and ideally extend share gap against the number two branded player.
brand 1/2	Private Label may be a viable consideration (or may supplement your existing production) – how strong are your existing growth plans? Are your competitors outpacing you?
brand 3/4	Private Label should be stongly considered or a comprehensive 'turnaround' strategy put in place – or you may be forced to exit the category. Do you have a unique niche to focus on instead?

Figure 14.6   In or out

issues of safety and reliability – particularly important for the new and young family segments.

Decide if you are 'in' or 'out'

Private Label is here to stay – formulate your response. It almost doesn't matter what it is. Any response is better than none. Figure 14.6 shows a few responses, depending on your market position. You'll note that we are saying that if you're number three or four, get out. If you're number two, think again. The future for most FMCG categories is one brand leader and one premium-led Private Label. Be sure you're the brand leader.

Prove you still have a role

Finally, this is an opportunity to ask yourself whether your brands really work. You need to re-examine your brands' role. Ask yourself, is there is still a role for brands? If there is, exploit those roles to their fullest. Does your brand truly meet needs like the ones below?

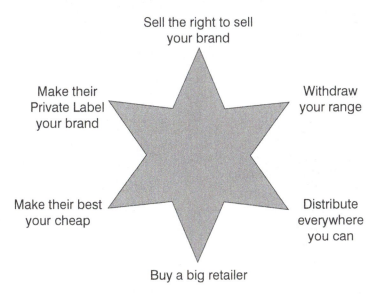

Figure 14.7 Actions

- Consumers may require assurance of quality. Do you consistently provide it vis-à-vis Private Label?
- Many products have strong historical brand equity. Is it still working for you in the way it did?
- Retailers need 'traffic builders'. Are your brands strong enough for such a role?
- Brands act as category signposts. Does your brand stand out enough to be such a signpost?
- Brands add innovation and excitement in store. Are you?

Summary and opportunities

Most companies are inherently conservative. They simply don't like change. However, you may have little choice, particularly if you're number two or lower in the brand hierarchy. You need to radically investigate the parameters of your business, from assessing whether you really do meet consumer needs to whether you are producing products in the most efficient way to how and where you should sell.

So are you in or out? Are you thinking radically enough to survive? You'll need to be!

get moving!	radical
We need radical thinking, radical solutions and radical implementation for tomorrow.	a. Split into groups. b. Come up with two very radical ideas for dealing with PL. c. Present and discuss.

Figure 14.8   Private Label management workshop exercise

- Opportunity 4: Make your brand a RADICAL BRAND. Start thinking completely out of the box about solutions. Write a list of 10 radical things you can do to beat Private Label.
- Opportunity 5: COPY THE COPYCATS. Produce products that mimic the Private Labels, but provide better value.
- Opportunity 6: Become a MULTI-FORMAT BRAND SELLER. Explore every distribution option out there, from the web to local. Explode your options. More about this later.
- Opportunity 7: If you can't beat them, BUY THEM. Retailers are a cheap investment. At the very least, buy a significant share of their shares and get on their board. You might be surprised to see how their attitude changes. Overnight.

Actions to consider

1. Sit down and have some extreme brainstorming sessions.
2. Nothing's not considered, however bizarre.
3. In fact, the more bizarre the better.
4. Involve your agencies.
5. Analyse your dependence on retailers.
6. Write a list of 10 radical things you can do to beat Private Label.
7. Investigate radical ways to change your distribution model and give you real future options.
8. Investigate radical ways to grow consumer loyalty.

15 Private principle 3: Tomorrow's global, social and environmental issues are your opportunities today

Here we look to the future – there are clearly a number of key global issues radically shaping our society today.

> Next to knowing when to seize an opportunity, the most important thing in life is to know when to forego an advantage.
>
> Benjamin Disraeli (1804–81)

Headlines

- There are clearly a number of key global issues radically shaping our society today.
- They will equally radically shape the role of the retailer, resulting in new ways to communicate, present and sell our products.
- Brands and retailers must embrace these changes to avoid stagnation.
- They're permanent, very influential and equally they're counter to a lot of today's accepted practices.
- Failure to change will lead to change being thrust upon you.

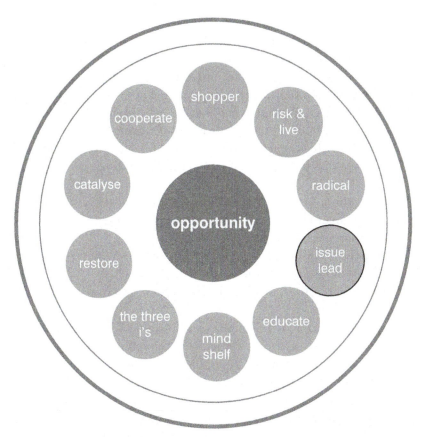

Figure 15.1   Lead the big issues

Trusting in the future

Grasp the 'real' future. The future gives us a very strong clue about where and how we can regain that trust – the trust we need to reinforce and re-establish our brands in our shoppers' minds. Maybe by knowing our future better we can better appreciate the real future of Private Label and therefore brands, and particularly by knowing the real future – not just a possible scenario. Stop, you say! We're not fortune tellers. But stop, we say. The 'real' future is staring you in the face today. You're already putting your toes in it.

What you're not doing is embracing it, putting your whole body in it. This is as clear a future prediction as there is likely to be as the world changes before our eyes and affects us now, tomorrow and for the next 50 years. Apart from the Industrial Revolution, there has never been a more blatant revolution happening around us. That revolution, of course, is the health revolution, and it's not just health, but all the macro global factors that contribute to its never-ending impact. It's a life revolution. It's a trend that is not only at its tipping point... but it's already well and truly tipped. And it will continue tipping for many decades to come. Its impact is a daily one, and it will impact us all every day for many years to come. This is the trend that didn't go away:

- We are getting more and more obese pretty well everywhere.
- We live in an era where our children uniquely have lower life expectations than ours.
- Many people believe that the world is getting warmer and warmer and more dangerous by the day.
- The daily rubbish we produce is in danger of burying us.

What has this got to do with retailers and brands? Well, the answer is a lot. The answer is almost everything. Ask yourself, have you genuinely tipped with the trend? You're the engines of consumption and demand and the world has over-consumed itself to near death. You are as responsible as anyone, and arguably more so, for some of these issues. You have a social, moral and business responsibility to embrace this way of life wholeheartedly, this life revolution. When it comes to these issues you should be **trusted** by consumers. To date there is little evidence that you are.

Fact 1: People get more obese on the whole because we've fed them too many over-processed, low-nutrition foods (but high margin), especially since the Second World War. We can have an extensive scientific debate on the subject, but the reality stays the same. There is considerable evidence that the countries with the highest levels of obesity generally have the highest levels of processed food, ie the UK and the United States. Coincidence?

Fact 2: The short-term profit obsession of retailers and brands has been at the long-term cost to society. Can we put our hands on our hearts and say all our product developments have been for the good of mankind? It's almost as boring as listening to the likes of Shell and BP continuously telling us how good they are for the environment, just before the next leak or explosion. Food and consumer goods have a positive and negative side. It's time to accentuate the positive. But to accentuate it, you must live it.

Fact 3: The production and selling of goods produces most of the waste of the modern world. It's our responsibility to control it and eliminate it whenever we can.

Fact 4: Control it before you're controlled. Unfortunately for brands and retailers, these issues have become political no-brainers. Now that the 'nasty' tobacco and alcoholic drinks companies are under increasingly political 'democratic' control, it's time for the big one – food. These issues are no longer quirky niche issues run by green warriors and Greenpeace campaigners. They're mainstream election winners. You just have to look at the rebirth of Al Gore to see this. Or will it be President Gore one day?

Greenwashing versus realizing the big issues

Greenwashing has become the new business philosophy. If we appear to be actually doing something, people will feel good about us. This boils down to companies telling us what we want to hear versus companies telling us what we need to hear. Just look at all the rubbish the oil companies have told us about their green credentials in recent years. Well, the proof is in the pudding and if BP's recent history is anything to go by, they'd have been better off saying nothing. The reality is that these big issues aren't part-time commitments. They're full-time changes in behaviour – changes that shoppers increasingly seek and demand as part of their shopping experience.

It is clear that there are a number of fundamental changes afoot in the world today that will increasingly impact the very nature of the business we do and the lives we all lead. It's not that complicated to understand the things that drive us and our futures. Just read the papers. Although you might not like what they say, they do tend to capture the issues we're really concerned about, because that's what sells them, because that's what we like to hear. Those issues aren't rocket science, although a lot of people are pretending they are.

It is our opinion that, with very few exceptions, most companies (brands and retailers) pander to the truth and the reality of the way the world is changing. They believe that token gestures are enough to convince consumers they're truly responsible. But by being partly responsible they are actually irresponsible. You have to eat the cake of healthy living, not just pick up the crumbs.

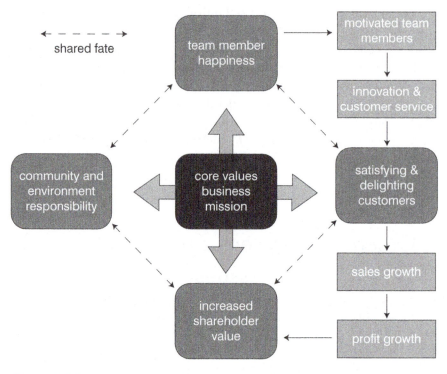

Figure 15.2   Innocent new business paradigm

And it can be done. Look at **Innocent** – a UK smoothies brand that's come from nowhere to be a major food brand – a brand that produces what it preaches. Innocent has always been in the ethics game – long before it became commercially desirable.

Recently the company published a book called *Stay Healthy. Be Lazy.* Consistent with its overall voice, the book sets an honest straight-forward tone. 'Are you lazy?' asks the book. 'Great, that makes two of us. But that shouldn't stop us from being healthy. By incorporating a few of the simple habits contained in the book, you can live a contented, healthy life whilst still having enough time to be lazy and eat the odd plate of chips.'

The simple, friendly approach translates across key brand touch-points. The company's unique 'cow vans', complete with horns, eyelashes, udders and a tail, are assigned personalities and even biogra-phies. The product packaging is also a clever representation of the brand. Unlike its fellow beverages, Innocent is simple and rather muted. The bottle is clear, with a simple product information band in one colour. The product stands out precisely because it is so different from the other loudly colourful beverages on the shelf. When a product has become a retail success it's important to stick to your roots and preserve what you were and what you meant to be.

Finally, it's important to note that this maverick brand gets shelf presence. Go into a typical in city Sainsbury's in the UK and next to the multiple Sainsbury's Private Label offerings you'll find only one brand... Innocent. Proof if you need it. **Issues work.** And work they will internationally, as Innocent expands into Europe, starting in France and Sweden.

Look at **WFM –Whole Food Market** – consistently voted as the world's best retailer. Why? Because they give shoppers what they want – an unparalleled choice of healthy fruit and vegetables, imaginatively presented. Founded in 1980 as one small store in Austin, Texas, Whole Foods Market is now the world's leading retailer of natural and organic foods, with 189 stores in North America and the UK. To date, Whole Foods Market remains driven by a very single-minded mission: 'We're highly selective about what we sell, dedicated to stringent Quality Standards, and committed to sustainable agriculture.'

They go on to say that they believe in a virtuous circle entwining the food chain, human beings and Mother Earth: each is reliant upon the others through a beautiful and delicate symbiosis. Nice words, and it seems they practise them. It's hard to find fault with Whole Foods, the supermarket chain that has made a fortune by transforming grocery shopping into a bright and shiny, progressive experience. Indeed, the road to wild profits and cultural cachet has been surprisingly smooth for the supermarket chain. It gets mostly sympathetic coverage in the local and national media and red-carpet treatment from the communities it enters.

> There's no inherent reason why business cannot be ethical, socially responsible, and profitable.
>
> John Mackey, the company's chairman

Under the umbrella creed of 'sustainability', Whole Foods pays its workers a solid living wage – its lowest earners on average $13.15 an hour – with excellent benefits and health care. No executive makes more than 14 times the employee average. (Mackey's salary in 2005 was

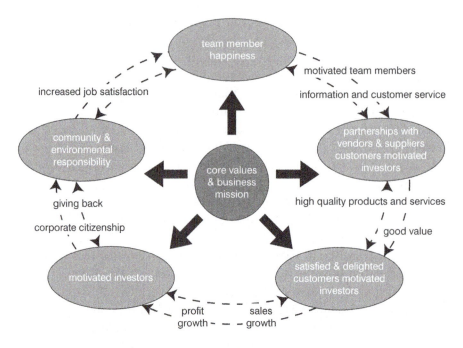

Figure 15.3   WFM conscious capitalism

$342,000.) In January 2006, Whole Foods announced that it had committed to buy a year's supply of power from a wind-power utility in Wyoming (Culturebox, 2006).

The big issues defined

So what exactly are these big issues we keep talking about? The big issues boil down in our view to:

- big global health issues;
- participation;
- lifestyle changes.

Let's look at these in more detail and hypothetically think how they may come to impact the very nature of selling – the very nature of your relationship with your customer.

Big global issue 1: health issues

This issue is, of course, constructed from a number of big issues in their own right, from rising obesity levels to the need for better nutrition in our diets to global warming. Thanks to Al Gore, global warming has become a very real issue. His recent documentary, *An Inconvenient Truth*, captured the public imagination and even made him an Oscar winner. It always was a major issue. Now it's an issue we can't avoid ourselves or for our children's selves. That issue has a direct impact on how we sell our products and particularly how we sell to the big retailers, the very place where Private Label has become the most entrenched. The supermarket is where shoppers can often most determine how big a carbon footprint they leave. What are they prepared to accept? Or not accept?

TWO-THIRDS OF A TYPICAL LANDFILL
IS OFTEN SUPERMARKET RELATED.

Consumers everywhere are asking themselves some very basic questions: about the real health of their food; about the origin of that food and whether it makes global sense. Would I be happier buying food that came from a local source or should I buy food that was sourced from the other side of the world? The chart shown in Figure 15.4 was published in 2005 and it showed even then that health was becoming a very big brand issue.

When you think about it for five seconds, the concept of buying butter from a cow in a field round the corner makes somewhat more sense than buying butter from 14,000 miles away in New Zealand. In fact, why do we even take five seconds to think about it!

LOCAL IS GOOD. LOCAL IS ECONOMIC.
LOCAL IS SUPPORTIVE, LOCAL IS ENVIRO FREE.

We would recommend that all food (and possibly all products) be given mileage stamps, so that you can know that your little slab of butter has 14,000 food miles or 25 food miles as its eco cost to us all. The greater the distance to travel to market, the greater the enviro cost. Of course, this is just as relevant to every product that travels, be it cosmetics produced in Japan or electronics from Taiwan. Local is indeed local these days. We don't mean countries. We mean counties, towns or villages.

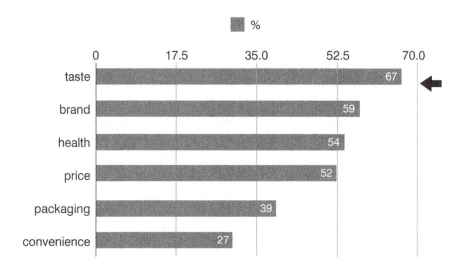

Figure 15.4   Unprecedented consumer focus on health in food (percentage of consumers who believe the following are important when choosing food)
Source: Nestlé survey of consumers in 2004

> As globalization continues to make our world seem smaller, local-ization will come to a head in 2007. We'll put great emphasis on sourcing everything from food to textiles. Decadent and excessive consumption will fall to the wayside as we stress quality, minimal environmental impact and support of local producers.
>
> Ann Mack, Director of Trendspotting at JWT

We know this sounds horribly unfair to some of those faraway nations. But life is changing and they will simply have to adapt like everyone else. The world simply can't carry on globalizing the way it has. Retailers have the ultimate power to influence this. It is, after all, they and they alone that encouraged such a growth in food mileage around the world in the first place as their global empires expanded.

Local products spend lower food miles. This is dramatically changing shopping behaviour. In the UK **local food markets** doubled in the last year alone (2006) as this approach became more attractive and responsive to the average shopper.

Why don't local food producers band together and deliver local food direct to households through web ordering? Tesco in the UK has shown how successful web ordering can be, with a significant part of its sales now attributed there. If you have enough scale, you can do it.

WEBFOODLOCAL.COM – JUST ORDER IT!

Then there's travelling to your retailer by car. Not an eco-friendly alternative. Apart from walking, there is of course the option of the web. As 3-D visual communications become the norm it will be much easier to sense what the offerings are without seeing them on a shelf. When you think about it, what actually happens when you see a product on a shelf? You look at it, turn it over and read about it. All of which can be simulated exactly on the web. It won't be long before we can smell it too (something IBM's actually developing). Then brands truly will make sense on the net as well.

The UK leads the way in terms of broadband penetration these days, with more and more money being spent on advertising directly on the web. There is a lot of evidence out there that there is genuine momentum building behind the shift online (*Times*, 5 January 2007, Robert Coles). Retailers ignore online shopping at their peril. It may even be safe to say that online shopping came of age this year. Why has it taken so long (or so short, depending on your perspective)? Simple. It has taken time because retailers had to build platforms for effective ordering and efficient delivery. It has also taken time because consumers have had to learn to trust the process of shopping by remote. And it has taken time simply because widespread access to broadband is only now really taking off.

THE AVERAGE UK HOUSEHOLD HAS 10 TONNES OF CO_2 AS A FOOTPRINT. ONE-THIRD OF HOUSEHOLD FOOD PURCHASES IS THROWN OUT.

The one thing that needs to be fully assessed in the future is whether all this is producing a net benefit. Or are online sales high-street replacement sales? There is some evidence that this is so. Next, a high-street fashion and online UK retailer, saw its high-street sales rise nearly 7 per cent, while its directory sales, of which more than half is online, rose nearly 10 per cent. It points to the likelihood that some online sites are creating a sales momentum of their own. Retailers cannot afford to ignore the impact of digital distribution anymore. Shoppers are becoming hooked on e-convenience and if you don't provide this option for your customers you will lose out. One way or another the internet is making life more interesting and challenging for retailers and brands. Those that have the ability to rise to the challenge will be those that win.

Over half the content of a dustbin is excessive packaging. Even after you've recycled, a significant amount of the rest is waste food which could have been composted if separated. We like to think we've made advances in this area. And we have. But there's a long road ahead. When was the last time you saw a supermarket or brand encouraging you to buy smaller portions and waste less food?

IN GERMANY SHOPPERS DESTROY/DAMAGE THE PACKAGE IN THE SUPERMARKET WHEN TOO MUCH PACKAGING IS PRESENT TO SHOW OTHER SHOPPERS HOW BAD IT IS.

In UK supermarkets alone £70 billion is spent every year. You'd only need a small percentage of effort and money going towards the issues highlighted above to reduce the tremendous waste and damage associated with the £70 billion. Everybody has to play their part, from shoppers changing their behaviour, to the brands actually producing good food minimally packaged, to the supermarkets making these issues banner customer-service-level propositions.

And it isn't just the supermarkets. From fashion to toys the story is the same... we have to be sexy and over-packaged to sell. This is complete rubbish in today's environment. In reality, if we can provide branding sexily through various methods from digital to physical, we can ease off on the packaging. We remember a number of years ago when **LEGO** introduced an adult range of LEGO construction toys to be ordered by mail order. How did they arrive? In black and white cheap disposable boxes. Did it affect their brand affinity? Of course not. It actually increased it as we recognize a responsible act when we see one. Yet if you look at the kids' toys market they're over-packaged to the highest degree. We don't mind if the one on the shelf is like this – but as a consumer, if we were offered a minimalist version when we left the shop we would certainly take it. I suspect we're not alone.

Some supermarkets are succeeding, some not. Tesco, Asda and the Co-op in the UK scored 'room for improvement' in a recent survey on green subjects. Sainsbury's and M&S were next best and Waitrose best, although even they had too many products with too many food miles. The role of supermarkets should be making the world greener for us all.

Brands are already moving in the green direction. Let's look at some brands (www.trendwatching.com) that are already experimenting with attaching 'life story labels' to their products, satisfying consumers who are ready to spend their money on whatever does the least harm. 'Bought locally, ordered online and delivered to your door.' That sums up what **Poptotheshop**s offers residents in South Wales. Poptotheshops, which was launched in late 2006, currently serves four high-street areas, which each sells between 3,300 and 4,500 products using the internet shopping service. The company's founder came up with the idea after being dismayed about being too busy to shop at local stores. Most local shops have shorter opening hours than the big chains like Tesco and Wal-Mart, which can make it hard to support local retailers. On Poptotheshops, customers can shop day or night, selecting products from the local butcher, baker, fishmonger, greengrocer and off-licence, before checking out in one go. Similar to online shopping at supermarkets, customers can save favourite products and specify when they'd like delivery to take place. Delivery is free for customers. Poptotheshops (PTTS) covers its costs (and will hopefully generate a profit) by charging retailers 10–15 per cent commission. Besides supporting the local economy and keeping the high street alive, PTTS also sees other benefits: independent stores often offer great local products and produce that aren't available in nationwide stores, consumers save time otherwise spent in supermarkets, and helping small retailers thrive decreases the control that supermarkets have over pricing, produce and suppliers.

Another example from the UK (where protest against the loss of local character of the high street has been the most vocal): the **Wedge** is a loyalty card with a difference. No store with more than 10 branches can participate. The card costs £20 ($39), half of which goes to charity. Initially the money will go to two local charities, but in future customers will be able to pick the charity that will benefit from their card. Wedge gives members special offers and discounts, usually 10 per cent off, at nearly 100 shops. Merchants hope that the Wedge card will give people an extra incentive to shop there rather than in the superstores.

Also on the rise are ever more sophisticated local indexes and search engines. They range from Google Local, which is taking on the Yellow Pages and TomToms of this world, to small players like San Francisco-based Green Zebra Guide, a combined shopping guide and coupon book that offers consumers savings of over $12,000 at more than 250 local organic restaurants, shops, spas, yoga and Pilates studios, independent bookstores, bike shops, museums and more. To add to Green Zebra's effect, many of the participating businesses are local independents whose brands aren't as recognizable as their larger chain competitors.

Singaporean inQbox (which stands for incubation in a box) is a small store in a Singapore mall that is stacked with well-lit, attractive shelving units. It rents out 'boxes' to small businesses and artists, providing them with retail and gallery space, and taking care of the daily hassles of retail. Prices for a box start at SGD 80 (€40/$50) per month, depending on size and location within the store. Vendors are selected carefully, and the store is popular with shoppers for its unique array of wares. Lots of shoppers means valuable mini real estate, so there's often a long waiting list for boxes.

As inQbox puts it, they aim to 'encourage creativity and entrepreneurship by providing individuals with a low cost and low risk platform to develop and incubate their talents further than just a hobby, home business or side interest'.

Also emerging are (STILL) MADE HERE ventures. These are local companies that take back production that's currently based in regions less concerned with eco and ethics. One example is **American Apparel**, which deals with ethical concerns in a radical way: by manufacturing its garments in… high-cost LA. American Apparel now operates the country's largest garment factory, employs more than 5,000 people and operates 145 retail locations in 11 countries. Workers are paid (on average) $12 an hour, almost twice as much as California's minimum wage. American Apparel isn't the only brand to do so: NoSweatApparel calls itself the pioneer of fair-trade fashion and footwear, setting (in their own words) an empowered, unionized workforce as the gold standard for fair-trade clothing. Also, Ujena offers one of the largest selections of swimwear in the world, yet still manufactures its products in the United States.

The second driver behind the (STILL) MADE HERE trend is using the local aspect as a story ingredient. Obviously, many of the aforementioned eco/ethics examples tell a story too, but the status/story driver encompasses more than these two angles. In fact, some of the local stories described below will translate into decidedly eco-unfriendly behaviour, as they turn local heritage into a worldwide selling point, causing pollution by long-haul transport to customers across the globe.

An obvious example of the link between locality and story/status is the perception of location-specific quality. Just because everything can be produced everywhere, it doesn't necessarily mean that (perceived) quality levels have been globalized, too. Some high-cost regions can afford to be expensive because of superior skills, rare expertise and/or a rock-solid brand. Which is why, contrary to earlier doomsayers, high-end brands like Italian Ermenegildo Zegna (nine factories in Italy), Swiss Rolex or British Vertu (luxury phones are assembled by hand at the company's headquarters in Church Crookham, UK) are manufacturing or assembling in their high-wage home countries, and not suffering from it. In fact, keeping in mind the story element, this is what they're selling, and what they've been selling for ages. And millions of consumers will gladly continue to pay a premium for these goods, as they tell a story of authenticity, of connoisseurship, of the owner knowing where in the world to source the best of the best for each product category. To believe in the outsourcing of anything and everything is to ignore consumers' desire to spend as much as possible on the real thing.

One more example of (STILL) MADE HERE and story ingredients: the founders of **Izzy Lane**, a new British clothing brand, rescue sheep from being sent to slaughter for being male, missing a pregnancy, being a little lame, being too small, being too old or having imperfections in their fleece. The ones that are bought by Izzy Lane live happily ever after in their Sheep Sanctuary: last year the company saved 400 lucky sheep. Combining their passion for animals, great clothes and Britain, these confirmed vegetarians have created a line of knitwear made of the wool from their flock of rescued sheep. Shetland skirts and suits are made from their flock of 250 Shetland sheep. Some of the knitwear is made from the wool of Wensleydale sheep, an endangered breed, with only about 1,800 left in the world. They have 250, most of which were destined for the meat markets before Izzy Lane saved them. The clothing is made locally by neighbouring craftsmen – the last worsted spinners and dyers in the Bradford area. The cloth is woven at an ancient mill in Selkirk using Victorian machinery that has been operating for over 100 years. For each Izzy Lane garment, the full provenance, from the fleece through the whole manufacturing process to the garment itself, is known. Now, what will garner the wearers of Izzy

Lane's clothes more status: the (obscure) label, or telling the heart-warming story behind their sweater?

And it's not just the small brands

Not so long ago, corporate America dismissed environmentally conscious consumers as hemp-wearing hippies with too little buying power to demand much attention. Now big brands are also discovering that it pays to go green. Apple Inc. launched 'A Greener Apple' campaign and pledged to remove toxic chemicals from its new computer products. Home Depot Inc. unveiled an Eco-Options stamp for more than 2,500 environmentally friendly products in its stores. The NBC soap opera *Days of Our Lives* staged a green wedding, complete with soy candles and a hemp suit for the groom. And Kohl's Corp. said it plans to convert most of its California stores to solar power.

'It's now sexy to be green,' said Bonnie Carlson, president of Promotion Marketing Association, a New-York-based trade group. 'It's very fashionable for consumers to say they're doing something to help the environment.' (*Chicago Tribune*, May 2007).

Use of organically grown cotton by retail titans, fashion designers, and small and medium-size companies resulted in a dramatic growth in global retail sales of products containing organic cotton between 2001 and 2005, according to a new report by the Oakland, California-based non-profit Organic Exchange. Organic production is based on a system of farming that maintains and replenishes soil fertility without the use of toxic and persistent pesticides and fertilizers and genetically modified seeds. During the four-year period, global organic cotton product sales increased an estimated 35 per cent annually, from $245 million in 2001 to $583 million in 2005. In the United States, such sales increased 55 per cent per year, from $86 million in 2001 to $275 million in 2005. The author of the report, 'The Organic Exchange Spring 2006 Global Organic Cotton Market Report', projects global organic cotton product sales to skyrocket to $2.6 billion by the end of 2008, reflecting a 116 per cent average annual growth rate. Consumers are no longer simply eating organically grown food – they are wearing clothes, using personal care products and outfitting their kitchens, bathrooms and bedrooms with products made with organic cotton. The five brands, according to Organic Exchange, using the most organic cotton globally in 2005 are (in order by quantity): Nike (Oregon), Coop Switzerland

how to lead tomorrow	issue lead
The big health issues are here to stay. Are you really doing anything about them?	a. Describe three actions you are or would like to take to deal with the health issues with your brands. b. Present and discuss.

Figure 15.5 Management action workshop exercise

and Patagonia (California), Otto (Germany), and Sam's Club/Wal-Mart (Arkansas).

As you can see, more and more brands are finding ingenious ways to use the big issues as a positive business force.

Big global issue 2: participation issues

Author Charles Leadbeater's opening keynote speech at a recent London conference centred around how innovation (a key focus of the conference) is changing its nature (ESOMAR's 2006 London congress meeting).

As he noted, we have **moved from mass production and mass marketing to mass participation**. This serves to emphasize how creativity is not a characteristic of large companies, nor is it an ordered, desk-bound process.

Increasingly, said Leadbeater, successful innovative companies are working with their customers to bridge the many gaps between what people really need and what they find in the marketplace. Much of this, of course, happens online, where examples like eBay, Wikipedia, YouTube and the whole computer games industry illustrate the trend.

Leadbeater argues that this means that several key elements of current management thinking are looking vulnerable or obsolete. In particular:

- the value chain – which is being outmoded by co-creation, in which the consumer actually is part of the value-adding process;
- the concept of a new product pipeline – which, even in big pharmaceutical companies (perhaps its last bastion), is being eroded, because innovation is no longer only by specialists in specialist settings;
- organizational hierarchies – which no longer help innovation ('never make the boss the owner of a new product project', he recommends).

So, will this be the end of big companies as we know them? No. There's room for all sorts, even traditional thinking and traditional organizations. But more and more we will see informal, interactive, consumer-participative organizations taking the lead in innovation.

There is overwhelming evidence of the progression of participation in the explosive growth of the big websites and allied technology (2006 estimates):

- Yahoo has a base of 420 million unique monthly visitors.
- Google has approaching 1 million advertisers and vendors.
- Pay Pal has 125 million+ accounts.
- Shopping.com has 40 million+ products in over 3,000 categories.
- Skype has 136 million+ registered users and may be the fastest-growing product in history.
- 60 per cent of internet traffic may be P2P (person to person) file sharing of unmonetized video.
- There are 57 million blogs, doubling every seven months.
- There were 1 billion camera-enabled mobile phones purchased within one year of launch.

And so on and so on.

We particularly need this sort of thinking applied in the brand/retail arena. Both have to evolve if they are to deal with the new necessities of the Private Label age. Brands have to become much more flexible, imaginative and creative than they have ever been before. Retailers really need to be seen to fully embrace customer needs and reshape their organizations accordingly. The web and technology will play an enormous part in that future.

Participation is the key for competing with Private Label in the future. If you really know and give shoppers what they want, they will buy you. If you ignore the issues that are meaningful to them, they will ignore you. And **ignorable = replaceable** in anyone's language.

Finally:

ROI = Return on Involvement

This is a phrase we will come back to. Making sure you're maximizing the return on involvement of your shoppers will become a number one priority for you.

Big global issue 3: lifestyle issues

Lives are changing fast and you need to keep up with those lifestyle changes. Despite the myriad of possibilities out there at the moment, maybe you can boil them down to just a few. We believe that the life of the future can take four distinct paths: we can choose to experience life to its fullest; we can choose to suspend life and ageing in perpetuity; we can reflect inwards to gain new strength outwards: or we can unlock our lives through feeling increasingly secure and sure.

These in turn can be built into four action-orientated positionings:

- **Enlightenism**. Increasingly, self-aware people seek to know themselves and what's good for their mind, body and the world they inhabit. The explosive growth in 'better' foods is direct real evidence of this lifestyle change. Fresh direct is here to stay.
- **Perpetualism**. Increasingly, ageing is perceived as a state of mind and body which can be suspended and sustained through consuming life-giving products. People want to live longer as evidenced by moves to better nutrition and cosmetic products to make us look and feel better. Age shuffling (40 is the new 20) is the new vogue.

- **Solitudinism**. In our ever more crazy, stressed world people seek moments of solitude where they can refuel, rethink and unlock their lives. And increasingly we live alone, thanks to the decline in marriage and the rise of divorce.
- **Securitization**. In an increasingly insecure world, people increasingly seek security for themselves and their loved ones.

Ask yourself if your portfolio (brands and retailers) takes account of these lifestyle changes. What have you done to reflect them?

One for all and all for one

By combining all the three major big-issue trends you can realize the opportunity. Realize the opportunity for brands to compete more effectively against Private Label. Realize the opportunity for the retailers' corporate brands to be more effectively tuned to their customers' future desires. Realize the opportunity for brands and retailers to work together for the common good. So let's all start by showing how we can really deal with the privatization of brands... how we can realize the brand opportunity.

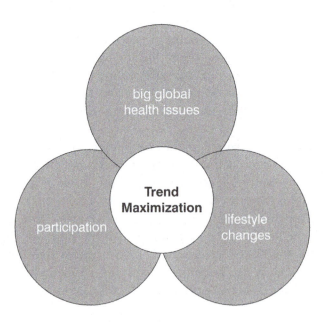

Figure 15.6 Trend maximization factors

Summary and opportunities

We need to go back to brand basics if brands are to find a place in an increasingly Private Label dominated world. Those basics start with redefining the brand and rediscovering the need to re-establish customer trust. Where will that trust come from? The answer is all around us in the big global issues that are driving the development of brands today. Only by completely embracing those issues will we fully realize our brands' competitive advantage.

- Opportunity 8: Make sure you're not a greenwashing company. Make sure you're a **REAL CHANGE** company.
- Opportunity 9: Become the market **BIG ISSUES LEADER** as well as volume leader.
- Opportunity 10: Maximize the new ROI: **RETURN ON INVOLVEMENT**. More about this later.

Actions to consider

1. Evaluate your greenwashing levels. Are you really being true to yourself and the world?
2. Conduct an internal audit on your influences on health issues, customer participation and lifestyle changes. Do you make a difference?
3. Construct action plans to make the difference real.

16 Private principle 4: Educate, navigate and inspire

Here we look at the new role of branding.

Figure 16.1   Educate all

Headlines

- The role of branding is changing.
- It's increasingly a role of education to help develop societal needs.
- Brands and retailers have a new macro responsibility they must embrace.
- Educating the shopper responsibly is a prime business prerequisite.

Become the educators

BY 2020 GLOBAL HEALTH EXPENSES WILL RISE BY 300 PER CENT

A decade ago, deeply integrating a socially responsible value proposition into a brand was a completely new idea embraced by entrepreneurial companies like Ben & Jerry's, Patagonia and Starbucks. Now there are over 100,000 pages on corporate websites dealing with corporate social responsibility (CSR), over 600 books listed on Amazon and more than 50 per cent of the Global 250 corporations issue corporate responsibility reports. Social responsibility is here to stay.

It is clear that today's lifestyles are out of control. Arguably, most of those out-of-control lifestyles have been fuelled indirectly by the supermarkets and multinational brands. Their obsession for growth has spiralled out of control. You can argue who is to blame, and in some ways it's all of us. We demand lower prices. We demand instant convenience. In return we get giant multinationals and over-processed foods, a never-ending development since the end of the Second World War. It is clear that it is time to stop, at the very least from a brand's strategic perspective. With the growth of global retail brands we have entered the era of the low-cost producer (LCP) in a big way. That low-cost producer is inevitably the Private Label brand. It's fine when a conventional brand can claim LCP status – but is it necessarily desirable? It's worth noting that the highest 20 per cent of spending in supermarkets accounts for 80 per cent of the profit. If that spending is directed towards a Private Label purchase, the brand has lost any residual bargaining power it may have had. One way to ensure that shoppers are pointed towards you is to **educate them positively**.

A new era of social consciousness is evolving throughout the world. People are increasingly embracing a new level of commitment to one another and to the environment, not just to themselves. This shift is creating a significant change among stakeholders (customers, employees, shareholders and suppliers) who are looking to brands to help define their role within society and for a purchase to count for something more than just an acquisition.

Ensure you have the armour to compete

Over the past 20 years, we have shifted from functionally centric brands to emotionally centric brands to values-centric brands. Today, brands must be inspirational in a socially responsible way. It is no longer enough for brands to define themselves in terms of what they are: they must make a statement – environmentally, culturally and socially – about what they want to be (Rachel Simmons). The evolution in the key attributes of leading car brands exemplifies this trend. We have gone from quality, value and safety (Volvo), to design and personality (Volkswagen Golf), to fuel efficiency/environmentally friendly (Prius). Some drivers literally use their car as a visual declaration about their concerns for the environment. As a Toyota Prius ad recently stated, 'green is the new black'. A series of

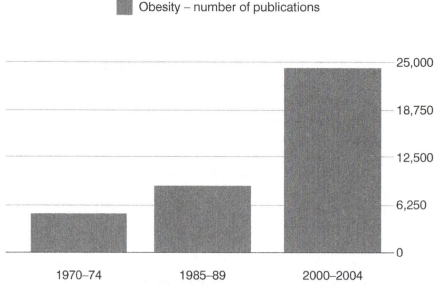

Figure 16.2 The ever-rising publicity wave
Source: NRC/Int

converging trends has meant that companies with high social brand capital (SBC) are tapping into new business opportunities and commercially booming. First and foremost, people are more socially and environmentally aware and are increasingly looking for companies that champion values they believe in when they make a purchase. People want to feel part of something bigger than themselves and brands are a natural place to find this sense of social belonging.

In addition, among a sea of brand choices it is becoming increasingly difficult to create competitive distinction through traditional product or service innovation. As Michael Porter and Mark Kramer recently stated, 'adding a social dimension to your value proposition offers a new frontier in competitive positioning'. Related to this trend is the fact that people are becoming more and more adept at sniffing out companies that are genuinely solving problems against those that are merely attaching their name to a cause to enhance their reputation. So the old cause-marketing model of trying to 'own' an association with a specific cause can actually generate more cynicism than success.

As a result, more and more companies are realizing it is the right time commercially, anthropologically and ethically to reassess their CSR programmes and build real market and social value by honestly realigning their core brand identity with deep and engaging social and environmental commitments.

A great example of a company that was ahead of the curve and has used its high SBC to become one of the best-known natural food brands and the category leader in organic yogurt is **Stonyfield Farm**. The value proposition of its products being healthy for the individual and for the planet is engrained in everything they do. From their packaging choices to their energy conservation policy to their support of family farms and organic agriculture to their 'Menu for Change' programme designed to improve the food in schools, the environmental and social commitment of their Stonyfield brand is consistently upheld. As Group Danone chairman and CEO Frank Riboud said, 'Stonyfield is much more than just a balance sheet – it represents an ethic.'

You need to fully understand the trends and accompanying big issues to truly prepare yourself for the battle ahead. In our recent book *How to Succeed at Retail* we talked about this in relation to the food industry. The food industry at the moment is a good example of an industry wide open to the influence of trends on its retail strategies. Paul Lincoln, CEO of the National Heart Forum in England, recently summarized the trends for the future as he saw them.

1. Junk food will become the new tobacco and there will be increased media and political interest in the junk food culture. There will be vastly increased monitoring and exposure of industry commitments and actions on products and brands.

2. Ever-tightening statutory regulation on marketing, health claims, labelling in Europe and increased prospect of litigation in the United States. Prospect of global food and health treaty in the wake of the ever-increasing worldwide chronic disease epidemics. Health care costs will continue to soar and governments will want to take action due to large extrinsic social costs of this type of food production and the damaging macroeconomic implications for their economies.

3. The food industry will more visibly divide into junk (health damaging) food producers and health-promoting food producers. Possibly the same for retailers? The companies will need to be clear about their future core business, market themselves accordingly and redefine their brand values. The social reform agenda is set. The critical issue is how the junk food orientated companies perceive the risk if they are going to adapt or fight change or stick with their core business. There will be much greater investment in R&D and product reformulation as consumer demand will increase due to higher health literacy.

Believe us, these issues are relevant to any food company's future. With issues like these, you had better make the right decisions! And take action to make your brand a better brand for tomorrow.

How to build tomorrow's loyalty?

These issues and the education of them will be increasingly tied into a brand's measure of future sustainable success – brand loyalty. There is much talk about the death of brand loyalty. But loyalty per se hasn't changed. People still prefer to buy the same reassuring brand again and again. Shoppers still want that important same thing... **something you can trust**. However, we would argue that the nature of building loyalty is evolving fast. The nature of buying the same brand again and again will be increasingly motivated by the big issues. Already we've moved away from the traditional factors that built most brands loyalty – product satisfaction.

	your brand today	your brand tomorrow
helps nutrition	+/-	++
reduces obesity	-	++
ecofriendly ingredients	-	+
ecofriendly packaging	-	+
organic	-	+
climate change impact	-	+
involved in people's lives and lifestyles	-	+

Figure 16.3 The big issues, today and tomorrow

yesterday's loyalty	today's loyalty	tomorrow's loyalty
brand repurchase as a result of product satisfaction	what helps me through the shopping experience in the most time if I can see you through the store more efficiently store cards	you're doing the right things for me and society

Figure 16.4 Loyalty evolution

In these days of increasingly perceived quality parity and brand/Private Label quality parity, other factors weigh in, from convenience to store cards. Loyalty is increasingly driven by the need for loyalty points rather than the love of any brand. Just look at the UK, with Tesco with 12 million loyalty-card members and Nectar with 14 million loyalty-card members (M&S and Sainsbury's).

We do, however, believe that tomorrow's loyalty will be more societally driven. Shoppers will be less selfish and more interested in supporting what they perceive as genuinely 'good' companies. Loyalty cards have represented loyalty to date. Ethics and sustainable policies will represent loyalty in the future. You could, of course, say that the mercenary will continue to win through, ie cards give me money. But we genuinely believe that a major psychological shift is occurring among the consumers of today – they are genuinely concerned about the way the world is going and they want to influence it by whatever small means they can.

Being serious about these changes will sort out the winners from the losers. Because serious you need to be. This isn't your latest line extension or product flavouring variant. It's a commitment to **total change**. Unfortunately, we don't really see that commitment out there in reality. There's a lot of talk and a lot of puff, whether it be Nestlé saying it is corporately moving in this direction or Cadbury's launching a new healthy chocolate bar. The reality is that ALL FOOD SHOULD BE HEALTHY. We invented and sustained unhealthy food. The trend must be reversed.

There is no such thing in the new world as unhealthy food and healthy food. There is healthy food alone. By just producing variants, food companies in particular are procrastinating against the inevitable. If they don't move here, shoppers will with their feet or governments will with legislation. These issues have become far more critical than the survival of a brand. They represent the survival of society as we know it.

MOST OF THE HEALTH SERVICES IN THE WORLD ARE LIKELY TO BE OVERWHELMED WITH DEALING WITH THE CONSEQUENCES OF A FUTURE OBESITY EPIDEMIC.

This is fact and not fiction and the headlines are starting to show the reality of that fact. Unhealthy living is no longer a societal option. Healthy living is a societal prerogative. Unhealthy living is no longer a brand option. Healthy living is the only brand option. Finally, this isn't just food. These and associated issues are relevant in any FMCG brand category, from electronics to padlocks.

Get real!

Coca-Cola's chief executive, E Neville Isdell, clearly frustrated that his industry had been singled out in the obesity debate, insisted at a recent conference that his diet products should be included in the health and wellness category because, with few or no calories, they are a logical answer to expanding waistlines (*New York Times*, March, 2007). **Are you kidding?** Empty calories would be a better description. The antithesis of healthy would be more accurate. While the $68 billion soda business in the United States remains alive, consumers are increasingly reaching for bottled water, sparkling juices and green-tea drinks. In 2005 the amount of soda sold in the United States dropped for the first time ever in its history. Coke and Pepsi plan to introduce new carbonated drinks that are fortified with vitamins and minerals – Diet Coke plus and Tava.

Two years ago, in a bit of a marketing gamble, **PepsiCo** launched a massive campaign that would place it in the role of educator (*The Advertiser*, August 2006). Recognizing that Americans were becoming increasingly interested in health and wellness, the company began masking its product pitches with more instructive information on the benefits of nutritious foods. The programme, called Smart Spot, was designed to help consumers choose healthier products while it subtly promoted PepsiCo-produced foods and beverages that met certain nutritional guidelines.

Today, more than 250 PepsiCo products sport a green Smart Spot stamp, which shows they contain at least 10 per cent of the recommended daily value of a targeted nutrient, have specific health and wellness benefits, contain limited amounts of fat, sodium and/or sugar, or also include healthier ingredients, such as whole grains. 'The Smart Spot products grew at more than two and a half times the rate of the rest of our portfolio in 2005,' says Lynn Markley, vice president of public relations for health and wellness at PepsiCo. 'Consumers are looking for healthier products. Clearly we're meeting the demand.' PepsiCo isn't the only company that has embraced the educational marketing concept. Several major brands in a variety of industries are using promotions to educate consumers not only about specific products but also entire product categories. As a result, consumers not only make well-informed buying decisions, experts say, they also become more receptive to product pitches because they are more trusting of the companies they do business with. 'Marketers can change people's behaviour by educating them,' contends Fred Senn, founding partner of the Minneapolis, Minnesota-based advertising agency Fallon Worldwide.

And there are many others. **General Mills**, in 2004, launched the interactive website BrandNewYou.com, where visitors get tips on calorie counting, portion control, and exercise. Consumers can learn about General Mills' portion-controlled offerings, such as 100-calorie popcorns and soups, and can download Betty Crocker low-fat recipes. Kraft Foods took a different approach to educational marketing by focusing on a niche market: South Beach dieters. In January, as this target audience looked for ways to start the year off right, the Northfield, Illinois-based company launched the Beach in a Box Tour. Kraft officials travelled to nine cities to inform consumers about how to prepare nutritious meals and maintain good eating habits while, at the same time, they were softly selling healthy Kraft products.

Yet again we must stress that the sort of things we describe above are moves in the right direction. However, they remain moves. None of these organizations has totally embraced these big issues. At the moment they tinker and hope it brings sales. Be careful. The tinkerers will be found out as shoppers start seriously selecting companies on their genuine commitment to the big issues. As big companies like Nike have already found, these big issues can have very damaging effects on their business when the world comes to correct you. Nike's originally negative policies on producing goods in the sweatshops of the Far East have caused more damage to the brand than they could possibly have dreamt.

Education is part of a much bigger process. But at least it's a start. **It is to be hoped that by educating your customers you may well end up educating yourself.** The key to a successful educational marketing campaign is recognizing the needs of the shopper. The more entertaining and creative the information, the more engaged customers will be, and the more likely they will be to trust that company's products. Some keys to successful educating include:

- Avoid information overload.
- Make it entertaining.
- Incorporate interactive elements.

- Point out the reward and show them the benefit.
- Practise what you preach.

Just a few questions to ask yourself:

- Which of your customers would enjoy knowing more about our product, and would be interested in accessing our product's life story, from an eco or ethics angle? How could we (literally) attach those stories to existing and new products? Can we start working on advanced labels like those that Tesco and Timberland (see below) are experimenting with?
- Is there a business opportunity in creating a new brand or turning one of our existing brands into a purely local play, including a compelling local story (and premium margins)? Should we partner with some of the new players in this field?
- Can we add story ingredients to some of our more obscure or virtual products, helping our customers tell stories to others? Should we create new products that do this, if most of what we offer is more mainstream?

Education is here to stay and examples are everywhere. Carbon footprinting has become a household term in mature consumer societies. You can safely expect consumers' desire to find out about the origins of a product to become a given. Questions no one ever asked a few years ago will become an integral part of the purchasing process. How was the product made? By whom? How did it get to its point of sale? What effects on the environment will it have after purchasing? UK supermarket Tesco plans to introduce carbon footprint labels on all 70,000 products it sells to allow shoppers to compare carbon impacts. Implementation will take a while: the company is currently investigating how to develop a 'universally accepted and commonly understood' measuring system.

Last year, footwear manufacturer **Timberland** (www.trend watching.com) started placing a 'nutritional label' on each shoe box, educating consumers about the product they are purchasing, including where it was manufactured, how it was produced and what effect it has on the environment. A nice touch is messaging inside the box asking customers 'what kind of footprint will you leave?' and providing a call to action for them after purchase.

Dole Organic lets consumers 'travel to the origin of each organic product'. By typing in a fruit sticker's three-digit Farm Code on Dole Organic's website, customers can read background information, view photos of the farm and workers and learn more about the origin of Dole products. What works for bananas works for eggs. Aptly naming their site wheresyoursfrom, UK-based Chippindale Foods was the first company to offer customers full egg traceability. Also check out intermediary MyFreshEgg, which aims to be bringing the same services to a host of farms and egg producers. Aceites Borges Olive Oil gives each bottle of olive oil a Numero de Lote (batch number), informing customers about the geographic origin of the olives, the pressing date, oil producer, place of pressing, litres bottled under the same batch number, date of bottling, degree of acidity, tasting score and tasting notes.

And now there's 'life story' labels. In Japan, millions of consumers have code-reading software on their camera-phones, which means that infinite amounts of information (including images and videos) can be 'attached' to products, satisfying even the most serious information-seeking consumers. Maybe not a bad idea to start mapping out your product life stories strategy as soon as possible?

To completely eliminate transit between source and table – and the need for egg traceability labels – **British Omlet** brings hens to consumers' gardens and fresh eggs to their table every morning. The company designed a hen kit for urban and suburban gardens, aimed at first-time chicken owners, families and eco-savvy individuals. How does it work? Omlet supplies organically reared and fully vaccinated female chickens at a cost of £365 (US $700/€550). The two-hen service comes complete with an Eglu, an eye-catching, 21st-century version of the henhouse. In its first three years of business, the company sold 10,500 Eglus and now also offers a larger version, the Eglu Cube, capable of housing up to 10 chickens.

Summary and opportunities

You can be great at dealing with the big issues, but you need to turn that effort into action. Education is key to catalysing your employee efforts and navigating them in the right direction. Education is key to securing your future long-term loyalty.

- Opportunity 11: Make your brand a BETTER BRAND. Totally socialize your brand and make it socially fit from top to bottom. Commit to total change.
- Opportunity 12: Become the BIG ISSUE EDUCATOR. You have a social and moral responsibility to educate everyone, from your employees to your shoppers, about the big issues we all face.
- Opportunity 13: Become the BIG ISSUE IMPLEMENTER. Change your total product line, your packaging, your communications and your distribution to reflect the new issues. Stop greenwashing. Start doing.

Actions to consider

1. Audit your 'big issue' involvement education levels.
2. Come to a point of view about how you can make your company a 'big issue' company communicator.
3. Develop plans to totally implement those issues in EVERYTHING the company does.
4. Develop internal communication plans and methodologies to educate everyone about the changes coming.

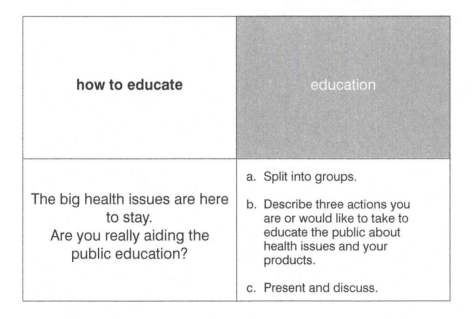

how to educate	education
The big health issues are here to stay. Are you really aiding the public education?	a. Split into groups. b. Describe three actions you are or would like to take to educate the public about health issues and your products. c. Present and discuss.

Figure 16.5 Management action workshop exercise

5. Re-brief R&D to ensure they take big issues on board and all the way.
6. Make sure your big issue communications are meaningful, not self-serving.
7. Teach yourself how to educate.
8. Look at Al Gore's film *An Inconvenient Truth* if you want to learn how to educate about a big issue.
9. Stop greenwashing, start doing.
10. Produce a 'big issue' handbook to show everyone internally what you're doing and where you're going.

17 Private principle 5: Winning 'mind shelf' is the name of the game

Here we look at the evolving shelf.

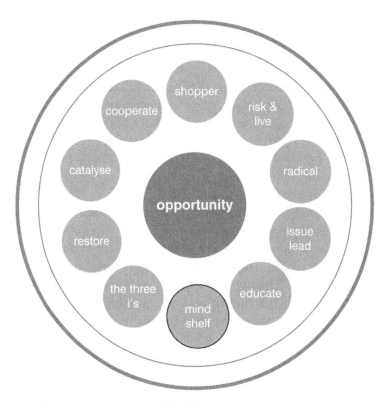

Figure 17.1 Winning mind shelf presence

Headlines

- It's not about mind space.
- It's not about shelf space.
- It's about mind shelf space.
- The brand has gone from a creator of mind space to a creator of mental images disproportionate to its shelf space.
- Make sure you have your share.

The fight for space

Who owns the shopper? The war for the shopper is being fought more than ever. And the two fronts of that war are the mind and the shelf. On the left side of the ring we have the brand, a sort of Muhammed Ali, fighting his opponents with the strength of his mind as well as his speed. On the other side of the ring we have Mike Tyson using brute strength to get his way. Yes, we're being a little over the top. But this is often the war as it's imagined and portrayed.

But of course, we're not boxing each other. We are instead trying to own space. But those spaces are very different, depending on whether we're a brand or a retailer. According to Corstjens and Corstjens (2000), retailers and manufacturers compete for a consumer's mind space. Mind space is about making consumers learn and remember. A successful consumer product builds up a web of experiences, associations and buying habits for the end consumer. These are intangible resources that the manufacturers hold outside the company, in the minds of the consumer and retailers.

The old battlefield of the fight for mind space which characterized the era of mass communication has increasingly become redundant. The shopper's mind and the retailer's shelf have limited capacity. As the concentration of retailers has grown, the shelf space has become an important marketing influence. Ever more sophisticated retailers actively market their own brands and use the shelf space to promote them. Shelf space has therefore become an important challenge to manufacturers.

However, arguably the battlefield with which retailers replaced it – the fight for shelf space – has also had its day. The shelf has become literally so full of overflowing choice that you can't see it anymore, let alone the brands that stand on it. These days there's only one battle that

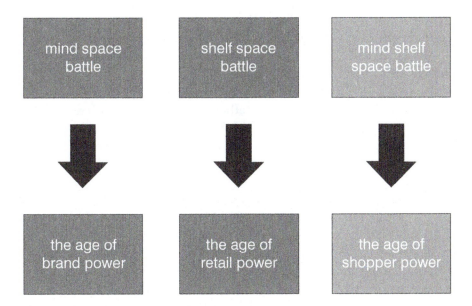

Figure 17.2 The battle for space

really means something and we call that the fight for mind shelf space. The brand has gone from a creator of mind space to a creator of mental images disproportionate to its shelf space – a creator of shelf mind space; a creator of brands that truly harness the power of the big issues we all face.

Once you've increased your mind shelf space in-store, increase it everywhere you operate, whether it be on the internet, through your own proprietary distribution, store in stores or even pop-up stores. In fact everywhere you sell. The shelf is no longer limited to the conventional store. It has become an everywhere, anyplace phenomenon – a challenge which potentially marginalizes the brand's importance.

A very new shelf of the future
starts to emerge

Get to the issues that really matter. Selling is what matters. And brands seem to have lost their selling edge. Traditionally, eye level has been buy level, and therefore selling level. But just go into a Sainsbury's and look at, say, the biscuit shelves, where the brands are proudly displayed on the lower shelves and the Sainsbury's products on middle-level shelves upwards. Who's catching the eye here?

Maybe we can change this by diverting buying into thinking. **In the future, think level will be buy level.**

We talked in our previous books about the need for brands to move to supplying wants for shoppers, rather than meeting their basic needs. When you want a product you seek it out wherever it may be. When you need a product you go to a commodity provider to meet that basic need. That basic but subtle difference is critical in re-establishing brand power.

> **The retailer supplies needs through Private Label.**
> **You supply wants through brands.**

Think about it. There is a difference. We will move from a society where people **'live to eat'** to a society where people **'eat to live'**. After decades as a byword for bad food, the UK need no longer be ashamed of its diet. British foods and drinks regularly win prizes in international competitions and a seventh of the world's top 50 restaurants are in the UK, according to *Restaurant* magazine.

This is just as true for electronics and fashion. Brands have no future in supplying basic needs. They have a future in stimulating our emotional appetites. They also need to re-stimulate our rational appetite through genuine product innovations, or even re-looking at boring old categories. Probably the greatest exponent of this is Apple, which is now redefining the phone with its new iPhone launch after redefining the music industry with its iPod. Food is also an area wide open to creating wants. Danone, the French yogurt maker, has taken the US market by storm with its 'Activia' brand, with active beneficial microbes included in the yogurt.

Let's also mention a Danish brand called **Aarstiderne**, which delivers boxes of organic vegetables, fruits, meat, fish and bread directly to the doorstep of customers every week or fortnight. In essence they've created their own mind shelf directly with the consumer without even being on the store shelf. Thirty thousand Danish households subscribe to the system of receiving a mystery box of organic food products on a regular basis. Customers pick a type and size of box, prepay one month in advance, and the content of the box is composed by Aarstiderne based on what's in season.

Farmer Thomas Harttung and local chef Soren Ejlersen started Aarstiderne with the idea of partnering with local households to change the general perception on farming, food and sustainability. By sourcing organic products from local farmers and growers, Aarstiderne aims to raise awareness of sustainability and food quality.

The boxes come with recipes and stories about growers, farms, the company, the food products and quality. The communication is honest and transparent – Aarstiderne lets the customers know how the farmers and Aarstiderne are doing, whether the news is good or bad.

Combining high-quality organic produce with the sense of surprise that accompanies each box, and creating a sense of community by sharing recipes and stories, Aarstiderne has both created a niche and filled an existing need in the organic food market. Similar concepts exist in the United States (Door to Door Organics), Sweden (Ekolådan), the Netherlands (Odin) and the UK (Riverford), to name just a few. Not an entirely new idea, but one whose time has come to be widely adopted!

Finally, why not consider changing your distribution shelf. German brewer **Karlsberg** (not to be confused with Danish Carlsberg) is convinced that it can get more women to drink beer. In countries such as the UK and Spain, roughly equal percentages of men and women drink beer (around 40 per cent). Surprisingly, this isn't the case in Germany, where women view beer as unhealthy, fattening or unsophisticated. They may have a point!

So Karlsberg is taking a different angle with its introduction of Karla. Stressing that beer is a natural product, Karla is being promoted as a healthy drink for women. The mixed drink is attractively packaged, and comes in two varieties. Both are low in alcohol content (1 per cent) and are a blend of beer and fruit juices. Karla Balance claims to provide 'peace and balance' by mixing hops with lemon balm, a herb well known for its sedative properties.

The other variety, Karla Well-Be, is also an offspring of the functional foods/nutraceuticals trend. Ingredients include soy-derived lecithin (which may positively affect cholesterol levels), folic acid (recommended for women considering pregnancy), and other vitamins.

Emphasis on health prompted an unusual distribution channel: Karla is sold through pharmacists. After a soft launch in 2005, Karlsberg recently teamed up with neutraceutical manufacturer Amapharm to distribute Karla to pharmacists across Germany. International expansion is in the works.

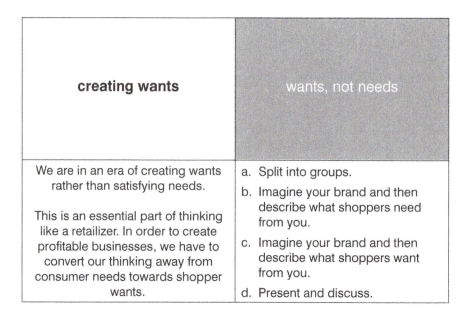

creating wants	wants, not needs
We are in an era of creating wants rather than satisfying needs. This is an essential part of thinking like a retailizer. In order to create profitable businesses, we have to convert our thinking away from consumer needs towards shopper wants.	a. Split into groups. b. Imagine your brand and then describe what shoppers need from you. c. Imagine your brand and then describe what shoppers want from you. d. Present and discuss.

Figure 17.3 Management action workshop exercise

Consistent, consistency

One of the keys to managing this mind share long term will be consistency. CEO Robert Polet, in a recent article in *Fortune* magazine (Fortune, 2007), eloquently put this in perspective for the Gucci brand, an 85-year-old brand survivor. He cites consistency as a key cornerstone for his brand. As he puts it, 'imagine the brand as friend. If that friend becomes inconsistent, the first time you say, "Hmm, strange". Second time it happens you say, "I'm not sure I feel comfortable with this person anymore because they're unpredictable." The third time you say, "I'm going to look for a new friend."' That's exactly what happens with a brand. If it is managed in an inconsistent way the consumer distrusts it and starts moving to another. That's how a brand dies. We'll talk more about this when we talk about the future store later.

Category disruptors

You can use this approach to mind shelf to literally break up and disrupt the normal rules of a category. As we know, today's shoppers are bombarded with thousands of products and services on a daily basis through advertising, in-store displays and store shelves, among other vehicles. The probability that a consumer will notice your product among the crowd becomes increasingly unlikely. However, it's not completely out of your control. But you need to be bold and radical.

The only way to get your product noticed is by disrupting your category's unspoken rules. There are two fundamental characteristics you must possess in order to 'disrupt' successfully. The first is having a rationale to do so. The second is feeling it's a natural thing to do – wanting to be different.

So how do you go about disrupting your category? First, review three elements of your product (**look, form and function**) and then decide which of these elements your product can disrupt, should disrupt and can afford to disrupt.

Look: Take a look at what your shelf neighbours are doing. Is there something you can do visually to make yourself stand out? Can you change the labelling on the package? Can you use colours that are not being used in the current shelf space? Can you position yourself on the shelf to stand out that much better? Can you be clearer and more legible about what you really offer? Can you give the shopper a health message he or she wants? Can you reduce your packaging clutter? Can you look more relevant to today's shoppers?

Form: Perhaps your product can be packaged in something other than the typical box or bottle. Review the structure of your package and determine if you can make changes, not only for disrupting the category but for the shopper experience as well. Can you go into a tube instead of a box, a bag instead of a tub? Often, by changing your packaging you can also change your store location and truly get away from the competition. Just think about how the introduction of pouches moved many refrigerated items to normal store aisles.

Function: One of the key ways to break category and achieve the status of signature brand is to review the function of your packaging. How can your product be packaged to achieve better use by the shopper? Recently a major sugar product has been repackaged in a plastic container with a lid so that consumers do not have to switch containers. By removing the sugar from the bags it made the product easier to purchase, easier to store and easier for brand recognition. Can you genuinely make your product easier?

Standing up, standing out and standing for something are the cornerstones of any brand looking to make a real difference in a relatively short time. Use these factors to disrupt your category and truly stand out.

Summary and opportunities

These days there's only one battle that really means something and that's the fight for mind shelf space. The brand has gone from a creator of mind space to a creator of mental images disproportionate to its shelf space; a creator of shelf mind space; a creator of brands that truly harness the power of the big issues we all face.

- Opportunity 14: Increase your MIND SHELF PRESENCE. In-store, make sure your presence and products are directly linked to the big issues society faces.
- Opportunity 15: OWN THINK SPACE AND LEVEL.

Actions to consider

1. Look at what you offer. Does it give you mind shelf presence?
2. Describe three ways you can change your products to give them greater mind shelf presence.
3. Find ways to own the think level.
4. Find ways to disrupt your category.

18 Private principle 6: Innovate, imagineer and involve

Here we look at how you can use the three i's to their fullest.

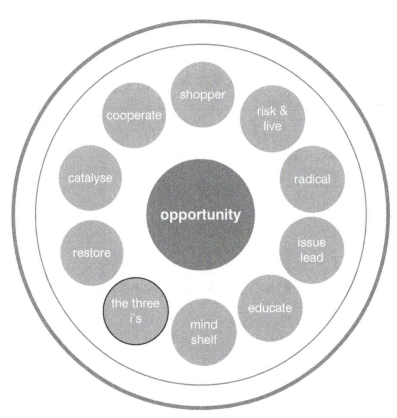

Figure 18.1 The three i's

Headlines

- Innovate like you've never innovated before.
- Bring back the power of brand imagery.
- Involve the shopper.
- Ideally do all three and combine their power.

i, i and i

This is where we creatively pull our strategies together to fight the Private Label variants and realize the opportunities – where we find ways to use the three i's to position ourselves creatively and effectively against commodity, copy and premium retail brands. Let's look at them one by one.

Innovation

Imagineer

Involvement

Figure 18.2   i, i and i

i number one... innovation

You can see the effect of innovation best in the CPG world where the rate of innovation is clearly closely correlated with the share of Private Label in that category. Jams, oils and sauces fail to hold it back (Figure 18.3). Low innovation has been their disappearing barrier to entry. Detergents and shampoos, however, stay Private Label independent. Their relentless search for innovation has made easy Private Label entry very difficult in practice. This argument can be taken even further when you start to think how brands should really innovate in practice. Yes, innovation is key. But it should be accepted as an everyday practice anyway. To realize the Private Label opportunity you may need more.

A recent study in 23 countries looked specifically at Private Label success in low-innovation categories (Kumar and Steenkamp, 2007). They found that **Private Label share is 56 per cent higher in categories with low innovation activity**. Seems like a good reason to innovate as much as possible. But one should bear in mind that you can even get Private Label in the highest-innovation categories. Remember our earlier description of the Apple threat from Private Label. So nobody's entirely immune, although innovation will provide a degree of security. For those brands in low-innovation categories it's clearly time to maximize your R&D efforts.

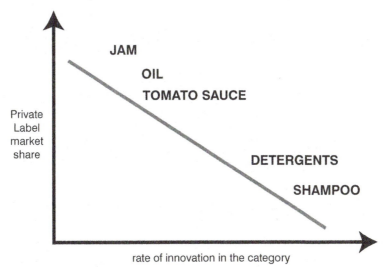

Figure 18.3 Value innovation is the best defence
Source: Jean-Noel Kapferer HEC

Figure 18.4 shows where the real opportunities lie for most brands in rebuilding volume by giving more for less and/or building **true value innovations** by providing shoppers with more for more. How does your new product development (NPD) programme stack up to this? The former is really a defence policy, the latter – pure attack. The only way you can truly make your brand consistently innovative is to offer far more for more.

When you look at your own product innovations, do you really meet this objective? Do your innovations reach the extreme of providing **far more for more**? Do they provide **true value innovations**? The chart in Figure 18.4, adapted and derived from Jean Noel Kapferer, makes it clear that brands need to innovate at this extreme to be truly successful against Private Label.

But look at your own innovations and ask, at a minimum, do they really provide more product for less cost than they did before the innovation or, even more ideally, do they provide more product for more price? The latter is your real target. Always **strive for far more for more**.

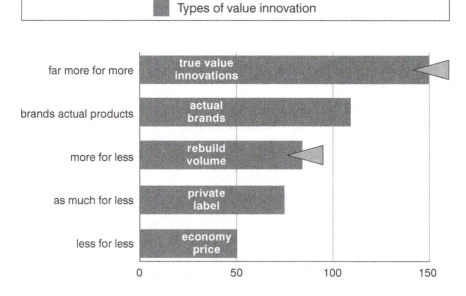

Figure 18.4 Innovation is the catalyst
Source: Jean-Noel Kapferer HEC

Let's look at this in practice. If we look at some recent innovations in the game machine industry (Figure 18.5), it's clear who's the ongoing winner: Nintendo. You can see why Sony is really losing the game. Yes, innovations galore. But boy don't you have to pay for them. With a price differential at least twice that of Wii you would expect an innovation mountain to greet you. Instead you get questionably useful innovations like Blu-ray packaged in a box that doesn't look that different from PS3. The new Xbox 360 partly avoids this mistake with well-priced innovation. But its packaging lacks inspiration. The low-priced-strategy entrant seems to have understood the market that much better. They came up with machines that were all about fun and not about technology overkill. They also realized that the simple TV control device that we all use could be utilized to become a game paddle that really allowed you to move around when playing. Just go out and try one and you'll see how addictive it is. They created real value innovation and gave people far more for more. That's why they're the runaway sales success in the sector.

Most people don't even get this far. They produce false innovations called line extensions and hope it's good enough. It's frankly not, and certainly not good enough to beat Private Label. As the head of a major Scandinavian retailer recently said to us: 'I'm sick of brands coming here and saying they've been in the business for a hundred years and know everything there is to know: "Here's our new line extension flavour variant. Give us more shelf space." I don't want this. I want innovation. I want food iPods.'

game machine	more product	more value	price level
Nintendo Wii	yes	yes	100
Microsoft Xbox 360	yes	partly	150
Sony PS3	yes	no	200

Figure 18.5   Value innovation winners

The lost innovation edge

Retailers are fantastic at selling things, but very few retailers are very good at developing things. Or so we thought. That used to be the raison d'être of the brands. But with their obsession for big-batch volumes they have often mixed up genuine innovations with the next flavour extension or volume variant package. It's a lot easier to produce variants on flavour rather than retool for a substantial change in product. Many FMCG companies have forgotten what originally made them big. When it comes to the retail arena, shoppers reach out for products, but they are often disappointed. Lots of companies have a brand these days, but few have a product. Or as Sir Martin Sorrel puts it: 'We have become so obsessed with the sizzle that we have forgotten the steak.' The brand is never the solution. The product is. In their book, *Blue Ocean Strategy*, authors W Chan Kim and Renee Mauborgne researched the effect of creating groundbreaking, creative new products, rather than variations of already existing products. Their conclusion was that 86 per cent of new product launches were variants of existing products and accounted for 39 per cent of total profit. The remaining 14 per cent of new products were real new products and accounted for a massive 61 per cent of total profit. Real products mean real profit.

The most successful grower of brands in the mass markets is arguably **Procter & Gamble**. P&G has built the biggest brand business in the world by understanding its competitive context better than anybody else. Its key to growth has been to constantly out-innovate not only the competition, but also itself. P&G's finest ability is to make continuous improvements to its brands through a constant series of innovations, adding small additional fighting features to its armoury, and sometimes creating entirely new product ideas and categories.

> Product innovation has been the cornerstone of our success in the past and it's the primary strategy for success in the future.
>
> pg.com

It has constantly sought to win each given shelf in each given market it operates in. Among other things, its innovations have been driven from the need to compete with, and understand, outstanding competitors and find ways to beat them. It is this drive for constantly out-innovating competitors that defines P&G as a company. Incremental never-ending change is the name of the game, and staying one step ahead is P&G's yardstick of measurement, and a very successful strategy it has been. P&G has over 16 brands exceeding sales of US $1 billion each, and is the global leader in four core product categories: fabric and home care, beauty care, baby and family care, and health care. P&G has used this innovation to good effect when creating word-of-mouth marketing. Its website Tremor.com lets teenagers be directly involved in product development and sampling. Hundreds of thousands of teenagers have used this site and their word of mouth is capable of reaching epidemic proportions, directly to key target audiences like friends and family.

> We should strive to be invited into consumers' lives and homes.
>
> Jim Stengel, Global Marketing Officer, P&G

Other big brand builders like Gillette have followed the same pattern for years. **Gillette**, like P&G, understands that product innovation must be constant, with noticeable (or at least marketable) improvements year in, year out. In today's market a company cannot count on consumer loyalty, and instead must constantly 'sell' the customer on product value. The Sensor was launched in 1990 and was the first major new product introduced by Gillette for 25 years. When BIC disposables threatened to turn the market into a cheap commodity one, Gillette responded with this apparently new shaving experience. There was initially only one blade and one lubrastrip, but step by step, blades and lubrastrips and more and more floating heads were added to produce what the company would like customers to perceive as the ultimate shave. Constant innovation has kept Gillette comfortably ahead of the competition – from Mach 3 to Mach 3 Turbo to M3 Power to Fusion. The incremental innovations from Gillette have kept the brand securely positioned as the global leader. The brand still maintains a 70-plus per cent global market share (Geneva, 2004) and quickly gains market leadership with every new product launch, a remarkably unique performance for such a high-consumption, everyday-use product. It has understood its competition from the very beginning and has always kept one step ahead.

Metro International is another successful example of how to out-innovate. In a world of free-flowing information and news on the internet, many newspaper businesses have been challenged. Tabloids have had an especially rough time. Because of the faster, more superficial and less quality-concerned nature of the tabloid product, readers more easily switched to the internet without feeling a large loss of quality. As a result, many tabloids have experienced a drop in sales and therefore a drop in advertising revenues, an evil circle that nobody seemed to be able to break – that is, until Metro International arrived on the scene with a radical new proposition, through out-innovating the competition in terms of pricing and distribution. It started giving its newspapers away for free on the streets and on public transport, something it could afford to subsidize through paid advertising. The first Metro newspaper was published in Stockholm in 1995. Now, there are 58 editions in Europe and international launches in 2006 include Bohemia, Moravia, Castellon, the Canary Islands, the Basque country, Mexico City and Croatia (Mandmeurope.com, 2006). According to the Metro website, the free daily is the largest and fastest-growing international newspaper in the world. Seventy daily Metro editions are published in over 100 major cities in 21 countries in 19 languages across Europe, North and South America and Asia. It's also now official! *Metro*, the flagship title of Metro International, has been declared the 'World's Largest Global Newspaper' by no less an authority than Guinness World Records.

Joint value innovation

Innovation and knowledge are the key. Innovation is no longer synonymous with new product development, but rather with how to become more innovative when satisfying and tailoring offers to customers. Companies that are not customer oriented and have a hard time understanding the needs of the market will, in the end, be dominated by companies that have superior knowledge. According to Doyle (1995), this is exactly what has happened in the grocery market and fast-moving consumer goods. Retailers with access to information about customer needs are thereby able to control that knowledge. This has become the professional core that adds value to their customers. The focus in marketing should therefore be on the core value-adding process of operations, innovation and customer creation and support rather than on the traditional marketing disciplines. The growth of Private Label is one of the single biggest issues in business today and as such demands a radical and creative approach to shopper (not consumer) marketing. Changing pricing strategy, doing a few more customized product innovations and promotions is possibly not going to change the picture in the long run. Reinventing the way we approach Private Label, the way the organization sees it and the way we deal with it, are the dynamic keys we need to push to move forward.

Joint value innovation is the name of the game in a way that transforms the shopper experience to build a new kind of equity. Not brand or consumer, but shopper equity. Brand owners and retailers need to get together and agree between them how they can leverage and apply shopper insight, deeper branded involvement and innovation across the whole value equation to achieve profitability and partnership, not just in terms of production but at every touch-point with the shopper. That means thinking about quality, price, choice, convenience and increasingly community in different ways, closing the gap perhaps between the way shoppers currently try to buy to deliver an altogether more rewarding shopper experience.

Innovation is, of course, part of the opportunity. The other two i's are equally critical.

i number two... imagineer

These people are using brands just as much as we use brands. They believe in brands. Don't be fooled.

Paul Polman, ex head of P&G Europe, talking about Aldi, Europe's largest hard discount retailer

Image remains a powerful brand force. The one thing that brands have, and Private Label does not, remains image. Billions of dollars have been spent over the years building those differentiated images. It may sound boring, but old-fashioned marketing and communications still play a powerful role. Brand studies almost everywhere have shown that consumers, when asked to choose between brands and Private Labels, tend to choose brands. A UK study in arguably the most Private Label sophisticated market in the world showed that consumers chose 49 brands first as the products they would miss the most from a supermarket shelf (Geronimo, 2005). The 50th was Tesco cheese. However, please note that Tesco with eight products had the fifth largest number of brands in the top one hundred. Obviously they're not far behind. It also ignores the fact that, as we pointed out earlier, **convenience rules**. And while we might like our brands, do we love them enough to cause us inconvenience if they're not on the shelf? You know the answer yourself.

Occasionally you see reasons for hope, and Sweden is one market where that occasionally shines through. A recent study by Lund University measured brand preference in Sweden among grocery brands and retailers. The number one retailer, ICA, came 34th! The 'in theory' most pressurized category (dairy) had the brand that came top – Arla.

While retailers have bigger and bigger corporate spends, they do not have the cumulative directed history that brands do. And they're not going to obtain it overnight. But they are becoming more powerful. Image advertising for a retail chain far outweighs any individual brand spend. In the United States 15 of the top megabrand advertising spenders are now retailers. In the first half of 2006 alone (adage.com, 2006), measured by millions of US dollars advertising spend, eight of the biggest spending brands are leading retailers in their own right. Additionally, their positioning, in our view, often isn't that clear. While the retail industry has imported marketing experience, they are not yet able to be as good as the brand giants out there. But they will be.

Brands have long been defined through their USPs or unique single-minded propositions – a system developed by the advertising industry to help them focus their creatives on producing targeted meaningful executions. We are far from convinced that Private Labels have well-developed USPs. There are mountains of evidence over the years to show that a good image leads to improved brand preference and greater sales. The best images are often the ones that are emotionally inspired, from Nike to Apple computers. Retail advertising does not have that same emotional clout. The need to talk price often brings it back to the rational and the boring.

While the power of this brand imagery has been diluted over the years, it is still a factor and still an influence. The problem for most brands is not how to create an image but how to communicate it. The decline of the world of mass media possibilities has led inevitably to the decline of the brand.

Let's take this argument on further and test your product against the three i's (Figure 18.6). Let's start by looking at the games industry we talked about earlier. Clearly we can see why Nintendo is winning the game. If you apply the three i's to your brands you stand a very good chance of staying ahead – staying unique.

game machine	innovation	image	involvement
Nintendo Wii	yes	yes	yes
Microsoft Xbox 360	yes	partly	partly
Sony PS3	yes	no	no

Figure 18.6 The three i's test

Another example is **Nivea Deodorant** in Germany. Private Label brands are 10 per cent of category value and 21 per cent of volume and have nearly doubled in share since 2000. At the same time, Nivea has also been able to grow share to 17 per cent value while operating at a price three times that of Private Labels. Deodorants, in comparison with all other categories in Germany, do very well on most of the key drivers of Private Labels. All Nivea communication in all categories (such as body care and shampoo, as well as deodorants) stresses the trustworthiness of the brand. This is backed up by independent tests showing that Nivea deodorants provide long-lasting performance – an important seal of quality for the German consumer. Nivea is also one of the most advertised brands in Germany and its deodorants benefit from the enormous equity created in the past. Nivea continues this strategy with new advertising creating emotional bonds between the brand and its consumers. Nivea also supports its quality claims by a constant stream of new product introductions. Each is supported by heavy advertising and promotional activity.

But the category doesn't do so well on two key attributes. Consumers perceive a high level of packaging similarity between manufacturer and retailer brands. They also believe that national brand manufacturers produce Private Label brands. Nivea counters these issues by being very alert when retailer brands start copying the appearance of national brands. They also introduce new products and variants at a pace that is difficult to follow. For example, Nivea recently launched a different form of deodorant, where tissues are applied to the skin to guarantee freshness. Finally, they do not produce Private Labels and proudly announce the fact. Nivea acts effectively on nearly all the key drivers of retailer brand success in Germany. It uses innovation and image in particular to maintain its competitive edge.

Our final example is **Walkers Potato Crisps** in the UK – a category with a Private Label share of 30 per cent in value. Yet Walkers has been able not just to repulse inroads from Private Labels but to grow their share significantly. How has this been achieved? Potato crisps, in comparison with all other categories, does very well on nearly all the key drivers of retail brands in the UK. Walkers has hit all the right buttons in the UK, from creating a high-quality image to maintaining a high level of trust towards Walker's to building a consistent marketing intensity to being truly distinctive. Specifically:

- very distinctive packaging vis-à-vis Private Labels ;
- short run – often seasonal – flavour introductions to 'move' the market and nurture an innovative image;
- new products – Premium Range and 'Traditional' Crisps – and wide range catering for different consumer segments;
- long-term consistent advertising and communication (eg 25 TV ads over 10 years featuring Gary Lineker, always emphasizing the quality and desirability of the brand);
- volume-driving promotions maintain product 'freshness' – a key perception of the Walker's brand.

This shows that managing your brand along the relevant drivers of Private Label success in your country will strengthen your brand in its battle against Private Labels. The three i's are the tools that will allow you to keep your focus.

i number three... involvement

Life is changing and it has a deep effect on our shoppers and the new ROI – RETURN ON INVOLVEMENT – we can expect from them. They are not the passive consumers of the past – passive serfs who did what they were told and shopped when told to by mass communications tools. Now they make their own decisions and you need to ensure your brand becomes fully involved with them, pre, post and during the purchase experience. You need to get closer to your shoppers and maybe one way of doing this is to start listening to them and start cooperating with them. You need to start 'listening to shoppers' more. Too many focus groups have their predetermined questionnaires which moderators are determined to get through, whatever it takes. This is not conducive to good research, which should be relaxed and stimulating at the same time. We should not treat shoppers as laboratory rats and we should avoid processes that provide average statistics. Average statistics give you average results. Throw away glass research mirrors and talk to shoppers about their lives and their shopping experiences – not just products. You might be surprised by what you hear. By listening to people more effectively we get closer to the true shopping nature of brands. Brands are living entities. Brands are holistic. Brands are not about stereotypes. Brands are about paradoxes. Brands are about talking to everyone. Brands are about emotions.

That participation can take many forms.

Shoppers want to be participants not just spectators. Shoppers want to be listened to. They want to know about what they're buying. They want to know they're buying the right thing. Right in terms of quality and right in terms of addressing the 'big issues'.

Shoppers want to be involved in innovation themselves. Innovation by the masses not just for the masses, but for themselves. Customer-made is the new mantra (Springwise.com).

> CUSTOMER-MADE: 'The phenomenon of corporations creating goods, services and experiences in close cooperation with experienced and creative consumers, tapping into their intellectual capital, and in exchange giving them a direct say in (and rewarding them for) what actually gets produced, manufactured, developed, designed, serviced, or processed.'

Here are a few examples:

- The **Nokia Concept Lounge** took place in the summer of 2005. The lounge invited designers in the Benelux to share ideas and design the next cool new phone. Not surprisingly, in a GLOBAL BRAIN world, entries came from all over, with the winner being a Turkish designer, Tamer Nakisci. His wristband-style phone (the Nokia 888) must have had phone manufacturers from China to Finland drooling. Remember, tomorrow's breakthrough designer, thanks to the spread and power of the internet, could just as easily come from equatorial Africa as California.

- The **Electrolux Design Lab 2005** attracted entries from 3,058 design students from 88 countries around the world, the top six countries being the United States, the UK, China, India, Brazil and Italy. Participants were asked to design household appliances for the year 2020. Twelve finalists participated in a six-day design event in Stockholm, including workshops, model building and a competition for cash awards, appliances and more.
- Another example of create and sell: LEGO's **LEGO Factory** has been around for a while, but it remains an inspiring example of how to truly unleash the GLOBAL BRAIN. Children and other building enthusiasts visiting the site are invited to design models (using easy-to-use, free downloadable software) and take part in competitions for LEGO prizes. A popular contest last year entitled winners to have their model mass-produced and sold in Shop@Home, receiving a 5 per cent royalty on each set sold.

Ideas come from many sources and you need to participate with those sources wherever they may be. Creativity is the product of collaboration at mass scale. Value chains become conversations, co-creating value.

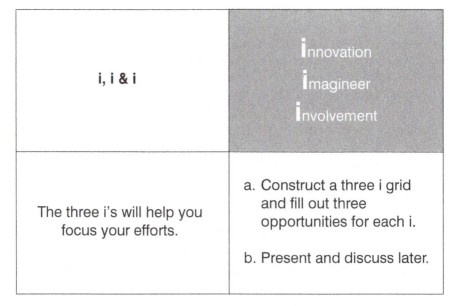

Figure 18.7 Management action workshop exercise

Summary and opportunities

- Opportunity 16: Innovate to the extreme by providing FAR MORE FOR MORE. Make your product the solution over making your image the solution.
- Opportunity 17: Seek BLUE OCEANS – innovations that leapfrog your present products and take you into new, fresh dynamic markets. TRUE VALUE INNOVATIONS.
- Opportunity18: CO-CREATE WITH YOUR CUSTOMERS. Get your customers directly involved in designing your products.
- Opportunity 19: Seek ways to be invited into your consumers' lives and homes.
- Opportunity 20: CO-CREATE WITH YOUR RETAILERS. Run JOINT VALUE INNOVATION PROGRAMMES.
- Opportunity 21: Maximize your RETURN ON INVOLVEMENT. Ensure your shoppers are participants, not just spectators.
- Opportunity 22: REJUVINATE YOUR IMAGE. Take your tired old image and give it a healthy boost through new dynamic new-age communications.

Actions to consider

1. Set up a three i's programme.
2. Evaluate your brands' three i's potential.
3. Are you delivering on innovation at a high enough level? Do you produce innovations that give far more for more?
4. Set up a programme to involve your customers.
5. Set up customer-made programmes and initiatives.
6. Maintain the development of your differentiated image edge.
7. Initiate a joint value programme with your key suppliers.

19 Private principle 7: Restore and reinvent the store

Here we look at the store revolution.

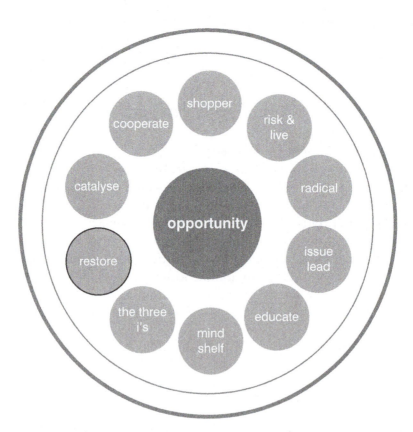

Figure 19.1   Restoring and reinventing the store

Headlines

- Today's store concepts are mostly designed for the passive consumer of tomorrow.
- They need to be redesigned for the active, informed shopper of tomorrow.
- They need to be redesigned for the 'lean' revolution in manufacturing that is descending upon us.
- They need to be redesigned for the changing nature of distribution,

The retail store of the future and how it would look

We bring two key factors of our wheel of opportunity into play here – the store and mind space. We have to reinterpret the battlefield for shoppers for the future. And we need to do a better job of this than Private Labels. To do this we must understand where we're coming from and where we're going. It's clear that the retail store of the future will be very different. It's clearer by the day that the place you can make a difference when communicating your brand is the store, where the real impact of communications is playing out its game. Media fragmentation outside the store, shoppers who increasingly decide inside the store, and the sheer number of communications respondents in-store daily point to the store being the real point of communications action, now and for the foreseeable future.

Maybe the supermarket of the future will have two forms:

> **first form**: packaged foods only for those who want convenience above all else;
> **second form**: fresh foods only (à la WFM) where choice, freshness and well-being rule.

Which one would you want to shop at?

There are many changes occurring in the fundamental nature of stores:

● **Only the fittest will survive**. We're clearly going through a shake-up and today's brands are not necessarily tomorrow's. Only the strongest will survive. Companies with strong brand identities will continue to have a retail future. As shoppers become more and more discerning about what they actually choose from the mountains of choice presented to them, natural selection will take over. A great brand with a clearly understood proposition is still going to stand out from the crowd. Whether the mass retailer allows them to stand out enough is another question.

● **The power shift continues.** In the foreseeable future there is little reason to believe that the age of brand power is about to return. On the contrary, we probably haven't remotely seen the full boundaries of the age of retail power yet. It's always worth remembering that while dinosaurs did become extinct, they took an awfully long time over it. And a lot of their natural competitors died out before them. Eventually the more nimble and flexible mammal won out – a creature that was infinitely adaptable in a way the dinosaurs weren't. However, in the here and now, retailers will continue to improve their profitability at the expense of manufacturers and there's obviously going to be a clear-out. Being number 2, 3 or 4 in a category is a recipe for future disaster in such a world.

● **There will be a few stars in each category.** You can see it already – categories are beginning to be dominated by two or three megabrands. This will be particularly evident at the international level, where sheer scale will make certain brands winners and others not. You can easily see a scenario where 50 retail brands rule the world. You can probably name them now. And you shoppers thought you had choice! Innovative niche players will still exist, but niche they are likely to remain. The same parallel will clearly happen on the manufacturer side. They will get bigger, merge, form alliances and so on if they are to have any say in their business futures beyond being a commodity manufacturer.

● **Formats will become more and more ubiquitous.** The formats of the giant retailers will increasingly look alike, wherever they are in the world. Local differentiation will diminish in large store formats, whether they be Aldi, IKEA or the giant electronic retailer Media Markt. Their global familiarity will be very consistent. That very ubiquity may well be your retail opportunity. If you can come up with a radically different way to sell and present your products, you'll stand out in a sea of blandness.

● **There will still be newcomers.** If you look at the history of retail, they come and they go. Look at Toys 'r Us, which ruled the toy world until recently. Now where is it? Look at Dixons, Britain's biggest high-street electronic retailer which closed its shops overnight to go on the web. And so on. Change will continue, albeit at a slower rate as the giants of the world become clearer and clearer.

> *Maybe the supermarket of the future will be a brand one only. Brands get together to provide the ultimate in brand experience under one roof. Maybe they simply buy one of the big players and convert them.*

● **Extremes will emerge.** According to Ko Floor in his excellent new book, *Branding a Store*, the shopping of goods will split into four extremes. The key question for brands is, where do you want to be? There's little point being in the middle as that is a road to nowhere. Choose your battlefield well – it will decide your destiny.

● **The in-betweenys have had it.** Price will polarize markets and medium-priced retail brands will increasingly disappear. Low price and high value will rule the waves. And premium brands with

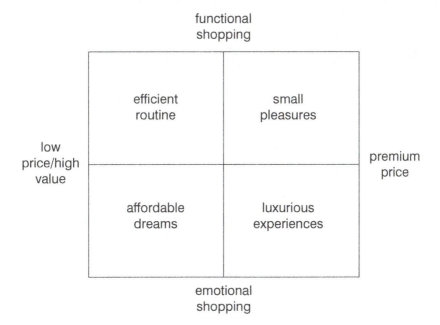

Figure 19.2 The future retail extremes
Source: Ko Floor – *Branding A Store*

unique products will continue to exploit their lucrative niches. No amount of Chinese copies is going to stop the Japanese from buying an original Louis Valliant bag.

MIDDLE OFFERS INCREASINGLY LACK CLARITY AND SELLABLE PROPOSITIONS TO THE SHOPPER

- **We all need to be an iPod.** As Steve Jobs of Apple eloquently put it recently, 'When I launch a product I assume it's redundant in six months.' Now we're not all Apple. But speed to market is increasingly critical. The brand that can rely on its hundred-year history as a reason for failing to innovate is going to find itself redundant and replaced.
- **Customer orientation will replace product relationships.** In other words, the store will fit the need and the shopping situation more than ever.

Petrol stations will become for people on the move,
toy shops for divorced fathers who want to see their kids,
fashion stores will become identity stores.

Design formats that meet SOCIAL NEEDS RETAILING. Identify shoppers' situational needs and provide shopping experiences/retail formats that meet them. Go to them. Don't expect them to come to you.

- **We shop everywhere or not at all.** We will increasingly expect our retailers and therefore our brands to have multi-levels of distribution channels from the web to the concept store to the supermarket to the pop-up store. Those that don't will lose out. Multi-channel retailing is here to stay. The start point for knowing which formats to use is to **rethink your relationship with your customers in terms of their circumstances rather than their attributes**. This is essentially the Tesco way forward and a very successful way it has been. When you do that, you start to realize you need to get your customer with multi-format retail from the home to the mass market. Ask yourself, are you really doing that at the moment and do you have innovative distribution systems that back up delivery of the product to the shopper?

Think of those circumstances as a crazy ride in your shoppers' lives, a ride where you are present when they need you. Not a ride where you are present when it suits you. If your shopper is best served by your being open 24 hours, then open 24 hours. If your shopper is best served by delivery direct to him or her, make sure you can. Or at least find partners from the post to Federal Express who can. Because if you don't, your competitors will, and the biggest competitor of all has key distribution advantages already – Private Label (Figure 19.3).

Maybe we never need to visit a supermarket again. Order from the internet. Special local centres allow us rapid pick-up of our orders at our convenience. We simply provide the order and the pick-up time or they'll deliver direct when it suits us at home, work, study, rest or play.

By meeting shopper circumstances a lot can change.

- **Freshness is critical.** Retail environments must strive with their brands to look fresh every day. That includes the coffee shelf in a supermarket as much as H&M. And we can truly be fresh all the time. Production is becoming leaner and leaner all the time as we move from a world of mass batch production to smaller and smaller mini-batch runs. More about this later.

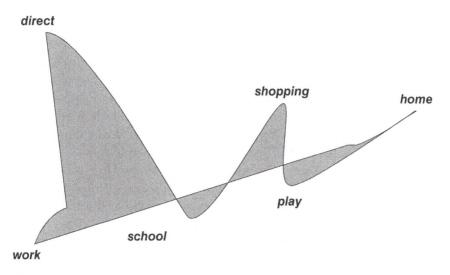

Figure 19.3 Meeting shopper circumstances

An overall revolution in supplying the shopper is afoot: a revolution in convenience retailing and a revolution in getting products to shoppers.

Daniel T Jones and James P Womack, authors of *Lean Solutions*, point this out when they make the point that stores are warehouses of slow-moving goods with very few high-moving goods. In other words, the proverbial long tail. They claim that on average 6 per cent of stock-keeping units (SKUs) account for 50 per cent of manufacturer volume. Taking this into account will make manufacturers move towards becoming much leaner suppliers of goods – moving from large batch suppliers to producing small quantities when you need them. They argue that, if handled properly, this process can be as efficient as the old batch system that has driven mass manufacturing capability to date.

They cite Toyota as the ultimate example of a company that has moved to this lean production model: a company poised to overtake General Motors as the biggest manufacturer in the world; a company with all the growth in the market; a company with enough cash flow to buy every other competitor out there.

Fresh every day

One of the inevitable consequences of this thinking is that, in theory, processed food can become fresh food. Convenient low-cost replenishment of products is now possible. Why do we have to have 12-month-old cornflakes when we can have week-old cornflakes? It does taste better after all.

Retailers are starting to embrace this new thinking. They are starting to realize that the very process of consumption has become more complex. Tesco in particular has rethought its relationship with its customers in terms of their circumstances rather than their attributes. That's why they have developed multi-formats from home shopping all the way to mass retailers. Tesco Direct, for example, now sells 8,000 product lines. It uses these multi-formats to capture more of its customers' spend and build a better understanding of their purchase behaviour – an approach it uses extensively today in the UK and an approach it will use to beat Wal-Mart in the United States.

You see the very same thing in 7-Elevens in Japan where so many of their products are now fresh and conveniently offered. Tesco has also understood that in addition to rapid replenishment you must know your customer intimately. Its loyalty cards allow it to uniquely do just that and get to the core of its customers' behaviour. This is where the convenience revolution is happening. And it's as applicable to selling food as it is to selling mobile phones.

It will change the very nature of retailing and you will see more and more retailers integrate home shopping with local stores. Our shopper will order from home. You will supply by picking up at store, and deliver to home, deliver to work or even deliver to local distribution centres, for example schools. We told you local was back!

Maria plans to visit her local store on the way home from work to collect some items for the family meal. Albert has some jobs to do around the house and he will stop at the local DIY to check if they have what he needs. He has already ordered some materials for direct home delivery. The children rarely use the 'shops'; they only go when it is a family occasion to look for something special. The family is happy to let the in-home systems monitor their needs and arrange solutions.

(*Source*: The future value chain, Capgemini)

Really, really understand the shopper

Private Label development is not solely influenced by factors such as quality, price, positioning etc but is also a function of retail structure and rooted shopping habits in a given country. Understanding how people shop is therefore an even greater prerequisite to determining their preference for Private Labels or brands. These facts are a clear signal that brand owners will need, now more than ever before, a better understanding of household purchase patterns and motivations in order to cultivate an enduring loyalty that will prevent the threat of Private Labels. In this context, going beyond traditional marketing approaches and preconceived ideas, to understand both 'consumers' and 'shoppers', will be the key to success.

Apple shows the way.

Case Study: Apple

I give [Apple] two years before they're turning out the lights on a very painful and expensive mistake.

(Retail consultant David Goldstein)

The use of a store can transform your brand. Apple computer has dramatically proved this point. Five years later, the earlier prediction has been proven completely and utterly wrong. Apple is now seen as one of the best retailing brands in the world and a very profitable one (*Fortune*, March, 2007).

Saks, whose flagship is down the street on Fifth Avenue, New York, generates sales of $362 per square foot a year. Best Buy stores turn $930 – tops for electronics retailers – while Tiffany & Co. takes in $2,666. Audrey Hepburn liked Tiffany's for breakfast. But at $4,032, Apple is eating everyone's lunch.

That astonishing number, from a Sanford C Bernstein report, is merely the average of Apple's 174 stores, which attract 13,800 visitors a week. (The Fifth Avenue store averages 50,000-plus.) In 2004, Apple reached $1 billion in annual sales faster than any retailer in history; in 2006, sales reached $1 billion a quarter.

You could say that Apple has landed – not only on our street corners and in our malls but also, for the first time, on the top 10 of *Fortune's* Most Admired Companies. Its peers have watched it upend industries from computers to music. But how did a high-tech wonder company become America's best shopkeeper?

People haven't been willing to invest this much time and money or engineering in a store before. It's not important if the customer knows that. They just feel it. They feel something's a little different.

(Steve Jobs, Apple CEO)

Back in 2000 the company was increasingly dependent on mega-retailers – companies that had little incentive, never mind training, to position Apple's products as anything unique. 'It was like, "We have to do something, or we're going to be a victim of the plate tectonics. And we have to think different about this. We have to innovate here."'

And innovate is exactly what they did. Here are a few examples.

They rented a warehouse and built a prototype of a store, and kept rebuilding it until they got it right. In other words, design it as you would a product.

retailer	annual sales per sq ft, 2006
Apple stores	$4,032
Tiffany & Co	$2,666
Best Buy	$930
Norman Marcus	$611
Saks	$632

Figure 19.4 Store profitability
Source: Fortune

They had a fundamental insight. They realized that the computer was evolving from a simple productivity tool to a 'hub' for video, photography, music, information, and so forth. The sale, then, was less about the machine than what you could do with it. When the first store finally opened, in Tysons Corner, VA, only a quarter of it was about product. The rest was arranged around interests: along the right wall, photos, videos, kids; on the left, problems. A third area – the Genius Bar in the back.

The chances of getting a computer fixed today are one in three. Their objective is to make it, by tomorrow, two in three and eventually as fast as the dry cleaner.

The most striking thing, though, is what you don't see. Clutter. Jobs has focused Apple's resources on fewer than 20 products, and those have steadily been shrinking in size. Backroom inventory, then, can shrink in physical volume even as sales volume grows.

Also missing, at the newest stores, anyway, is a checkout counter. The system Apple developed, EasyPay, lets salespeople wander the floor with wireless credit-card readers and ask, 'Would you like to pay for that?'

The store does not feel like a cult. A club, maybe, in the sense that owning a Mac means joining something. Apple wants the purchase to be the beginning, not the conclusion, of a beautiful – and, it hopes, profitable – friendship.

> Apple has changed people's expectations of what retail should be about.
>
> (Candace Corlett of WSL Strategic Retail in New York)
>
> Yes, it's Apple and Apple's a little different. But it's well worth remembering that until 2000 Apple had never been a retailer. Its first years were a dismal failure and what it's done is applicable to the selling of anything. It's up to you. Apple was threatened by the exact same thing that threatens you. But it's certainly not worried about them now.
> The Apple case study is a good way of showing you how to win. You need to look everywhere there are great ideas.

In our previous book *How to Succeed at Retail* we outlined, through 25 case studies, 25 very different ways to succeed. Look at them and ask yourself, is there anything you can take from them that's applicable to your and your brands' battle with Private Label? This is where the real opportunity lies – an opportunity that allows you to totally rethink your future.

retail brand winners	winning strategy
YOYAMART	understanding the situation
GOOH!	reinventing the boring
INNOCENT	retaining innocence throughout
HOLLAND & HOLLAND	making more of more
REI	living the brand experience
ZARA	react rather than predict
BOSE	try, try and try again
TCHIBO	creating an unchallenged 'star'
OLIVIERS & CO.	creating wants, not needs
APPLE	merging buying with trying
EASYJET	creating choice

Figure 19.5 Winning retail brands

retail brand winners	winning strategy
RED BULL	rewriting the rules
PROCTER & GAMBLE	the moments of truth
GILLETTE	constant innovation
ASSA ABLOY	solve a problem
PERONI	challenging perceptions
H&M	four seconds to get them
COURVOISIER	revitalization
SENSEO	brand co-creation
STARBUCKS	being in the people first business
GUINNESS	changing the shelf
SUPERQUINN	customer obsession
WHOLE FOODS MARKET	ethics in action
KARMALOOP	turning shoppers into fanatics

Figure 19.6 More winning retail brands

Involvement retailing

The Apple case in particular points us to the real retail future – the involvement of the shopper in the purchase of the product. A number of interesting retail concepts that are trying to use this approach are cropping up globally now – an approach which is a highly differentiated one for a brand. We call this **involvement retailing**.

For retailers targeting the sensation-seeking consumer, goods and services are no longer enough. Increasingly, retailers will differentiate themselves by using experiences to sell the dream – as well as the product. Some retailers will mix context and commerce to such an extent that retail and experience become indistinguishable. Experience retailing will go beyond entertainment, education or interaction to engage customers in a more meaningful way where the experience or activity becomes an authentic part of their life. This will help establish a sense of community with the customer and create repeat business by literally bringing the brand to life. The retail venue will become a place to spend quality time – and, increasingly, a place to spend money to spend time. These retailers will expand the definition of their businesses such that the experiential environment will become as much a selling point as the merchandise itself.

Take **Le Labo**, a new perfumery in New York City, which offers an interesting twist on ready-made fragrances. Le Labo certainly looks like a lab, but it's not all smoke and mirrors. The boutique perfumer operates like one as well, mixing its scents on the spot. The idea is to ensure maximum freshness and focus on the quality of the raw ingredients rather than spending money on fancy packaging or multi-million-dollar marketing campaigns. When customers buy one of Le Labo's 11 scents, a matured essential oil blend is mixed with alcohol and water to create a finished fragrance. The process is designed to take about 10 minutes, ample time for visitors to browse shelves of raw ingredients in the 600-square-foot shop. The matured oils are composed by one of eight perfumers, all of whom work for fragrance suppliers: Alberto Morillas, Annick Menardo, Daphne Bugey, Maurice Roucel, Frank Voelkl, Françoise Caron, Michel Almairac and Mark Buxton.

By keeping the essential oils refrigerated and blending at the very last minute, Le Labo ensures that the fragrance is fresh at the time of purchase. Le Labo is a relatively new (2006) independent perfume house that commissions different perfumers to design their fragrances. Le Labo's perfumes all bear names of building blocks followed by a number to indicate how many other building blocks went into the formula.

Another example is **Starbucks**, which continues to blur the line between product innovation and business model innovation. Recognizing that it's not enough simply to roll out new coffee products every six months, the company is searching for new ways to build out its entertainment offerings (ie selling CDs in stores, promoting movies like Akeelah and the Bee). Starbucks is now looking to extend its brand experience with the opening of a temporary arts and performance coffee house in New York City. They have tentative plans to open similar 'pop up' salons in San Francisco, London, Beijing and Boston sometime in the future. The concept builds on coffee houses' history of being informal venues for arts and entertainment, and the salon will feature both up-and-coming and established artists.

Finally, **The Shop at Bluebird** in London – a constantly evolving mix of fashions from leading designers, plus accessories, furniture and books. Housed in a huge, stunning space which was previously the Bluebird Food Market, The Shop at Bluebird is a unique shopping experience and a must-see for retail design aficionados. Digital Wellbeing Labs are presenting their next collection 'Into The Woods...' in collaboration with the Shop at Bluebird, King's Road, Chelsea. 'Into the Woods...' showcases the sometimes weird and wonderful relation between technology and nature through a selection of products, software and art. The collection includes a range of digital products using natural materials to encase and interact with electronic components, or software that is based on mathematical rules discovered in nature. Clearly involves someone!

Summary and opportunities

By reinventing and in a sense restoring the store to the centre of your brand strategy you can produce a real competitive edge to your Private Label competitors. Your edge will be a real understanding of shoppers and their circumstances and a desire to involve them with your brand.

- Opportunity 23: GO WEB in a big way. Consider changing all (or the majority) of your business to the internet for direct selling.
- Opportunity 24: Open a BRAND ONLY supermarket selling brands at discount. Or buy a retailer and convert.
- Opportunity 25: POLARIZE PRICE. Become low price or high price. Eliminate all mid-price brands. They don't have a shopper future.
- Opportunity 26: Design formats that meet SOCIAL NEEDS RETAILING. Identify shoppers' situational need and provide shopping experiences/retail formats that meet them. Go to them. Don't expect them to come to you.
- Opportunity 27: Rethink your relationships with your customers in terms of their CIRCUMSTANCES rather than their attributes. The Tesco way forward.
- Opportunity 28: Sell your products when it suits your shoppers. Not when it suits you. SELL TO SUIT. Wherever that may be and whatever it takes.

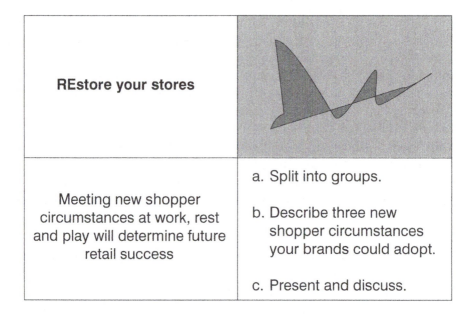

REstore your stores	
Meeting new shopper circumstances at work, rest and play will determine future retail success	a. Split into groups. b. Describe three new shopper circumstances your brands could adopt. c. Present and discuss.

Figure 19.7 Management action workshop exercise

- Opportunity 29: Get LEAN AND FRESH. Move to production systems that give you fresh products in small batches rather than ancient products in large batches.
- Opportunity 30: People need to understand it's not what you buy that's important – it's what it allows you to do. SHOW WHAT YOU ALLOW.
- Opportunity 31: If your present retailing efforts are non-involving, change them. Embrace the new concept of INVOLVEMENT RETAILING.

Actions to consider

1. Are you anticipating and adapting to the retail stores of the future?
2. Understand those changes and plan how they might affect you.
3. Understand the nature of the future shelf and adapt your strategies to take account of it.
4. Rethink your relationship with your customers in terms of their circumstances rather than their attributes.
5. Look at your involvement retailing potential.

20 Private principle 8: Catalyse your communications and brand from till to TV

Here we look at how you can redirect and recatalyse the power of your communications.

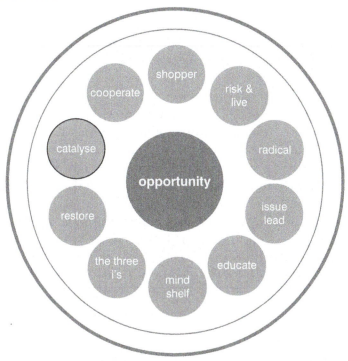

Figure 20.1 Catalyse your communications

Headlines

- It's not about mass communications.
- It's about catalytic communications.
- It's about making things happen at the point of action.
- It's about making things happen to drive shoppers to the point of action.

Creativity is all – but where should it be?

In a sense we put all of our rings of opportunity together here, as they are increasingly connected. Those rings are about communication. The nature of that communication is dramatically changing and evolving from being a two-dimensional passive form of communication to an increasingly three-dimensional, interactive agenda-forming mode of communication.

The use of the medium itself will change and evolve to make the new agenda useful for brands. TV remains the most effective media communicator around, despite all the fragmentation that surrounds us. TV is the medium that produces the best and most direct link to our shopper. But traditionally that medium may have been in the wrong place. That medium has to, and inevitably will, move from the couch to the store and the till.

One of the newest and, in a sense, least developed of the so-called new media is in-store TV – a medium that to date has been an extension of the traditional medium of mass communications TV. The growth of this medium has been slow to date, for two main reasons. First, retailers tried to own the medium and then sell space to the brands. Somewhat unsurprisingly, brands have felt that giving retailers even more of their budgets is hardly a way to increase their relative power. Second, the medium has been slow to innovate. Putting on the same old ads you see on conventional TV is hardly forward thinking. If this medium is to have a real future it must have real content.

However, the retail TV companies out there are not all the same. Some realize the opportunity. A very interesting and very independent company in Sweden called RTV has started to explore this area more precisely than any other company we've encountered. Most in-store TV companies are store-owned and are certainly not independent – a source of misapprehension to many FMCG companies. As a result, the medium has never really been developed to its fullest. Maybe the time has come. Maybe the shelves are literally stacks of boxes waiting to fly off the shelf. RTV has realized that this medium is about the packaging – what's on the TV – the **content** with which you can be truly informative, emotional and interactive in a way boring old two-dimensional content can never be. As a result, they are busy building themselves into 'catalytic communicators' – the medium that transforms shopping behaviour into purchasing behaviour – the shopper into a buyer.

This catalytic approach to communications is the way forward – catalytic in the sense that the communications and media action take place at the point of action, the point of purchase. As we have said on many occasions, we have moved from the world of mass production and mass communication to a world of mass participation. In this new world, people watch TV more than ever. But where are the people? They're out shopping. Retail is the channel where people are. Those same people demand product knowledge and brand participation. In-store TV is a medium that can deliver this proposition effectively – the medium that can catalytically convert our shoppers into buyers.

But it's not just TV. As the digital revolution takes off, it will be more and more critical to connect the websites to the stores. At the moment an increasing number of key categories are pre-searched for info before the shopper reaches the store. Wouldn't it be great if his or her new knowledge was reinforced by strong digital communications at the point of purchase? This will increasingly be the case as TV becomes a more effective point-of-sale (POS) medium. Delivering brand messages through various digital applications also helps to differentiate the retailer in a competitive marketplace.

That was the bottom line of a talk delivered recently by Frank Beurskens, CEO of **ShoptoCook**, in Las Vegas at the Content Strategies & Awards Summit. The Buffalo, NY-based firm is a leading developer of interactive digital customer service solutions.

'Discoverable media' is a term coined by Beurskens to describe interactive in-store media that enable shoppers to learn about meal solutions and other product-related how-to information, and obtain relevant promotional incentives. Interactions take place through fixed kiosk-type devices or mobile digital devices mounted on the handles of shopping carts. A potential option is to channel discovery interactions over advanced mobile phones.

The problems facing manufacturers and retailers today are driving demand for discoverable media, according to Beurskens. For the former, the key challenge is media fragmentation, which increases the cost and complexity of delivering brand messages. For the latter, problems include channel blurring, big-box proliferation and trade-dollar accountability.

> Digital interactive technology is changing the way we shop, work and live. The days where marketers 'shout' at consumers by persuading their purchase decisions through 'push' strategies is giving way to productive 'pull' strategies where the consumer seeks out a desired brand regardless of price.
>
> Frank Beurskens

He has developed ShoptoCook's software, which includes Meal Planning, Wine Pairing, Item Locator, Price Check, and Health & Wellness. Its basic Answers Center gives shoppers a unique opportunity to discover new and exciting solutions to their shopping dilemmas. They can print their favourite recipes, accompaniment ideas, and coupons. The Answers Center is typically located near the supermarket's meat, seafood, produce, wine and cheese departments.

> We offer branded manufacturers a media channel that places their message where most meal planning takes place – in the perishable aisle. We use kiosks as a vehicle to promote branded ingredients in the context of a meal solution for a shopper.
>
> Frank Beurskens

ShoptoCook is installed in over 200 AholdUSA divisions of Giant and Martin stores located throughout New York and Pennsylvania.

More sophisticated features of the Answers Center include: Recipes on the Web, which allow integration with a retailer's website, and Private Branding, which allows retailers to customize the interface by store location, seasonality, and promotional events with retailer-specific logos and graphics.

> We're continually trying to provide information and resources for supermarkets to offer expert advice in everything from all the products they sell in the perishable department, to every bottle of wine they have interest in, to every item related to health and wellness. All of it is geared to one goal: if you want to build loyalty, help solve the shopper's problems. Loyalty is about problem solving; it's not just about selling.
>
> Frank Beurskens

For example, an average 200-store retail chain prints 1.5 million recipes annually from ShoptoCook's Answers Center. An average shopper views 40 recipe photos and 2 recipes in detail for every recipe printed. Furthermore, the average shopper spends 1.5 minutes per visit at the center, reflecting a high degree of engagement.

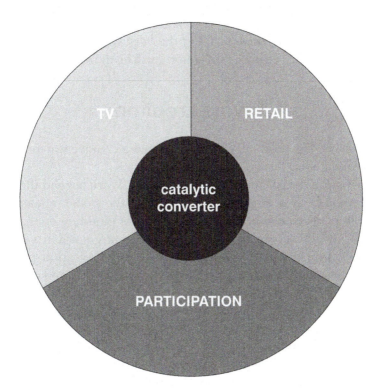

Figure 20.2 Catalytic conversion

Build yourself a private room

You need to think up new creative ways to deal with Private Label and turn it from a threat to an opportunity. This needs new radical thinking in new environments, not the same old boring, staid formulas of old. To help you along the path, why not build your very own private room and invite the competition in? Literally transform one of your conference rooms into a three-dimensional Private Label world. Use the walls to bring that experience alive.

Show the totality of the experience on the walls:

- the private retail brands;
- your brands;
- a Private Label integration wall;
- your private manufacturing capability and rationale.

Use this room as a meeting point for all your key discussions on Private Label, for all your education and training purposes, for all your retailer and key supplier meetings, for all your creative brainstorming sessions, for all your co-creation sessions. Let the very subject of Private Label surround you. The response, we believe, will be more creative.

Private creation

When was the last time somebody suggested a creative way of dealing with Private Label? Never! Probably so.

Form a creative task force with your agency. Work beyond the brand itself. Remember you're dealing with T-Rex – the global retailers – the brand eaters. You need brilliant solutions – not plodding ones. Private Label should be set up as a key competitor target when you have communication discussions with all your communication partners. Saatchi & Saatchi X now does this routinely, with all its brand clients. All agencies should adopt a similar line.

Branding has gone from being rational to emotional to spiritual. Consumers have gone through all the stages in Maslow's hierarchy of needs – from the fulfilment of subsistence needs to higher-order ones – leading to new demands on brands. Now, when so many consumers have arrived at the high levels of self-esteem and self-realization, they also want their brands to be there with them, as well. The brand supplier must, then, create a belief system which underpins its overall commitment to the customers through, for example, the brands. That is why the big issues will become ever more critical, as the big issues are the links that will increasingly tie brands, retailers and society together.

You have to be creative in as many directions as possible and, where possible, get your brand away from the Private Label threat. Take **Heineken**, for example. Heineken co-developed the 'beer tender' with a small-appliance manufacturer from France (SEB), an at-home tap that accepts 4-litre kegs of Heineken. It has been an enormous success despite its high price and has completely changed the nature of the distribution, apart from reinforcing the brand image. Consumers now can have real Heineken beer on tap at home when they want.

Then there's **Gapa**, a brand that combines the big issues with alternative distribution options. Gapa, which is Swedish for 'open your mouth' (very useful for your phrase book), is preservative-free and sold in cheerful containers in Sweden's second largest supermarket, as well as in four trendy restaurants, a smart move for reaching parents who enjoy taking their babies out for dinner. In the United States, several entrepreneurs have developed similar concepts. Californian **Homemade Baby**'s certified organic and kosher food for infants and toddlers is freshly made each day. Stressing an important selling point of gourmet baby foods, Homemade Baby claims that 'when babies learn what real food tastes like and how good it makes their little tummies feel, they are on their way to making good food choices for life'. They'll need to, given our previous discussion about obesity.

Californian tots can also dine on fresh organic baby foods from **Bohemian Baby**, available for those aged 6–15 months. Bohemian Baby offers home delivery within LA. On the East Coast, **Evie's Organic Edibles** delivers freshly made foods within Manhattan. Parents can select dishes from menus that vary weekly and are designed to help stimulate developing taste buds. Most of these brands are relatively small and regional start-ups, founded by parents who couldn't find foods they wanted to feed their babies and toddlers. We haven't spotted any of the major manufacturers venturing into fresh or frozen baby food, so now's the time to start your own line.

You need to develop creative tools that will help you facilitate that process. You need to involve your creative suppliers fully in such a process. You need to involve your shoppers in the development of that creativity directly.

Customize the creative reaction

The talk that does exist about dealing with Private Label tends to centre around conventional mass solutions like raising quality, improving innovation and lowering prices. Surely we can be more creative than that. Figure 20.3 shows just a few thoughts for dealing with each private variant.

What this means in practice is producing radical solutions for radical battles. Aren't you sick of Private Labels copying you? Why not lampoon them and out-copy the copyists? As they say, there's no greater form of flattery than mimicry. Rachet up. Copy better. Private Label can hardly complain about copycats, given their history.

You can even outdo the premium Private Label by doing things radically differently. **Nespresso**, from Nestlé, has radically changed the way coffee can be sold in Europe. It sells expensive Nespresso coffee machines to prestigious retailers and supplies coffee through capsules, sold in sleeves of 10, by phone, fax, internet or 42 worldwide Nespresso boutiques. It has sought out customer circumstances and moved to meet them. It has generated a quarter of a million hooked-in customers and

objective	price variant	creative strategy
being real about the variant	commodity	ignore
discourage copying	copy	copy the copycats
premium plus	premium	outdo the premium

Figure 20.3   Customize the creative reaction

$600 million sales, growing at 30 per cent per annum in a stagnant coffee market. It's not worried about Private Label, or retailers in general.

Keep them creatively surprised

If you look at **Aldi**, it offers a selection of exciting non-grocery products as '**surprise buys**'. These items, which change every Thursday, are there while stocks last. They include products like notebook computers. All Aldi has done is copy **Tchibo**, which has developed this approach to become Germany's third biggest retailer and one of the fastest-expanding retailers in Europe.

What started off as a branded shop selling coffee has become a major retailer selling key consumer items. Every week Tchibo offers its customers consumer goods – so-called non-food items – under the company's own brand, TCM. Whether the current theme is the kitchen, garden, sport and leisure, clothing or jewellery, the diversity of thematic worlds and the number of articles mean that in the course of a year there is bound to be something for every customer. The composition of weekly thematic worlds is based on ideas which are developed to suit current trends, long before sales get under way. To do this, the product managers concerned monitor developments in the most varied markets from many different perspectives. Important information is supplied on a regular basis through cooperation with trend spotters and market research companies which analyse long-term developments in society and their influence on shopping habits. This means that Tchibo can adapt to the current desires and needs of its customers, cater for changes in their lifestyle and fulfil their expectations of modern technology.

Initially the range consisted of one or two items, but it soon extended well beyond 'food and drink'. Then, in the mid-1980s, phase sales began, with product offers linked to a central theme that changed every two weeks. Since 1994, phases have changed in a weekly sequence and through its TCM brand, Tchibo now sells everything – from watches to bicycles to skiwear to saucepans to underwear – that their customers would find useful, practical and desirable. Today, 'a new experience every week' consists of around 15 thematically linked items.

Tchibo has transformed a simple coffee-bar concept into a dynamic consumer goods retail concept. By offering a new experience every week it has developed a unique, thriving retail brand experience.

A simple FMCG brand has become a retail star in its own right. Why not you? Why don't you surprise your shopper? And the competition? When was the last time your brand surprised anyone? Did the unexpected?

Consumers are exerting increasing control over their media environment. They multi-task, they time-shift, and they are able to talk to – and about – brands as never before.

To survive in this environment, advertisers must find new, creative ways of reaching their target audience. At the same time, the internet has made it possible – perhaps mandatory – for organizations to look for new, collaborative customer experiences. This new perspective offers huge potential for advertisers to harness customer feedback through brand interaction, dialogue, engagement and empowerment – more relevant, interactive experiences that can deliver greater emotional impact. There's no stopping creative consumers getting involved in co-creating goods, services and experiences influencing brands. Consumer co-creation can be a powerful tool.

You need to understand how engagement and co-creation work together within the overall marketing mix. How should brands set out to engage with customers and how can they involve people in co-creating new ideas? How can brands, users and media owners capitalize on this new mindset? What are the opportunities or threats for brands and businesses as consumers exchange reviews of their products and services in blogs and social forums? Find the best way to rewrite the rules – make engagement and co-creation work together.

Finally, we can also creatively surprise people where they're not expecting you. The 7 million or so inhabitants of **Second Life**, the three-dimensional online world, have spent millions of dollars on digital makeovers, clothing and other goods and services for their avatars. But will the game's players buy anything for themselves? Retailers and manufacturers like Reebok, Adidas, American Apparel and 1–800-Flowers.com are setting up shop in Second Life, hoping that users will steer their avatars to these stores and buy goods to deliver to their real-world addresses. So far, retailers say, they have low expectations, but some believe that the experiments could yield important lessons on how people might operate in the online realm. One of the more successful commercial applications within Second Life has been Reebok's virtual store, where users may create custom versions of Reebok shoes for their avatars, and for themselves. According to Benjamin James, who leads the San Francisco office of Rivers Run Red, the agency that created Reebok's Second Life store, the site distributed more than 27,000 pairs of digital shoes in its first 10 weeks. James said he did not know how many of those people clicked through to Reebok's website to buy physical reproductions of their avatars' shoes, but he said the effort, which began in October, was indeed helping to sell the real items. 'This allowed people to get comfortable with their product in the virtual world,' he said (*New York Times*).

Strive to improve your retail positioning

There are retail bands out there with good images. But on average the images are not as developed as conventional brands. To get better, Private Labels need to be better at the science of positioning. This is an opportunity for brands if they change their brand positioning to be more retail orientated. This approach will force brands to think more like their retail competition and more effectively link the shopper to the brand through the power of retail thinking. In other words, **retailize**. And more directly, challenge the retail brands. We discussed this in our previous two books and recommended the increasing use of retail-orientated selling propositions (RSP).

The **RSP** briefing form:

- **Shelf**: What new thinking have you developed? Are there new shelves you should be on?
- **Context**: What new thinking have you developed to better compete?
- **Shopper**: What new thinking/insights have you developed about your shopper?
- **Product**: What have you reimagined and will it work in a retail environment?
- **Retail**: Describe your revolutionary selling situation.
- **Communications**: What communications approaches do you recommend to excite your shoppers and drive them to your shelves?
- **Organization**: What changes and structures are you putting in place to optimize your organization's retail capabilities?
- **BRI**: a simple phrase that captures the essence of your Big Retail Idea. It should be a vibrant, flexible stimulating call to action.

We need RSPs aimed at shoppers, not consumers. These RSPs must be involving, entertaining and inspiring. We need to move to a more focused effort where your consumer USP is refocused towards being a unique selling proposition for the shopper... the RSP. The product as well as your communications is an important part of making the RSP work.

Get closer

Many retailers have been able to interest consumers in their stores and Private Label ranges. This approach was prompted by the 1990s trend towards Private Label as a store differentiator and the consequent need to take risks in carving out a unique positioning. This approach to product development was later mirrored in some new approaches to branding – approaches you can learn from directly. This has been particularly apparent in the United States. The closeness of these stores to their shoppers – as well as the borrowing of some ideas from up-and-coming challenger brands such as Snapple or Ben & Jerry's – resulted in marketing campaigns and in-store promotions that are novel (and sometimes downright quirky). Some of the best examples of novel branding come from Trader Joe's, the Aldi-owned US specialty supermarket chain. Such brand-building activities can offer new opportunities for retailers. For example, in mid-2006 Wild Oats was able to start selling its Private Label products on Amazon.com, opening up a new revenue stream that was not previously available to it.

It is essential for famous brand manufacturers to work with supermarkets, and it can be beneficial to leverage supermarkets' loyalty databases. However, it would be unwise to rely on the retailers' ownership of consumers for direct marketing and consumer insight – particularly in cases where brand objectives clash with the retailers' own Private Label programmes. In this context it makes sense for companies to build their own consumer databases, both for direct marketing purposes and in order to gain unique insights into consumer behaviour. The internet offers an excellent way of achieving this goal, allowing brand owners to communicate directly with consumers without the intervention of retailers and other intermediaries. Particularly as consumer trust in traditional advertising is eroded, building a compelling web presence can be an excellent way not only of raising consumer awareness of a given product, but also of building consumer databases.

Creatively extend in-store

As brands we must seek creative options through all the communication possibilities. Ensuring stand-out at point of sale is a priority. With limited product-specific marketing budgets, packaging is one of the most important ways in which Private Labels can gain consumer attention. Packaging also plays a significant role in quality perception, which is an area that some Private Labels still need to address. Retailers are increasingly investing in attention-grabbing packaging that offers shelf-stand-out, as many examples show. Spanish retailer Mercadona has recently introduced a new Gel ChampuparaHombre, branded under the Private Label name of 9.60. In France the sub-brand Carrefour Kids was extended to Bain de Douche Extra Doux in 2006.

Another method of using packaging effectively is by being different from the prevailing colours in a particular aisle or fixture. This tactic has been adopted by brands such as Unilever's Dove that have attempted to build a 'wall of colour' when their own product variants are merchandised together. Other point-of-sale promotions relevant to Private Label include:

- In-store displays. Like packaging, in-store displays are a key way to grab attention in the crowded store environment.
- Sampling. In order to alleviate consumers' fears over Private Label quality, sampling is a very useful activity. This is particularly important when retailers have introduced premium Private Label ranges at higher-than-usual price points.
- Guarantees. In order to further reduce the risks of trial, US supermarkets typically offer a money-back guarantee on their Private Label products.

Getting them to love you

To be truly number one, you have to be known. You have to be loved.

Eric Kim – CEO, Samsung

Very finally, we can truly catalyse our communication efforts by getting more people to love us. The growth of Private Label is one of the single biggest issues in business today and, as such, demands a radical and creative approach to retail thinking and shopper marketing. Changing pricing strategy, customizing packaging or doing a few more promotions is not going to change the picture in the long run or unlock the potential that Private Label presents. Shoppers accept Private Label and they still want brands, although it's just not enough to be talked about, respected, trusted or even admired any more. Going forward, those brands and retailers that win will be those that shoppers fall in love with. That deep emotional connection will mean that shoppers will leave the store if the product is not in stock, or go out of their way to visit a specific store if they can't get what they want. Simply put, brand owners and retailers will win or lose with Private Label based on whether or not they manage to inspire loyalty beyond reason.

For Saatchi & Saatchi X that means helping brands along the journey from respected trustmark to Lovemarks™. This way of thinking transforms the way shoppers currently try, buy and experience products, brands, services and even retail environments, to deliver an altogether more emotional, more rewarding experience, creating drama for the shopper around the things that they really care about. It means thinking about the value equation – quality, price, choice, convenience (and increasingly community and sustainability) – in different ways and using mystery, intimacy and sensuality, the very essence of Lovemarks, to tell stories, excite the senses and provide small but meaningful gestures of goodwill at every touch-point with the shopper.

Brands have run out of juice. More and more people in the world have grown to expect great performance from products, services and experiences. And most often, we get it. Cars start first time, fries are always crisp, dishes shine. A few years ago, Saatchi & Saatchi looked closely at the question: What makes some brands inspirational, while others struggle? Their answer was Lovemarks. They claim Lovemarks transcend brands. They deliver beyond your expectations of great performance. Like great brands, they sit on top of high levels of respect – but there the similarities end. Lovemarks reach your heart as well as your mind, creating an intimate, emotional connection that you just can't live without. Ever. Take a brand away and people will find a replacement. Take a Lovemark away and people will protest its absence. Lovemarks are a relationship, not a mere transaction. You don't just buy Lovemarks, you embrace them passionately. That's why you never want to let go. Put simply, Lovemarks inspire loyalty beyond reason.

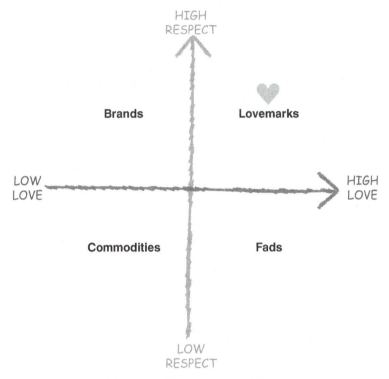

Figure 20.4   Saatchi & Saatchi X Lovemark™

At the core of every Lovemark is Respect. No Respect? It's not a Lovemark. It's as simple as that. Check out the Love/Respect axis and see just where your favourite brand is sitting. A Lovemark's high Love is infused with these three intangible, yet very real, ingredients: Mystery, Sensuality and Intimacy. Mystery draws together stories, metaphors, dreams and symbols. It is where past, present and future become one. Mystery adds to the complexity of relationships and experiences because people are drawn to what they don't know. After all, if we knew everything, there would be nothing left to learn or to wonder at. Sensuality keeps the five senses on constant alert for new textures, intriguing scents and tastes, wonderful music. Sight, hearing, smell, touch, taste. Our senses work together to alert us, lift us, transport us. When they are stimulated at the same time, the results are unforgettable. It is through the five senses that we experience the world and create our memories. Intimacy means empathy, commitment and passion – the close connections that win intense loyalty as well as the small, perfect gesture. These are often remembered long after functions and benefits have faded away. Without Intimacy people cannot feel they own a brand, and without that conviction a brand can never become a Lovemark.

Lovemarks can be found everywhere, but to connect with consumers three places matter most: on screen, online and in-store. For decades, screens were Irreplaceable and Irresistible whether in television sets or cinemas. In the 21st century the family of screens has many more members, whether on mobile phones or computers, personal digital assistants (PDAs) or digital billboards. But the proliferation of screens is not an excuse to get more complicated. It is the way to get closer to consumers by creating Lovemarks and Loyalty Beyond Reason. The online revolution has given consumers an extraordinary new way to connect with the products they care about. Online they can prove that they own the brand. Online they can show their Loyalty Beyond Reason. And online they have new opportunities to act as Inspirational consumers and passionate advocates for the brands they love. This is why Saatchi & Saatchi X created lovemarks.com: to celebrate the engagement the online medium offers consumers. Finally, Mystery, Sensuality and Intimacy are transforming the in-store experience. Stores will host the next creative revolution as they become Theatres of Dreams. Lovemarks in store activate the drama of the brand where it matters, by looking through the eyes of shoppers. The store is where over 80 per cent of shopper decisions are made and an amazing 50 per cent of brand switches happen.

Summary and opportunities

- Opportunity 32: CATALYSE YOUR COMMUNICATIONS. Make your communications work harder at the point of action – the store. Turn your shoppers into buyers.
- Opportunity 33: Seek HIGHLY CREATIVE SOLUTIONS. Make your agencies put their creative resources against this target.
- Opportunity 34: MAKE THE COMPARISON. Spend effort, time and money showing shoppers the brand difference. Don't take it for granted. Your product advantage has turned to parity. You must restore the advantage.
- Opportunity 35: Find ways to SURPRISE the competition and the shopper, as well as yourself.

- Opportunity 36: Get SHOPPER CLOSE where you can, starting with the web.
- Opportunity 37: EXTEND and OPTIMIZE creativity in-store.
- Opportunity 38: GET LOVED. Use Saatchi & Saatchi X's Lovemark™ approach to help you be loved by shoppers even more.

Actions to consider

1. Review your communication plans to see if they allow you to fully optimize your big issue positioning.
2. Look for a new in-store medium as a more effective facilitator of the brand message and the medium that translates shopping behaviour into purchase behaviour.
3. Build a 'private room' where you can fully understand and creatively develop your position.
4. Use creativity as your main tool to turn the Private Label threat into the Private Label opportunity it should be.
5. Use creativity to develop customized solutions for private variants.
6. Where Tesco Finest exists, why not produce your brand's finest at exactly the same price? And sell it in competitive retailers.
7. Why not do 'taste the difference' tests with pop-up stores, just like the old Pepsi/Coke wars?
8. They have the finest... you launch the **very finest** variants.
9. Use pop-up stores to do a 'brand health check' to show the world how much more nutritious your products are. Check first that it's actually true!

21 Private principle 9: Collaborate and cooperate through co-opetition

Here we look at more ways to collaborate in the future. Let's face it, most Private Label brand strategies and executions are here to stay. Brands must either cooperate with each other or with retailers.

Figure 21.1   Collaborate and cooperate through co-opetition

Headlines

- Above all, co-opetete.
- Co-opetete with your competitors.
- Co-opetete with your suppliers.
- Co-opetete or die.

Co-opeteting

In most modern business theories, competition is seen as one of the key forces that keeps firms lean, drives innovation and ensures happy consumers. However, this kind of thinking has been challenged by people such as Adam Brandenburger of Harvard and Berry Nalebuff of Yale School. In part using some of the ideas of game theory, they suggest that businesses can gain advantage by means of a judicious mixture of competition and cooperation. Cooperation with suppliers, customers and firms producing complementary or related products can lead to expansion of the market and the formation of new business relationships, perhaps even the creation of new forms of enterprise. They chose the term co-opetition for this concept (a blend of cooperation and competition), which they used as the title of their 1996 book explaining their theories, a book which has become a bestseller. The theory of co-opetition is particularly relevant in the era of retail power. In our case there are two possible routes: co-opetition with other brands and co-opetition with your retailers.

Brand co-opetition

Brands need increasingly to make retailers know the limits of their aggressive strategies. OK, they can get bigger and bigger and have more Private Label. But being a plodosoraus led to extinction, as size meant slowing up. They have to realize that having both brands and Private Label is the long-term best route to profitability. The supermarket model, like the brand one, is a growth model. They never take their eye off the objective. The UK has lost nearly 10,000 (food, confectionary and tobacco) independent retailers in the past 10 years as a result of this drive for growth. It may well lose its brands next. But there are ways for brands to match that scale.

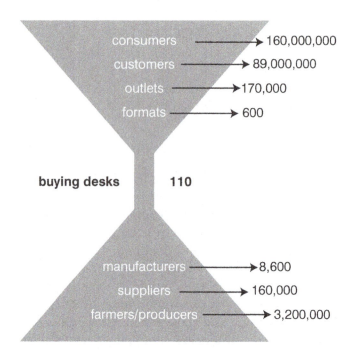

Figure 21.2 European food supply chain

Become a selling giant! There has been much talk about this. But maybe the time has come. Maybe the big brands should get together and increase their scale to one where they have more influence on the buying and selling process. However, they will need to enter a radically new spirit of competitive cooperation to be truly successful. They have to see the real competition as the Private Label, not necessarily the brands. In overall share terms, that is precisely what they are.

If you look at the retailer alliance set out in Figure 21.3, the retailers are already moving in this direction. Not satisfied with being big enough already, they are forming international alliances to get even bigger – alliances to increase their buying power even more. So why aren't brands? Seems logical to us.

Brands have to fight back. The recent acquisition of Gillette by P&G has often been said to be a first step in this brand-giant consolidation process. But it's not out of the question that two, three or even four of the major food companies could get together to become very big selling alliances. The Kraft–Nestlé–P&G alliance will be with us sooner rather than later.

Figure 21.3 Retailer buying power alliances

The other way to get bigger is to acquire… a retailer. Why not? You're both selling. Your distribution is being taken away from you. Why not get back into it? Become a mass retailer. **Buy one and make it for brands only at competitive prices.** Or co-opetete with other brands to ensure that you have the buying necessary power. A retailer is a retailer and brands are retailers. You're in exactly the same business – selling. As they seek to encroach on your territory, encroach on theirs. Retail space is going to get cheap over the next few years as the web attracts buyers online. If the UK is any example, there could be 40 per cent of high-street space up for grabs. **Look out for space bargains.**

If you look at the big private-equity groups, at the moment they are busy circling the big retailers like Sainsbury's, Boots and Carrefour. They have done their homework and realized that these retailers are very cheap, especially when you value their property assets. It's somewhat ironic that one of these retailers, Carrefour, is under pressure – the second biggest retailer in the world. Carrefour in French means crossroad and we may well be at a crossroad. Of course, you don't have to buy the lot. Ten per cent will give you a board seat. And then watch how they treat your brand once you're on the board. We promise you, you will notice the difference.

Finally, think of brand co-opetition as a way of making the brand point. If there is an issue that brands feel strongly enough about, they should all take the same path. If somebody copies you, sue them whatever the cost, be they a retailer or a Private Label supplier. Your intellectual development property is yours alone. Without it you have nothing. This should become a 'must' for any brand owner and should automatically happen.

Very finally, you can extend this brand co-opetition all the way to the web. Why don't brands set up a website and service for groups of like-minded individuals to ask questions of others in their brand community? Clearly, a key source of questions will be dealing with Private Label. This site would offer a structured 'one-stop shop' of established and next-generation web communication tools for professional groups to connect, collaborate and co-create, ie tap into the 'wisdom of the crowd'. It could provide structure and search tools for popular questions to be asked and answered, and the responses shared. Just a thought.

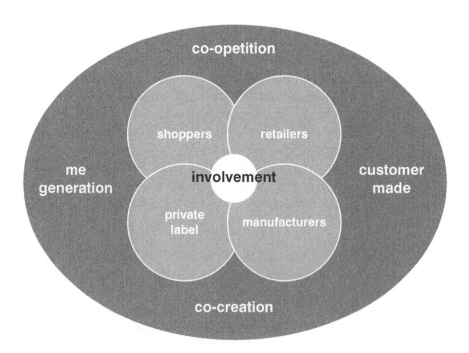

Figure 21.4 Everyone cooperating

Retail co-opetition

The definition of retail co-opetition is slightly different. Simply put, it is the co-operation between retailers and manufacturers that will jointly grow the essence and business of both partners while stimulating the category as a whole.

Brands should use their creativity as a force to encourage co-opetition. They should arrange creative sessions with retailers where together they creatively explore the category and what's possible. In essence, **co-create the co-opetition.** What's possible in terms of innovation? What's possible in terms of promotion? What's possible in terms of joint efforts? What's possible in terms of category-growing cooperation? What's possible in terms of **joint value innovation**? These forums are critical if we are going to demonstrate to both parties that they are better off with each other than not with each other.

Shown in Figure 21.6 is a small list of why brands and retailers should be helping each other. We're sure you could make this list even longer. When you look at these very different offerings you wonder why a war seems to be going on. But there again, you could say that about most wars. Their reasons for being are often completely illogical. This is clearly the case here.

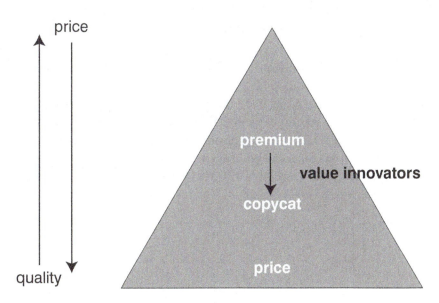

Figure 21.5   Joint value innovation

brands need retailers	retailers need brands
distribution	image
selling power	choice
competitive context	innovation
promotion	margin
growth	growth
shopper knowledge	consumer knowledge

Figure 21.6 We need each other

Summary and opportunities

- Opportunity 39: Become a BUYING GIANT. Form alliances where you can to raise your power.
- Opportunity 40: SUE THE MIMICS. Don't put up with Private Label copying for any reason. Always challenge mimicry all the way.
- Opportunity 41: Learn to genuinely CO-OPETETE. Brands need retailers and retailers need brands.
- Opportunity 42: Develop a PRIVATE LABEL FORUM – a cooperative website where you can all learn from each other.

Actions to consider

1. Become a retailer by buying one.
2. Buy a board seat on your major retailer and see your relationship improve.
3. Seek anyway you can to co-opetete.
4. Produce special unique products for each retailer.
5. Seek joint value innovation options and opportunities.

22 Private principle 10: Shopper solutions steal share of wallet

Here we come back to money. Yes, we all want to make a profit – an even greater share of the wallet. Providing shopper solutions will help us steal that share of wallet. Our ultimate objective is win–win–win. Win the retailer, win the shopper, win the brand owner. Win, win, win. But be careful of the downside.

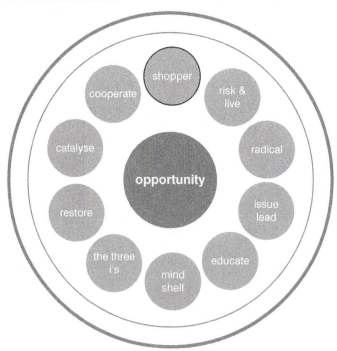

Figure 22.1   Shopper solutions steal share of wallet

Headlines

- We have become a world of shopaholics.
- You need to lead the trends.

Money, money, money

Many big ideas have struggled over the centuries to dominate the planet: fascism, communism, democracy, religion. But only one has achieved total supremacy. Its compulsive attractions rob its followers of reason and good sense. It has created unsustainable inequalities and threatened to tear apart the very fabric of our society. More powerful than any cause or even religion, it has reached into every corner of the globe. It is consumerism. We have become a world of shopaholics. We are bombarded by advertising from every medium which persuades us that the more we consume, the better our lives will be. Shopping is equated with fun, fulfilment and self-identity. Consumerism has taken over our lives almost unnoticed. Shopping has become a recreational activity. We're well beyond the time where shopping was just a way of transacting what you need in life. It's now all about identity and status and recreation and companionship, even about meaning in people's lives.

It's also killing the planet. Merely switching to 'ethical' shopping may not be enough. We need to shop less. We throw away our own body weight in rubbish every seven weeks.

To quote a famous song, it all comes down to money. But getting to that money, that profit, has to be increasingly linked to some of the changes we've detailed so far. Social changes have to work with shopper circumstance changes. Sometimes it's small examples that show us where this change takes us.

Take school lunches. They are a hot topic across the world: from British celebrity chef Jamie Oliver's Feed Me Better campaign to Two Angry Moms trying to improve school lunches in the United States. Both are aiming to get junk food out and bring whole foods in.

In the Netherlands, children traditionally go home for lunch, and school cafeterias are an anomaly. These days, however, more and more Dutch children are 'staying over' for lunch at school. Soda and chips are gaining ground, and childhood obesity is on the rise. Two entrepreneurs came up with their own solution to the lunch problem:

Lunch4Kids. Packaged like a McDonald's Happy Meal, each lunchbox contains sandwiches, a drink (milk or juice), a piece of fruit and a snack (yogurt, a cookie, a baby cucumber etc). Parents order online, specifying which foods their youngsters will leave untouched, and anything to which they're allergic. The lunchboxes are delivered to participating schools every morning, and invoices are sent directly to parents. This keeps things simple for schools: nothing to administrate or refrigerate.

Besides the obvious advantages of balanced meals and healthy variety, there's also a high convenience aspect to Lunch4Kids. Parents don't have to worry about what to pack, or panic if they've run out of fresh bread or juice boxes. According to parents who participated in the trial run, this alleviates morning stress and makes breakfast a time to enjoy with their families. Lunch4Kids was soft-launched at five primary schools, and parents and schools aren't the only ones that like the concept. Large food brands, including Unilever and Danone, are itching to get in on the action. We can't blame them – this business idea incorporates some of the biggest and enduring trends around, from an obsession with health and craving convenience to the power of design and customization/personalization (trendwatching.com). And it avoids the Private Label competition!

We have entered a world where a triple win is uniquely potentially possible. Win the brand supplier, win the retailer and win the shopper. Private Label has to a large extent made us realize that win. But Private Label is only part of the story, albeit a very visible part. Throughout this

re-create perception	re-create difference	reinvent new difference	increase involvement
make the quality comparison to PL direct	upgrade ALL main products	new innovations in new categories	web street mktg events direct

Figure 22.2 Shopper defence summary

book we have talked the story of opportunity rather than threat. It's clear, when you take this stance, that your total perspective changes. And a world of opportunity opens up before you. Let's look at all those opportunities together. The ones that allow you to win–win–win. When you look at them as a totality it becomes very clear that brands and retailers are not necessarily in conflict. You both seek the same solutions and the same opportunities for your shoppers. Work together and that's what you will achieve.

The key to working together is understanding that price is not necessarily the only game in town. In the past five years you have seen people wake up to things like sustainability, regionality and provenance. Before that their first question would have been: 'How much is it? 'In recent years consumers have become more concerned about things like health and ethics rather than convenience and price,' says Geraldine Padbury, Senior Analyst IGD (*Daily Telegraph*, 2 June 2007).

Shoppers want better labelling, they're worried about sugar and salt content and environmental concerns are making them look more closely at food miles. 'Retailers have seen a perceptible change in customer attitudes even in the last 12 months,' says Judith Batchelar, Director of Sainsbury's brand. 'Price has not been the most talked about issue as people have become more interested in sustainability and social issues. Our fair-trade business has more than doubled in the past year. Customers are much better informed and they're prepared to pay more for products with a story. They're interested not just in taste, but in provenance, where their food has come from and how it got there.'

Moreover, developments at the premium end help to raise standards throughout the food chain, so mass market products are also improving.

Ideas, ideas, ideas

If you're going to stay ahead and make money, you need to lead the trends. One of the world's biggest advertising agencies has named the top 70 products, trends and services it thinks will take the world by storm in 2007. Top of the list is technology that will allow free phone calls over the internet. Next-generation games consoles, such as the Nintendo Wii, social networking businesses and tiny technology all make it into the top five. 'Trends are illustrated by the products and services that exemplify them,' said Marian Salzman, Chief Marketing Officer of JWT Worldwide, the firm behind the report. 'By examining what resonates with consumers, we can identify the larger patterns that will shape our lives in the years to come.'

Here is the list of all 70 predictions. Do any of them make sense to you? Maybe they should if you want to compete in this future world:

1. Free telephone calls over the internet
2. Wii and the next-generation gaming systems
3. The business of social networking
4. Pop-up stores, restaurants and bars... installation style
5. 'Shrinky Dink' technology (TVs are flat and hidden, iPods are down to half an ounce, speakers are smaller and less visible, and so on)
6. The rise of nanotechnology
7. Sustainable construction/green buildings
8. Hydrogen fuel cell technology
9. Veggie-bus: school buses running on biodiesel fuel
10. Transfat fallout
11. Reality-show talent searches
12. Ohio State's freshman basketball phenomenon, Greg Oden
13. Fear of agri-terrorism
14. Halal foods
15. Participatory advertising (user-generated advertising and music video competitions)
16. Premium-drink bars
17. Organic fabrics
18. Stem cell research
19. Iceland
20. Hybrid dogs
21. Locally sourced produce
22. Churchonomics: religion as big business
23. Reunions of donor insemination siblings
24. Hitting the off-button: demanding downtime
25. Indian cross-over actress Aishwarya Rai
26. Home schooling
27. Natural building materials such as stone and wood
28. 'Binge chilling'
29. Personalized diets
30. Brand 'tarts'
31. Modernized tradition

32. 'Chindia'
33. 'Alpha mums'
34. Internet TV
35. 'Citizen journalism'
36. RSS feeds
37. Fresh Direct
38. Google domination (Google as acquirer, and Microsoft as Google follower)
39. Mobile video
40. Rachael Ray
41. Inconspicuous consumption
42. *X-Factor's* Leona Lewis
43. *Dreamgirls'* Jennifer Hudson
44. Environmental causes
45. Companies going green
46. Barack Obama
47. Soft, natural hair
48. Microgeneration (generating one's own energy)
49. Party planning for teens
50. Paying for user-generated content
51. Higher-waisted pants
52. iPhone
53. Co-branding (think Nike plus Apple)
54. Amy Winehouse
55. The rebirth of raves
56. Energy-saving lightbulbs
57. Sacha Baron Cohen
58. Mash-ups (music, websites, everything)
59. Japanese apparel chain Uniqlo
60. Promoting 'Brand Me'
61. Ensemble TV casts (*Ugly Betty*, *Grey's Anatomy*, *Heroes*, *Criminal Minds*)
62. Multilingual cinema
63. 'Kidults'
64. Transformers (the movie)
65. Web-based microfinancing
66. Generosity
67. Al Gore, the environmentalist
68. Unstrategic alliances (Paris and Britney, Tom and Brooke, Bush Sr and Clinton)

69. Europeans getting fatter
70. Age shuffling (40 is the new 20, for example).

Companies are increasingly tapping into these trends to help them appeal more in the future. Clichés, by definition, are born out of truths. So while it may seem a little tired to say that 'the only constant in business today is change', we should not ignore the fundamental truth of this statement. Making sense of change is, after all, key to business survival and business growth, particularly for a business serving the constantly changing needs and wants of consumers. In our view, trends are a way of making sense of change. As consumer attitudes and behaviours continuously evolve, trends provide a framework for labelling, structuring and understanding these changes. When they are well observed, validated and communicated, trends become a powerful tool for stimulating consumer-centric business growth. Yet too often trends fail to act as the growth catalyst that they should be. A lack of clarity, unstructured thinking, insufficient evidence and turgid delivery can all constrain trends work, said Nadine Critchley, Consumer Excellence, Strategic Generating Demand Unit, Nestlé, Switzerland, at ESOMAR's Annual Congress, London, September 2006. This approach has been developed for creating a trends programme that has really inspired business growth within Nestlé.

Summary and opportunities

So go out there to win, win and win. The key is to really know your shoppers and constantly bombard them with new, meaningful innovations. Those opportunities will literally come from everywhere. But in order to focus their applications, think of four cornerstones for your future. Do you truly involve shoppers? Do you meet their shopping circumstances? Are you a truly shoppable brand? Do you produce value innovations (preferably working with your partners)?

- Opportunity 43: Look for ideas everywhere.
- Opportunity 44: Adopt a multi-tier strategy. If it grows the Private Label business it will certainly grow yours. More of this in Part 4.

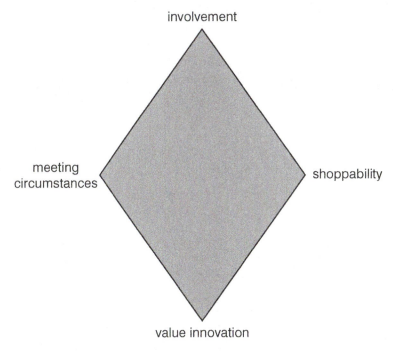

Figure 22.3   The future shopper cornerstones

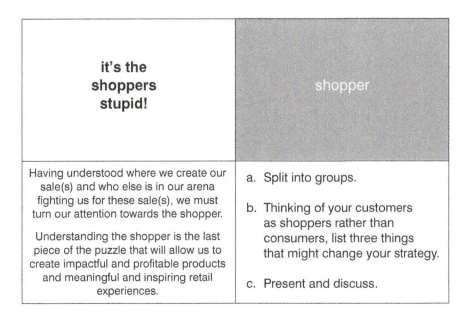

it's the shoppers stupid!	shopper
Having understood where we create our sale(s) and who else is in our arena fighting us for these sale(s), we must turn our attention towards the shopper. Understanding the shopper is the last piece of the puzzle that will allow us to create impactful and profitable products and meaningful and inspiring retail experiences.	a. Split into groups. b. Thinking of your customers as shoppers rather than consumers, list three things that might change your strategy. c. Present and discuss.

Figure 22.4   Management action workshop exercise

Actions to consider

1. Review your new idea-generating capabilities and increase them.
2. Do some shopper research. You probably haven't to date.

Part 4

Retailizing the retailer opportunity

Here we show retailers how to fully realize the brand opportunity that the growing Private Label phenomenon has given them. In essence, retailizing your retail brand.

**Wal-Mart Private Label is the biggest brand in the world
six times bigger than Coca Cola!**

Realizing the retailer opportunity

To stock or not to stock: that's the question.

Whether 'tis nobler not to make the shopper suffer the pain and dilemma of out of stock products, or to take up arms against the manufacturers, and by winning mind space end them?

To delist: to self promote; no brands; and by rejecting brands to say we end the low profits and the selling orientated market that stores are heir to.

'Tis a situation devoutly to be wish'd. To destock, to self promote; to control, perchance to sell more own brands!

Ay, there's the rub – for in that low choice store, what shoppers will come, once we have shuffled out the major brands?

(Corstjens and Corstjens, 2000)

23 For every opportunity there's an even bigger opportunity

> Too many people think only of their own profit. But business opportunity seldom knocks on the door of self-centred people. No customer ever goes to a store merely to please the storekeeper.
>
> Kazuo Inamori

The rise of the responsible retailer brand

It's also time for retailers to seize the real opportunity of Private Label, beyond the opportunities already realized. Simply put, instead of using it for essentially becoming bigger and bigger they should use it to become a new type of retailer – a retailer mature enough to deal with the long-term consequences of the world and a retailer mature enough to deal responsibly with the partners and suppliers that make them what they are. You can carry on using Private Label as a tool to increase your competitive edge continuously. But we say be careful. The customer, ie the shopper, is undergoing profound change and unless you use Private Label to embrace that change, you may find yourself in a customer-less future. The new breed of knowledgeable shopper will embrace the organizations that reflect their personal beliefs. They will reject the ones that are in it for themselves. Brands have made this mistake for years and are busy trying to rectify the situation now. Make sure you don't keep them company. The ultimate person that you have to please is your customer, as our Japanese quote clearly shows. He and she are the ones to please. Not you. In a sense we've come full circle and reinvented the world as we were in those far-off days we mentioned earlier. We believe retailers are in danger of forgetting this as agendas of world domination increasingly drive them. Remember our thoughts at the beginning. Retail brands, a long time ago, moved to brands and eventually returned to retail brands. A new cycle may be emerging before our eyes: the era of responsible brands. There isn't one winner here. By its very nature a responsible brand is a retail brand and/or a conventional brand.

> Next to knowing when to seize an opportunity, the most important thing in life is to know when to forego an advantage.
>
> Benjamin Disraeli (1804–81)

Like Mr Disraeli, you need to look at Private Label with new glasses and possibly forgo the short-term opportunity for the greater long-term

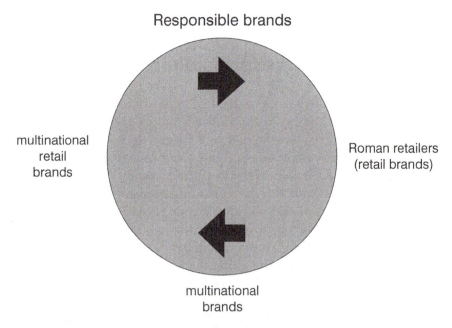

Figure 23.1 The rise of the responsible brand

one – an advantage for now for an advantage tomorrow. Profit today for sustainable growth tomorrow. This is, of course, counter to everything a retailer has done historically. 'Think three days ahead and tomorrow will look after itself' needs to become 'look 30 years ahead and tomorrow will arrive today'. Such thinking will require a revolution among today's retailers or tomorrow's potential retailers.

(A note to brands: You may choose to skip this section. Don't! What we are saying is just as, if not more, relevant to you.

A note to retailers: Read Part 3 first.)

What's new and what's next?

The first challenge and opportunity for retailers as they build their Private Label brand portfolios is first to develop a better relationship with their customers, beyond price reasons. Essentially the question is: if the price is the same, would a customer purchase a store brand in preference to a manufacturer brand? To date, very few retailers can answer that question and even then only for a limited number of categories. As we have indicated, we believe that price per se is not enough as we go forward. You will need something more, and that something more represents a significant challenge.

The second challenge is to manage your very diverse portfolios efficiently in a very consistent manner which allows you to further develop and differentiate your corporate retail message. That management to date has been very effective. But some of these portfolios are becoming unwieldy. Tesco Private Label alone has over 12,000 lines – a number that vastly exceeds any individual brand. Now that Private Label brands represent some of the biggest brands in the world, they will need to be on top of brand management like never before. Additionally, the increasing internationalization of their brands not only realizes manifold opportunities, but numerous headaches. Remember, brands didn't get good at international brand management overnight. It was a long and often slow and painful process. Don't make the simple mistake of thinking you know it all already. You don't.

The third opportunity and challenge is to use your Private Labels as a means to an end. That end is becoming a retailer capable of evolving to deal with the societal needs of tomorrow – the big issues as we described them earlier. There is an argument that no single brand can be seen to really meet social needs as a whole. However, given their scale and choice of offerings it is in theory possible to evolve a retailer who is seen as caring and sympathetic to people's and society's needs. This has already happened to a small extent with the emergence of Whole Foods Market (WFM), a retailer recently voted the best retailer on the planet. We mentioned this retailer earlier, but we would like to say more about it now.

WFM – a way forward

> Simply the best merchandized anywhere.
>
> Sir Martin Sorrell, CEO, WPP

Founded in 1980 as one small store in Austin, Texas, **Whole Foods Market**® is now the world's leading retailer of natural and organic foods, with 189 stores in North America and the United Kingdom.

We think it's worth repeating some of their claims – claims that seem to be constantly praised everywhere. WFM was recently voted the greatest food retailer in the world by *The Grocer* magazine's panel of experts in the UK.

Whole foods. We obtain our products locally and from all over the world, often from small, uniquely dedicated food artisans. We strive to offer the highest quality, least processed, most flavorful and naturally preserved foods. Why? Because food in its purest state – unadulterated by artificial additives, sweeteners, colorings and preservatives – is the best tasting and most nutritious food available.

Whole people. We recruit the best people we can to become part of our team. We empower them to make their own decisions, creating a respectful workplace where people are treated fairly and are highly motivated to succeed. We look for people who are passionate about food. Our team members are also well-rounded human beings. They play a critical role in helping build the store into a profitable and beneficial part of its community.

Whole planet. We believe companies, like individuals, must assume their share of responsibility as tenants of Planet Earth. On a global basis we actively support organic farming – the best method for promoting sustainable agriculture and protecting the environment and the farm workers. On a local basis, we are actively involved in our communities by supporting food banks, sponsoring neighborhood events, compensating our team members for community service work, and contributing at least five percent of total net profits to not-for-profit organizations.

> Staggering range of innovative lines and good food. This is food shopping as a pure leisure activity.
>
> Simon Bell, Retail Director, Leathams

This is Private Label at its very best. A retail brand at its very best. A brand at its very best. This is a brand beater any day. This is a brand as good as any brand out there. The big retailers of the world may well throw their hands up in horror and say 'we couldn't possibly be this'. We say you can and you must. This is the future of responsible global retailing. In reality, the big global retailers play around at this concept without really putting their feet in the water. It's about time to change. If you look at WFM's explosive growth, it's no accident and it's a very powerful wake-up call to what today's shoppers and therefore today's society are demanding from the retailers of tomorrow. Those demands are going to get louder and louder.

Traffic lights for health

And let's not forget the politicians who are increasingly demanding such a response from the retail and brand owners community. If you don't change, you will be changed. Legislation will transform your business. The UK government would like to bring in their traffic signalling system for packaging labelling. It will transform consumption, with Private Labels and brands dramatically changing market-share positions as shoppers, for the first time ever, realize what's good for you and what's not. No brand or Private Label is secure from this dramatic shift in consumers' perception of the products they are sold. And it certainly won't stay as a UK phenomenon. The EC will follow rapidly and the United States is already looking into it.

Just one look at a food label should help you choose a balanced diet, but views differ on what consumers need to see on the front of packs of

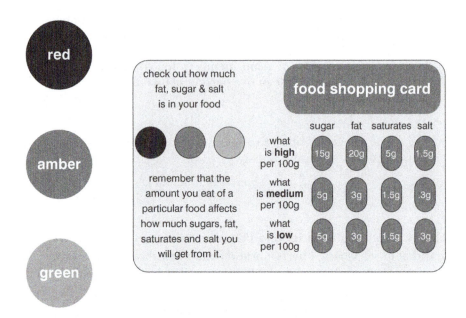

Figure 23.2 The UK traffic lights system

processed foods. The Food Standards Agency (FSA) in the UK thinks it should be red, amber and green. It has spent £2 million promoting traffic-light labels for the front of food packs. These show crucial nutritional information, such as levels of fat and salt, at a glance, and the FSA wants the food industry to adopt them for processed foods. The FSA surveyed 2,676 consumers in 2005. It found that shoppers are more likely to work out the nutritional content of products using the TL (traffic lights) system.

However, the food and retail industry in the UK wanted to introduce its own system – the GDA. The GDA label, developed by the Institute of Grocery Distribution, is based on the maximum levels of key nutrients we should have in one day. But without traffic light colours, they don't indicate whether products have high, medium or low levels, only the amount of each nutrient per portion and its percentage of your GDA. Whatever that means! The GDA campaign has spent £4 million promoting its front-of-pack label based on GDAs only. More than 20 food companies, including Tesco, Unilever and Nestlé, have rejected traffic-light colours and are backing the GDA campaign organized by the Food and Drink Federation.

Last year, the Which? consumer lobbying organization (www.which.co.uk) surveyed 636 people. Each was questioned about one of four label types (the TL and three GDA variations). While both GDAs and TLs helped people identify healthier products, 97 per cent spotted healthier versions of similar foods using the FSA's TL label compared with 87 per cent using the GDA campaign's favoured label. And far more people could gauge levels of nutrients in food using the TL label; 50 per cent correctly identified levels of fat, saturated fat, sugar and salt compared with only 5 per cent using the GDA label. As there's no consensus among manufacturers and supermarkets on which labels to use, the FSA has appointed an independent team of experts to review front-of-pack labelling schemes.

The fact that this increasingly public war has risen to the surface reflects badly on the UK food and retailing industry. The TL system is clearly a better system and all they've achieved by continuing to fight it is increased consumer and media scepticism as to their real motives. Hardly a way to restore brand trust!

The traffic lights system will herald the biggest change in mass consumption patterns that has ever occurred in the UK food industries' history. No brand or retailer will be immune. Surely it would be better to get your strategies in line with this inevitable change.

When you look at what's actually happening out there, frankly it's not much, compared with what will need to happen. And it won't just affect food. This wave is about all products, from making clothes more sustainable to producing electronics that biodegrade.

Just for example, let's take a few moments to think about the waste from clothes. A Cambridge University report called *Well Dressed* recently said that the one-trillion-dollar global textile industry must become eco-conscious. The report explores how to develop *'sustainable clothing'* – a seeming oxymoron in an ever-changing fashion world.

> Our research shows that customers are getting very concerned about environmental issues and we don't want to get caught between the eyes.
>
> Mike Barry, head of Corporate Social Responsibility at Marks & Spencer, one of Britain's largest retailers

We produce new fashions at a horrendous rate thanks to brands like Zara, H&M and Gap, which have made global fashions increasingly possible for the masses at prices they can afford. However, there's a cost, and that cost is an increasing mountain of used clothing. Around the world the concept of second-hand clothing is seen as a student/poor man's pursuit, or the sort of thing we give to charity shops to send off to the developing world. This has to stop. And there's a model out there that shows how to stop it. That model exists in Sweden, where buying second hand is a way of life for everyone – rich and poor. **Stadmission** is a particularly good example of a store that has turned charity into a powerful society-positive business.

What's the real benefit?

Retailers have to balance the success of Private Label against their overall success. They need to answer some very basic questions:

- Is Private Label more profitable than a brand?
- Does it improve my bargaining power and leverage over brand manufacturers?
- Does it really change my overall image?
- Is it what my customers really want?
- Will it keep me ahead of the game?
- Would my business be a better business if brands didn't exist?

Summary

Private Label still represents a major opportunity for retailers. But it needs to mature as an opportunity to reflect future shopper needs and corporate vision. The challenges are significant; the rewards even greater.

24 Retailer Private principles 1 to 5

We talked earlier about the big issues. They and the other principles are just as relevant to you.

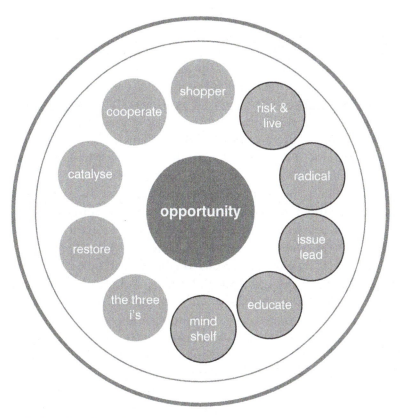

Figure 24.1   The first five principles

Accept too

Back to our wheel of opportunity. Retailers? Why should they be concerned about Private Label? It is, after all, they who have driven Private Label to its present high levels. But all is not what it seems, and retailers need to address a few fundamental issues to develop Private Label further. Those issues simply boil down to:

- learning how to really brand;
- ensuring they don't become boring;
- harnessing the big issues;
- learning how to co-opetete;
- harnessing the power of innovation;
- learning how to deal with customers circumstances better.

Changing the mentality

A major problem is how to change the organizational culture from the trading focus to the brand-building focus. ROS (return on sales) specialists don't become ROI specialists overnight. They need to learn about the brand owners' internal processes: how they educate their workforce about their brands; how they get everyone on board; how they get them to live and breathe their brands; how they run international business. It is not good enough to just put them on a shelf. You must do more. Much more.

Part of that process should be embracing lessons from the brands. Produce brand visions that will truly stimulate your customers and even more importantly your employees. As any great brand will tell you, the real brand starts within. The real brand starts with the employees. They have to embrace the brand and be enthusiastic about it. They have to be educated about it. Retailers should consider producing manuals that are then disseminated and cascaded across employees in vigorous internal communication campaigns.

Retailers sometimes give the impression that they have nothing to learn from brands. The truth couldn't be more different. Brands can teach retailers something they really need to know: how to sustain their long-term image and continue to develop it in a cohesive manner. It's not clear to us that retailers do this as well as they could, at the moment.

Move beyond price

The Private Label game is no longer the singularly simple game of just offering a price advantage. Consumers have quickly moved on to expecting better price as their genuine right – however, the traditional tenets of what makes strong brands and aspects which allow consumers to make informed decisions still hold. The real trick is in providing the brand message in a simple, compelling manner with a reinforced functional benefit. And, most importantly, to do it at the point of purchase. After all, that is where Private Label is winning the battle. The truly successful Private Label will stand, like a brand, for a multitude of factors. Price is only one of them.

And you can even get someone to haggle the price for you. Americans who are in the market for new automobiles, but don't want the headaches of searching or haggling for the best price, now have an alternative that can help them sidestep the usual dealership woes – **No Haggles**, a new car-buying service that promises to save customers time and money by negotiating all of the details of the purchase on their behalf (Springwise.com). Started by former car dealership managers, No Haggles negotiates with dealerships in a customer's area to negotiate price, financing, warranty and trade-in allowance, when necessary, for a small fee.

Customers contact No Haggles directly by phone or e-mail with information about the make and model of car they are looking for, including any desired add-ons or special features. No Haggles shops at local dealerships for the customer to find the vehicle at the best available price and facilitates the entire transaction. At no point is the customer contacted by anyone but their No Haggles representative, who even participates as a signing party on the buyer's agreement and can provide the customer with a detailed report of the negotiations. The representative is right there through all steps of the sales process, including delivery and inspection of the vehicle.

While certain dealers have long offered no-haggle pricing, No Haggles is unique in that it's not affiliated with any particular brand or seller. Customers can use the service to negotiate sales on any make or model. No Haggles currently serves customers throughout the United States, but the best-deal-without-haggling concept could easily be duplicated or expanded upon. In fact, the company is already running a test market programme with the largest US auto insurance company to further serve its customers.

Stop being so secretive

You would almost think the retail trade was embarrassed by Private Label. Look how difficult it is to get a comment from a retailer about the role of Private Label in their brands. Especially in Sweden! What's the big secret? You're either successful or not. And if you are, you shouldn't be ashamed of it. We increasingly live in a world where transparency is the key to success; transparency with customers; transparency with suppliers; and transparency with yourself. You have used Private Label to date as a key factor in reinforcing your customers' trust in the corporate brand. If your Private Labels are to be truly sustainable, they also need to be trustworthy individually in their own right. Can you put your hand up and say that each of your sub-brands is the 'best in class' when it comes to the big issues we face? Are you 'best in class' when it comes to consumer transparency?

RETAILERS NEED CUSTOMER TRUST. THEY ALSO NEED
BRAND OWNER TRUST.

Embracing the big issues

Sustainability is profitable for our company.

Wal-Mart

Embrace the big issues in a big way. The big issues we outlined earlier are as pertinent to retailers as anyone. There's a lot of talk about their involvement, but the action often doesn't meet the rhetoric. A recent UK survey showed that at least one of the major retailers used 13 plastic bags to take away 39 products: 3 per bag – hardly eco friendly. It is all too often the case that healthier food lines are more expensive. And the low-cost or economy-range Private Label foods are much less healthy than their more expensive counterparts. The market has changed over the past two or three years.

In today's hypercompetitive markets, companies in categories such as computers and retail struggle to establish and maintain a competitive advantage. Given that consumer expectations are evolving, many of these companies are turning to green, to differentiate their offerings by being greener than their competitors. As the basis of competition shifts to the green space, companies seem to be continually upping the ante by trying to outdo each other for being the greenest company in the category.

> Retailers will have to change their business models in order to keep in lockstep with this movement because, ultimately, it's going to be legislated, and they're not going to have a choice. Much like Sarbanes–Oxley or Y2K, it would be a very prudent thing for big retailers to begin the programs now.
>
> Fred Crawford, Managing Director at Alix Partners

Interestingly, green competitiveness is having an unintended consequence: green competitive pressure is accelerating the rate of change within these categories. Industry leaders such as Wal-Mart and Tesco, and Dell and HP – already engaged in intense battles for consumer hearts, minds and share of wallet – are playing tit for tat when it comes to green (Wordpress.com). As the demand for green products has accelerated, companies have increasingly used ethics and the environment as a hook to market products, with little or no verification of the data being reported.

Marketers increasingly touting the greenness of their products have contributed to the confusion about which environmental claims are true, leading some industry experts to warn of 'green fatigue'.

> In the past, the market was driven by price. But so much value has been stripped out by going down the price route, customers have cottoned on to that.
>
> Steven Esom, Managing Director of Waitrose

Analysis by the UK National Consumer Council says that most bargain-basement lines contained significantly more salt – and slightly more sugar – than even the supermarkets' own-brand counterparts, and there are fewer healthy food promotions in supermarkets where poor consumers are likely to shop. This is hardly taking the 'big issues' seriously. In the survey, nearly all scored poorly on communicating healthy-eating messages and some relied too heavily on their website or magazine, but were unable to answer direct queries. Health is a lifestyle in its own right. Make sure you're part of it in a meaningful way.

> Consumers who rely heavily on economy ranges are clearly being short-changed.
>
> Lord Whitty of the NCC

Multi-tier Private Label strategy

If you can get shoppers to buy Private Label organic foods and other premium products, it will certainly increase total sales of store brands. But perhaps more importantly, deploying such a multi-tier Private Label strategy will also increase loyalty to the store.

Those were some of the results of a new major US Private Label consumer study conducted by Catalina Marketing, a provider of behaviour-based shopper research, and Daymon Worldwide, a broker of Private Label products. The goal of the study was to create a robust understanding of the Private Label shopper and to gain insights to drive sales growth.

The companies formed a research team that dug into retail databases to access the purchase behaviour of over 100 million households. The team was able to quantify the upside sales opportunity as well as the effect of Private Label on consumer loyalty to the chain. They concluded that Private Label had moved beyond the limited role of providing low-price alternatives to nationally advertised brands. Beyond the role of enhancing margins, the new role of Private Label is much more powerful. Private Label can literally define the image, personality and the most powerful point of differentiation among retail chains and retail channels.

Pam Boynton, Director of Marketing at Daymon Worldwide, said, 'In the 1980s and 1990s, Private Label began to follow the brands. In the 21st century, what we're seeing is that Private Label is starting to lead the brands and that's an exciting place to be at this point.'

The study examined four tiers of Private Label products: National Brand Equivalents, Premium, Value, and Organic. According to Elmore, offering multiple tiers of Private Label is essential to meeting consumers' needs. Over half (55 per cent) of shoppers buy Private

Label in two or more tiers. They found that consumers engaged in all four tiers are the most valuable ones. A one-tier consumer spends $934 annually, while a four-tier consumer spends over $5,000 annually. In fact, they were more than five times more valuable than someone buying in just one tier.

To find out whether multi-tier purchasing correlated with loyalty, the study used Catalina's Loyalty Quotient, which scored each household to determine their share of wallet at a chain. For example, a high loyal spends over 80 per cent in a chain. The study determined that consumer engagement in multiple tiers increased along with loyalty. Just 27 per cent of the non-loyals buy Private Label in more than one tier. However, 58 per cent and 64 per cent of your medium to high loyals spend across multiple tiers. People who buy only the National Brand Equivalent tend to be least loyal to a chain. The most loyal customers are those purchasing multiple tiers of Private Label. One-tier consumers spent almost $3,000 annually, yet the four-tier consumer spent over $6,800. This is 2.3 times more, even among the most committed shoppers in your chain. The study proved that 'the low-hanging fruit of opportunity is to expand category penetration with your existing Private Label consumers'.

Here are some other key findings:

- In the past year, Private Label outpaced overall store growth by two to one. This was driven largely by differentiating tiers. Concerted marketing efforts have driven the growth of Value, Premium and Organic Tiers well above the rate of National Brand Equivalents.
- The Premium Tier contributed 9 per cent of the total Private Label dollars across the study group. Yet the Premium Tier contributed as much as 16 per cent of the Private Label dollars in one or more of the chains. That's a seven-point increase in importance and helps you understand how high is up when Premium is your key differentiator.
- The Value Tier held a share of 4 per cent across the industry, yet the best-in-class retailer was at 20 per cent of Private Label sales. A five-times improvement helps you understand that if Value is your differentiating tier, that's how high up you can go.
- The Organic Tier had a 2 per cent industry share, but the best-in-class retailer was 7 per cent. This is a new and emerging product for households.

The study also examined National Brand Equivalents and considered how big the opportunity was for Private Label sales. If the National Brand buyers would buy into just one more (Private Label) category, it would generate an incremental $159,000 in sales per store per year. So you might assess your Private Label strategy by understanding which categories are the entry points for your consumers.

The study identified the five core categories that drive National Brand Equivalents. In order of importance, they are paper products, frozen vegetables, soft drinks and water, cheese, and proprietary remedies. The strategy here is to get consumers more engaged within the tiers where they currently buy.

Finally, of course, such a multi-tier strategy is just as relevant to brands.

Crowd clout

The power of groups, the clout that crowds can exercise to get what they want, is nothing new (trendwatching.com). What is new, however, is the dizzying ease with which like-minded, action-ready citizens and consumers can now go online and connect, group and ultimately exert influence on a global scale. Call it group power, call it CROWD CLOUT. This crowd clout should worry retailers.

> CROWD CLOUT: 'Online grouping of citizens/consumers for a specific cause, be it political, civic or commercial, aimed at everything from bringing down politicians to forcing suppliers to fork over discounts.'

So, why is CROWD CLOUT likely to become such a force?

- First of all, a billion people are now online. We cannot emphasize this mind-boggling statistic enough. Whatever web-based business you're planning to set up, you now have a potential audience. And this audience can be reached with virtually no marketing budget to speak of, as good ideas will spread instantly, thanks to the blogosphere.
- Second, this huge online audience actually shops online. In the United States, consumers spent more than $200 billion online last year (including travel), while Europeans shelled out €100 billion on online goodies and services. Online sales in Asia are in the tens of

billions of US dollars, too. (*Sources*: Forrester, Shop.org and eMarketer.)

- Third, as the past few years have seen an all-determining shift from 'visiting' to 'participating' (if not grouping) in the online world, many consumers may now be up for more active and involved business models like CROWD CLOUT. Consumers are now both the audience and the participants.

- Last but not least, an entire infrastructure of personal profiles and blogs is now in place (for example, MySpace boasts about 150 million profiles, Facebook counts 18 million registered users, while UK-based Bebo has over 8 million users), potentially giving consumers a direct, private outlet to itemize and tag their intentions – and giving them readily accessible lists of friends to group with. Smart intermediaries or even the social networking sites will jump on this opportunity and facilitate the aggregation process. Also keep an eye on the proliferation of social commerce sites (pick lists, voting mechanisms and TWINSUMERISM included): StyleHive, CrowdStorm, Yahoo Shoposphere, ThisNext and Kaboodle are just a few of the many sites exquisitely positioned to be future CROWD CLOUT leaders.

So who is putting intention to good use? Look to China for CROWD CLOUT initiatives that are moving closer to a reincarnation of letsbuyit.com. Of particular interest is the *tuangou* ('team purchase') phenomenon, which involves strangers organizing themselves around a specific product or service. Think electronics, home furnishings, cars and so on. These like-minded people then meet up in real-world shops and showrooms on a coordinated date and time, literally mobbing the seller, negotiating a group discount on the spot. Popular Chinese sites that are enabling the crowds first to group online, then to plan for actual real-world shopmobbing, are TeamBuy, Taobao and Liba, which was recently acquired by 51tuangou.com. Combined, these sites now boast hundreds of thousands of registered members, making money from ads and/or commissions from suppliers who are actually happy to have the mobs choose their store over a competitor's.

Oh, and one more fun example from India: **Offers For Shoppers** is an online coupon site, dipping its toes in the CROWD CLOUT pond by letting customers tag any interesting offer, and thereby revealing their intentions. When the number of potential buyers reaches a pre-determined total (a number that vendors consider a bulk buy), customers are notified and offered a take it or leave it bulk price. This is clearly one to be copied by the social shopping sites that are now mushrooming in the United States.

Another initiative to watch: French **CrowdSpirit**. Currently in beta-mode, the company hopes to go full circle on crowd-innovation: participants not only submit ideas for consumer electronics, but also take part in every stage of the product life cycle, up to purchasing the end result. In the first stage of the project, the focus will be on products with a market price below €150 ($190). How it will work:

> Step 1: The community sends ideas, fine-tunes them and votes for the best one.
> Step 2: The best ideas and their product specifications are jointly defined with CrowdSpirit's research and manufacturing partners. Community investors start financing the product development.
> Step 3: The first prototype is tested and fine-tuned by the community.
> Step 4: Customers purchase products thanks to the CrowdSpirit supply chain. The community takes care of product support and recommends products to retailers.

A tentative launch is planned for the summer of 2007. May we humbly suggest that every B2C (business to consumer) industry, from travel to food and beverage, experiment with this model? If only to get a feel for the innovation prowess of 'ordinary consumers'.

Summary and opportunities

The big issues are as relevant to retailers as brand owners. In fact they may be more relevant as the world becomes more anti big retailer. Private Label is the mechanism to face this challenge effectively.

- Opportunity 45: THINK AHEAD. ACT TODAY. Start thinking more long term instead of your usual short-term obsessiveness.
- Opportunity 46: GO BEYOND PRICE. You need value way beyond price for the new future. Make sure you have it.
- Opportunity 47: Revise and improve your BRAND ARCHITECTURE. The present brand structure is for the past. Make sure you change to anticipate it.

- Opportunity 48: LEARN FROM BRANDS now you are one.
- Opportunity 49: Be TRANSPARENT about your Private Label success.
- Opportunity 50: Make CROUD CLOUT work for you before it works against you.
- Opportunity 51: Make your brand a BETTER BRAND. Totally socialize your brand and make it socially fit from top to bottom. Commit to total change.
- Opportunity 52: Become the BIG ISSUE EDUCATOR. You have a social and moral responsibility to educate everyone from your employees to your shoppers about the big issues we all face.
- Opportunity 53: Become the BIG ISSUE IMPLEMENTER. Change your total product line, your packaging, your communications and your distribution to reflect the new issues. Stop greenwashing. Start doing.
- Opportunity 54: Investigate your MULTI-TIER strategy and optimize it.

Actions to consider

1. Think about the impact of Private Label from an international perspective. It is increasingly a multi-border operation.
2. Produce a Private Label toolkit which not only explains the true nature of Private Label to your organization (the facts and the myths), but also clearly lays out principles and rules for dealing with it.
3. Show that toolkit to your suppliers so they actually understand what you're trying to accomplish.
4. Do a Private Label audit of your brands to fully evaluate how well you stack up against your key Private Label competition.
5. Big issues are here to stay. Let's be clear about that. Why not make it part of your retail make-up? Show you are actually doing something good for all and try to involve the community in a straightforward way.
6. Audit your 'big issue' involvement.
7. Come to a point of view about how you can make your company a 'big issue' company.
8. Develop plans to totally implement those issues in EVERYTHING the company does.

9. Develop internal communication plans and methodologies to educate everyone about the changes coming.
10. Re-brief R&D to ensure they take big issues on board.
11. Make sure your big-issue communications are meaningful, not self-serving.
12. Avoid getting CLOUTED

25 Retailer Private principles 6 to 10

We talked earlier about the store of the future with reference to brands. Those observations are, of course, just as critical for retailers. The new formats, the new strategies, the new fights for space are the same battles for you as a retailer. And there are others...

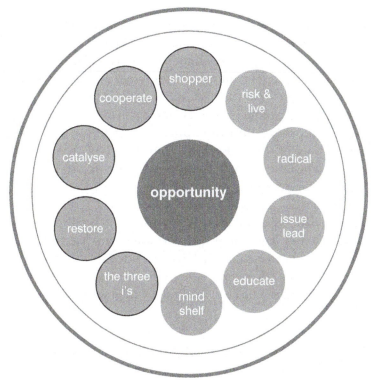

Figure 25.1   The next five principles

The intention economy

Accurately dubbed the Intention Economy by Doc Searls, it all comes down to letting consumers make their buying intentions known, inviting one or multiple suppliers to bid for their business (trend-watching.com).

To quote Searls: 'The Intention Economy is built around truly open markets, not a collection of silos. In The Intention Economy, customers don't have to fly from silo to silo, like a bee from flower to flower, collecting deal info (and unavoidable hype) like so much pollen. In The Intention Economy, the buyer notifies the market of the intent to buy, and sellers compete for the buyer's purchase.'

Simple as that. In The Intention Economy, a car rental customer should be able to say to the car rental market, 'I'll be skiing in Park City from 20–25 March. I want to rent a 4-wheel drive SUV. I belong to Avis Wizard, Budget FastBreak and Hertz 1 Club. I don't want to pay up front for petrol or get any insurance. What can any of your companies do for me?' – and have the sellers compete for the buyer's business.

If this catches on, we're going to be living in a very different retail world – one where the shopper really is totally in charge. Now, even though there are a growing number of intermediaries helping individual consumers to get a quote or offer based on their intentions, this space remains wide open. In fact, most of these 'information brokers' focus on only one product/category (mortgages, cruises, plane tickets), making it a hassle to find the appropriate site for each individual intention. Many of them also work (too) closely with a limited set of suppliers, so the bidding process becomes somewhat scripted, with less than spectacular discounts as a result.

So while there's cruisecompete.com for getting a quote from cruise travel agents, and Priceline, which lets customers name their own price and then matches it with the (pre-set) minimum prices that airlines, hotels and rental car companies have provided to Priceline, this space remains wide open for intention-brokers who can handle a variety of intentions per customer, and genuinely operate on behalf of those customers.

For true inspiration, take a cue from these 'intention 2.0' firms that are shaking up the traditionally not-so-transparent world of real estate in Finland, the UK, the Netherlands and the United States.

- **Igglo**. Finnish real-estate site Igglo lets potential buyers 'pre-order' houses that aren't on the market. Igglo has photographed every building in Helsinki and several other Finnish cities, and combines these photographs with satellite images and maps. Every property is listed, not just those that are currently on the market. Their tagline is: '*Your house is already on Igglo.*' Potential buyers can earmark a building, street or neighbourhood they're interested in, and post offers online. This lets potential sellers find out how desirable their property is, even if they weren't actively considering selling. Buyers also receive an alert when a property in their earmarked building or area comes up for sale. If demand and supply meet, Igglo handles the transaction for a lower fee than is charged by regular real-estate agents (less than 2 per cent). Lower fees are made possible by the fact the Igglo agents don't get involved until buyers and sellers have found each other. Consumers like it: the site attracts more than 50,000 visitors a week, and the company is now working on European expansion.

Is it so difficult to imagine shoppers who pre-order healthy lifestyles from caring retailers?

- **Zillow**. On the side of intentions and consumer sellers, there is also US-based Zillow, which lets home owners take the initiative, by allowing them to set a Make Me Move price without actually putting their house on the market. Once owners set a price ('*that magical number you just can't refuse*'), potential buyers can contact them anonymously via e-mail. It's then up to the owner to decide whether they really want to sell. Here too, intentions are key: if homeowners are thinking about selling in the near future, the service helps to start gathering interest. Or they may have long-term plans to sell, but could be motivated to do so sooner if the right offer comes along. What match-making start-up will go all-out and combine Igglo and Zillow-like intention-services to create a beyond-transparent real-estate super site?
- **Eventful**. There's more, though: how about listing an intention to go see an artist or band if he, she or they would only come to a certain country or city? Enter Eventful, which not only enables users to find and post local events anywhere in the world, but also lets them demand events and performances in their town and spread the word to make them happen. At last count, there were

more than 126,000 demanded events on Eventful. This should help persuade well-known artists to change their regular touring schedule now and then, and should definitely create a long-tail-style bonanza for niche audiences, and thus niche artists, niche events and niche performances.

Once shoppers really start buying and thinking about buying in very different ways, Pandora's box has really been opened and nothing will be as it was. It's not that much of a stretch of the imagination to see consumers listing an intention to buy only from retailers who are genuine about the big issues. It might be a small list at the moment. But it will end up being a very large list.

Learning how to innovate

Consumers are very picky when it comes to buying new products. As a result, upwards of 80 per cent of all new consumer packaged goods are rapidly off the shelf because of poor sales. Last year 33,000 new products were introduced in the United States. Nearly 18,000 were food and beverages, while the rest were health and beauty care and general merchandise items, according to researcher Mintel.

It's generally believed that such a high failure rate doesn't apply to Private Label products. Analysts say the success rate of new products is much higher for store brands for three reasons:

- Retailers own the shelf and can keep products in stock longer.
- Retailers are closer to shoppers and understand their needs.
- Retailers can very quickly produce products in growth categories that tap into changing tastes and trends.

According to analysts, retailers wait until a certain minimum threshold of sales of a new product is attained before reaching out to a Private Label manufacturer to produce a store brand in a given category. For example, stores are launching more of their own upscale and specialty products nowadays as consumers have shown they will pay for such goods. For instance, a line of products that will be sold only at Kroger's stores, bear the brand name of Disney's Magic Selections and feature more than 100 health-oriented food items resulted from an alliance between the Walt Disney Co and Kroger. The line will encompass 12 categories, including water, juices, milk, fruits, vegetables, pastas, soups, breads, yogurts, meats, cheese and portion-controlled snacks such as ice cream and biscuits. It is the first time Disney has licensed a food retailer to sell its own store brand of products.

But the sizzle of Private Label extends beyond traditional food these days. Target is looking to grow its Private Label business in health and beauty categories with its new Bath & Body department, which includes 20 new brands. Whole Foods offers its shoppers the Mineral Fusion line of natural cosmetics in its Whole Body department. Costco has 112 products in its Office Impressions line of office supplies. Safeway's new organics line of more than 150 items accounted for $160 million in sales during its first year.

All of these retailers are launching and succeeding with such creative lines of Private Label products because they are simply meeting consumer demand. According to a recent nationwide survey, the popularity of Private Label grocery products is growing among American shoppers.

The Ispos MORI research also revealed:

- Consumers in the middle-income ($30,000–75,000) and high-income (over $75,000) brackets are much more likely to buy a larger amount of Private Label in the coming year than those in the low-income (under $30,000) bracket.
- Almost half of those interviewed said their regular shopping basket now contains one-quarter or more store brand products. For all consumers in the study, the average amount of Private Label they buy is 32 per cent.
- The popularity of grocery store brands is spreading a halo effect to non-grocery Private Label products in trade channels apart from supermarkets. About one-fifth of consumers said they frequently buy Private Label products in the health and beauty, home office, household, and home improvement categories. Three of four respondents said their overall past satisfaction with non-grocery-store Private Label products will likely prompt them to buy more such products in the coming year.

Having painted this positive picture for Private Label, it's not all rosy. Frankly, retailers have not been good brand innovators to date. Why is this? Simply because they haven't really put the investment behind innovation to make it work. It's often too easy to mimic somebody else rather than be genuinely different, as copycat Private Label variants clearly demonstrate. To a large extent they are happy to leave those risky innovations to the brands. They are happy to be non-radical in their thinking. MISTAKE numero uno!

Brands have succeeded because they have, throughout their histories, taken innovative leaps and risks. Most fail, but when they succeed they make a real difference. Which was the last retailer brand you could accuse of being innovative? Which is the last innovation risk you remember a retailer taking with a brand? This despite the fact that shoppers clearly expect the Private Label of the future to be innovative. Our S&S X survey clearly showed this to be so.

The interesting thing is that there is a clear and consistent dissonance between retailer, shopper and brand owner expectations when it comes to innovation (Figure 25.3). The retailer in the United States and the UK thinks that 100 per cent of the time, Private Label is as innovative as a brand. Their shoppers think so half of the time and the brand owners

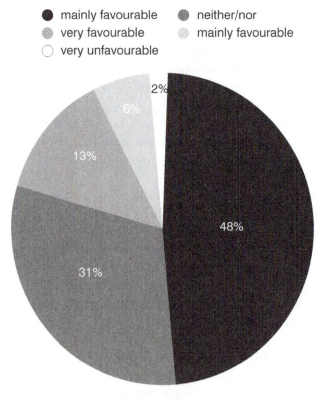

Figure 25.2 Private Label favourability
Source: ISPSOS US adults

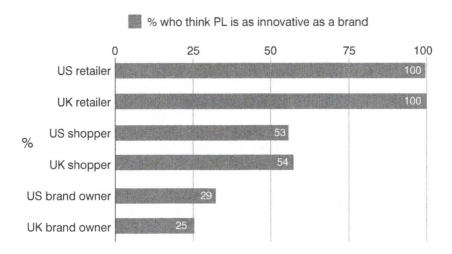

Figure 25.3 Private Label innovation
Source: S&S X report

think so a quarter of the time. We can put this gap down to retailer ignorance or brand owner ignorance or arrogance. That doesn't really matter. What matters is that this gap exists.

Shoppers clearly think that innovation requires investment and, most of all, it requires creativity. The problem for a retailer is that it's all too easy to copy innovation rather than create it. Maybe retailers should look at some of the world's leading cultures and categories when it comes to copying. With few exceptions, it leads to blandness and cheapness on the road to commoditization.

The road to great innovation was never easy. That's why most people fail. The rewards, however, are great. Take a category and think up 25 crazy ideas to get you going – 25 crazy radical ideas. Here are 22 ideas for the dairy category, or do you just want to sell a commodity?

1. Organic foods with real organic ingredients (proved and tested)
2. Make your own dairy products – mix and match
3. Heavy lite products – lite products with some depth
4. Good health labels – instead of warning labels
5. Truly transparent products – we tell you exactly what you get
6. Dairy bars – retail outlets
7. Dairy on the go – pop-up stores on the road
8. Beautifully simple products – we take the complexity out of food
9. Power dairy products – high energy drinks

10. Portion packs
11. Products designed by you
12. Bone-growing products
13. Spicy dairy
14. Milk-soaked meat
15. Dairy on the go
16. One-cal milk drinks
17. Zen products for well-being
18. Brain food
19. Tubed butter and flavoured variants
20. Scandinavian dairy for the world
21. Black dairy products – dairy with a whole new taste and feel
22. iMILK.

And once you've come up with these ideas, radically implement them in radical ways. You can always, of course, take the Apple route. Here's a company famous for its innovation that doesn't think it's innovative. It believes instead that it redesigns products. The iPhone is the latest example of this – a product innovation clearly waited for by consumers, but not by manufacturers, who have failed to develop their innovations far enough.

Or take the Samsung route, where every Monday they declare their products to be in a state of perpetual crisis and in need of innovation. This constant attack on innovation has transformed a traditionally boring brand into one of the world's leading innovators in the space of five years.

Learning to involve

Remember you're not in charge. According to Godin (1999), it is the selfish consumer who has control, not a marketer, in this new marketing reality. This consumer doesn't care about the manufacturers, products and brands if his or her problems are not solved. Traditional marketing management and brand management try to keep customers as prisoners, while marketing based on permission and mutuality tries to give customers concrete reasons for drawing their attention in terms of information, education, entertainment or even cash.

As we have said earlier, involvement is a key factor for the future – a factor innovative brand owners are diving into. **Involvement retailing** is just as pertinent to retailers as brands. Take a brand like **Karmaloop**, a Boston-based clothes internet retailer that brings innovation direct to its customers. Karmaloop helps give their partner brands rapid entrance into the fickle 18–30 early adopters market. With an e-mail list of a million young online shoppers, Karmaloop is able to get its brands in front of these tastemakers where they spend time – online. Take **P&G** with their Tremor project where they have formed a community of teens. Tremor is a marketing service – powered by the Procter & Gamble Company – that develops teen word-of-mouth marketing programmes by recruiting teens to help develop exciting and relevant product ideas and marketing programmes that teens want to talk about. Tremor works with companies in industries like entertainment, fashion, music, food and beauty. Their members are directly involved in the creation and launch of these companies' ideas and programmes to build word-of-mouth among teenagers. In only two years, this focus group cum sample/coupon-dispersing network signed up 280,000 US teens, ages 13 to 19, who actively promote new products to their peers, and may be asked to place coupons and product samples in living rooms, schools and any other relevant locations.

Apple, as we described earlier, is the arch proponent of getting customers involved. That obsession has resulted in Apple becoming the most efficient retailer in the United States in five years! It had considerable problems until it realized it's about more than the product. It's about what products do and what products let you be. All retailers, from mass FMCG to clothes, should take that on board. Apple takes this to the extreme and lets 75 per cent of its floor space be devoted to non-product areas that lets shoppers know more: areas that educate – areas that entertain – areas that involve. The result is a massive ROI from its floor space, not only ahead of the competition, but ahead of everyone else. The result is the best **Return on Involvement** in the retail industry. And the company that essentially reinvented retail. Can you reinvent retail?

people need to understand it's not what you buy that's important – it's what it allows **you** to **do**.

Figure 25.4   Apple positioning strategy

Learning how to imagineer

Learn how to make great brands with great images.

> A product is something that is made in a factory; a brand is some-thing that is bought by a customer. The products can be copied by a competitor; the brand is unique. A brand can be quickly outdated; a successful brand is timeless.
>
> King in 1990

We go back to this earlier quote because it clearly shows the real other gap between manufacturer and retailer brands: image. When retail brands can master producing great images they will become the true brand masters and we will definitely have returned to our Roman forums. If you look at Interbrands' 2006 annual valuation of the world's greatest brands, there's not one mass FMCG brand in the top 100. IKEA comes in at 42, followed by Gap at 52 and Zara at 73.

What great retail ad can you remember? What retail ad have you seen and you thought to yourself, that changed me? What retail ad have you seen that you would describe as timeless? Your obsession with the rational delivery for your benefit images has precluded you from developing the more emotive images which produce the really great campaigns – the ones that stand the test of time.

You're also in too much of a hurry. The two quotes from Samsung, arguably the most successful brand builder of recent years, make it clear that time and consistency are key. And love!

> Having created a splash, Samsung now has to ensure
> consumers feel attached to its brand. It normally takes
> decades to grow a brand. We achieved success in coming
> from nowhere to be one of the top contenders, but in some
> ways that was the easier challenge.
> To be truly number one, you have to be known.
> You have to be loved.
>
> (Eric Kim – CEO, Samsung)

> Once you embark on a brand, you have to keep at it.
> You can't just do it one year and then because
> business is not so good, not do it the next year.
> If you do that, whatever you
> did the previous year was waste.
>
> (Eric Kim – CEO, Samsung)

Relationship marketing

We are increasingly influenced by relationship marketing management. Today, when we have moved into the information age, information technology will be part of the tools that enable the relationships to develop. Communication is not just a matter of persuasion-push; it will be replaced by permission-pull, when companies and their marketers communicate with their prospects. In the management of relationship marketing, communication based on image creation that can enhance the benefits – economic, functional and psychological – identity and lifestyle – sought by the consumers is of importance. The Saatchi & Saatchi X Lovemarks™ that we mentioned earlier is an interesting approach to realizing that image.

We believe that one of the reasons retail chains have gained power in the marketing channel is that they have understood this need and also tried to satisfy it in terms of their own brand alternatives. They are trying to create new value for their customers through cheaper, more innovative brands at the same time as they have obtained higher profitability and position vis-à-vis manufacturers. The value is, in a sense, created with customers and not just for them, as is the case for manufacturer brands. There needs to be more of this thinking as we move forward. Broadcasting messages and marketing communications is not enough. Inter-communication based on involvement is needed.

Actually, this is like returning historically to the roots of merchandising. Manufacturers were, then, just producers and retailers were the final link and had direct contact with the end customer. Retail brand management needs to follow this development more than ever, and become influenced by the new marketing paradigm – relationship marketing. This new paradigm is a strategic company philosophy leading to a new approach for retail brands (and arguably conventional brands). Brands are seen to be parts of the building and cementing of relationships with customers and parts of overall strategic decisions. Today, we also need continually to become more customer orientated, and that means building brands for customers in a mutual sense!

Keep it simple

So why have retailers been able to drive the Private Label agenda successfully across shop shelves in Europe? The answer lies in the fundamental tenets of human behaviour and motivation. Essentially, retailers have latched on to the basic consumer need for simplicity. Work done around the world has found that consumers are spending less and less time shopping for certain categories. In the non-food arena, this reduction has been quite dramatic. A staggering insight is that in three out of four categories where Private Label is growing, consumers are looking predominantly at a functional benefit rather than the emotional attributes of a brand. A dishwasher product has to clean, and if the Private Label performs 'as well as the leading brand' it is an easy buy. We've gone back to the rational. By satisfying these basic needs, offering a singularly focused functional benefit – at a lower price – Private Labels have managed to create singular message-based marketing devices to attract those consumers who seek one thing in their shopping decision making – simplicity.

Consumers still carry a multitude of brands in their heads and make purchase decisions using a complex set of rules. For some categories these rules converge very quickly as they browse through retailer shelves, and if their purchase decision is based on seeking a simple functional benefit, Private Label wins hands down. What is even more interesting is that over time these Private Label relationships begin to carry brand values and consumers gradually begin to transfer the retailer brand equity onto their Private Label brands.

If one product fails, the whole brand suffers.

Learning how to brand

One of the problems that retailers face in building retail brands is simply the sheer complexity needed. Long-term investments are needed in people, skills, quality control, marketing, consumer research and supplier relationships. None of these are easy.

Some of the big retailers have started to deal with this, with varying degrees of success. But they have a long way to go. Even Wal-Mart with a $500 million communications budget, placed alongside the multi-billion dollar efforts of the big branders like P&G, seems insignificant.

The web is clearly going to change the nature of retail and branding and somewhat faster than we originally thought. One of the major impacts will be within retail space (*Daily Telegraph*, 23 February 2007, Stores to Shrink).

> Retailers are to cut the size of their stores and move away from the high street.
>
> John Clare, CEO Of Curry's and PC World, UK

It's clear that the growth of online shopping has meant that retailers no longer require the same floor space. Only three years ago it was forecast that internet sales would account for 10 per cent of UK electrical sales eventually! Now they estimate that 60 per cent of their store customers visited their websites first. IMRG predicts that online sales will top £42 billion in 2007 in the UK alone. The threatened revolution of the internet bubble is here now. And as a result, the need for additional retail space is declining. It's interesting to note that half the new UK retail space came from one retailer which, in theory, accounted for only 13 per cent of your wallet: Tesco. Clearly things are afoot.

All the real increases in retail sales in the last three years in the UK have been online.

Dealing with change

Finally, the retailers also have to deal with changes in their supplier relationships as a result of them focusing on their retail brands and building their own brand power. It doesn't take a genius to see that in many cases those relationships truly suck, whatever is said publicly.

Manufacturers have not historically been very interested in retail brands, since it has been considered better to invest in their own brands. Manufacturers also wanted to be independent. Nevertheless, studies show that retail brands can offer retailers, wholesalers and manufacturers strategic relations and advantages. Through inter-organizational relations, a win–win situation may arise. More importantly, retailers are honing their Private Label strategies by focusing on the aspects that were traditionally the weapons of mainstream manufacturer brands to drive growth. In doing this retailers are now:

- working with manufacturers to expand and develop their product lines;
- investing in marketing research, product development, marketing and merchandising;
- creating multiple brands, logos, looks and prices;
- co-branding products.

The battlefield for increased discontent between both parties is only likely to grow in the short term. Make sure you avoid such a battle. Learn to co-opetete. It is just as important for a retailer as it is for a brand in the long term. CO-OPETITION STARTS WITH YOU. It's in your short-, medium- and long-term interests.

Dealing with reality

The presence of conflict and cooperation is a fact in the retailing industry. Suppliers and retailers can have common goals, but also disparate ones. These differences must be confronted, otherwise the relationships will stagnate and both sides will lose flexibility and the potential to develop. Therefore it is important to handle conflicts in a constructive way. The extent of this conflict widens considerably according to geography. In theory, retail chains and manufacturers should become more integrated and develop joint strategies. They are, after all, serving the same target audience… the shopper. In the United States, this has already happened, while it tends to be more difficult in Europe. The large French retailers in particular tend to resist this level of cooperation. In the UK, however, retail chains, for example Tesco, also increasingly work more closely with manufacturers.

Summary and opportunities

- Opportunity 55: Become a part of the INTENTION ECONOMY before it goes around you.
- Opportunity 56: Design formats that meet SOCIAL NEEDS RETAILING. Identify shoppers' situational needs and provide shopping experiences/retail formats that meet them. Go to them. Don't expect them to come to you.
- Opportunity 57: Rethink you relationships with your customers in terms of their CIRCUMSTANCES rather than their attributes. The TESCO way forward.
- Opportunity 58: Sell your products when it suits your shoppers, not when it suits you. SELL TO SUIT, wherever that may be and whatever it takes.
- Opportunity 59: Become a RISK INNOVATOR, the true sign of a real innovator.
- Opportunity 60: Consider REDESIGNING innovation – putting products that already exist out there in a very different way, not just copies of them.
- Opportunity 61: Create TIMELESS brands like the real brands.
- Opportunity 62: Maximize your RETURN ON INVOLVEMENT. Ensure your shoppers are participants, not just spectators
- Opportunity 63: CATALYSE YOUR COMMUNICATIONS. Make your communications work harder at the point of action – the store. Turn your shoppers into buyers.
- Opportunity 64: Seek HIGHLY CREATIVE SOLUTIONS. Make your agencies put their creative resources against this target.
- Opportunity 65: CO-OPETITION STARTS WITH YOU. It's in your short-, medium- and long-term interests.

Actions to consider

1. Are you anticipating and adapting to the retail stores of the future?
2. Understand those changes and plan how they might affect you.
3. Understand the nature of the future shelf and adapt your strategies to take account of it.
4. Produce brands that drive shopper wants.
5. Truly understand your shopper.
6. Truly understand their intentions.
7. When it comes to innovation, create, don't copy.
8. Consider redesign.
9. Remember you're in perpetual crisis. Deal with it.
10. Maximize your Return on Involvement.
11. Strive to make timeless brands.
12. Sit down and have some extreme brainstorming sessions.
13. Be radical.
14. Involve your agencies.
15. Review your communication plans to see if they allow you to fully optimize your big-issue positioning.
16. Look for a new in-store medium as a more effective facilitator of the brand message and the medium that translates shopping behaviour into purchase behaviour.
17. Build a 'private room' where you can fully understand and creatively develop your position.
18. Use creativity as your main tool to grow Private Label.
19. Use creativity to develop customized solutions for private variants.
20. Seek any way you can to co-opetete.

Part 5

Conclusions

Here we come to some final conclusions and put it together... hopefully!

Tesco has over 12,000 Private Label product lines and a store within striking distance of pretty much every UK postcode.

26 Realizing the opportunity together

Innovation should come from brands and Private Label. We have no agenda to push Private Label beyond what our shoppers want it to be. Knock on our door and ask us how we can help you build your brand.

Justin King, CEO, Sainsbury's, IGD Trade Briefing, 7 June 2007, London

The above quote says it all. You have to realize the opportunity together, or not at all. Win, win, win. We have entered a world where a triple win is uniquely potentially possible. Win the brand supplier, win the retailer and win the shopper. Private Label has to a large extent made us realize that win. But Private Label is only part of the story, albeit a very visible part. Throughout this book we have talked the story of opportunity rather than threat. It's clear, when you take this stance, that your total perspective changes. And a world of opportunity opens up before you. Let's look at all those opportunities together. The ones that allow you to win–win–win. When you look at them as a totality it becomes very clear that brands and retailers are not necessarily in conflict. You both seek the same solutions and the same opportunities for your shoppers. Work together and that's what you will achieve.

To fully understand the full opportunities out there, however, we may need to think of four interacting forces, four forces that work together to bring innovation – joint value innovation – to the market (Figure 26.1): brand owners, Private Label manufacturers (who may be

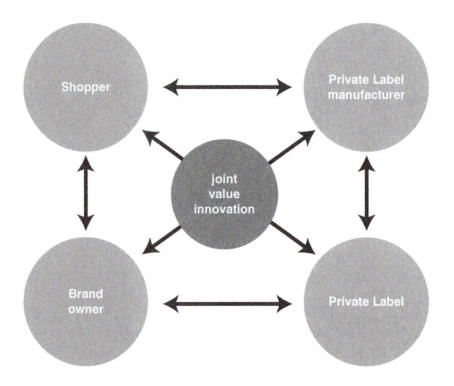

Figure 26.1 Win, win, win and WIN

the brand owners as well), retailers and shoppers. In a sense, all should be working together in the pursuit of joint value innovation. It's in ALL their interests.

The formula isn't that complicated. We all need each other. Are there ways for all the parties to better cooperate? Are there ways for all the parties to better create? Are their ways for all four parties to help sustain our society? In theory, there should be 64 opportunities at least. Four to the power of 3 equals 64!

- Shoppers need retailers.
- Retailers need shoppers.
- Shoppers need brands.
- Brands need shoppers.
- Retailers need brands.
- Brands need retailers.
- Shoppers need retailers.

- Retailers need shoppers.
- Shoppers need brands.
- Brands need shoppers.
- Retailers need brands.
- Brands need retailers.
- Private Label needs you all.

Let's look at all the opportunities we have identified so far. All 65 of them!

Brand opportunity summary

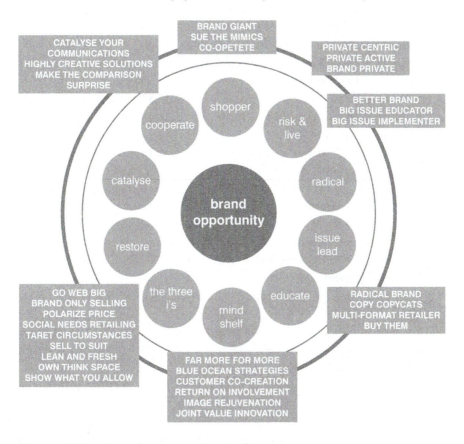

Figure 26.2   Brand opportunity circle

- Opportunity 1: Become PRIVATE CENTRIC. Significantly change your organizational structure to reflect today's private world. The Private Director becomes your most critical communications director internally and externally.
- Opportunity 2: Become PRIVATE ACTIVE. Make all your resolutions for dealing with Private Label proactive ones. The days of being reactive have gone. You need to take the initiative in everything you do.
- Opportunity 3: Make the shopper seek the BRAND PRIVATE OPTION, not a private brand/label option. Make the shopper realize again and again why brands are different and special. And very private to them.
- Opportunity 4: Make your brand a RADICAL BRAND. Start thinking completely out of the box about solutions. Write a list of 10 radical things you can do to beat Private Label.
- Opportunity 5: COPY THE COPYCATS. Produce products that mimic the Private Labels, but provide better value.
- Opportunity 6: Become a MULTI-FORMAT BRAND SELLER. Explore every distribution option out there from the web to local. Explode your options.
- Opportunity 7: If you can't beat them BUY THEM. Retailers are a cheap investment. At the very least buy a significant share of their shares and get on their board. You might be surprised to see how their attitude changes. Overnight.
- Opportunity 8: Make sure you're not a greenwashing company. Make sure you're a REAL CHANGE company.
- Opportunity 9: Become the market BIG ISSUES LEADER as well as volume leader.
- Opportunity 10: Maximize the new ROI: RETURN ON INVOLVEMENT.
- Opportunity 11: Make your brand a BETTER BRAND. Totally socialize your brand and make it socially fit from top to bottom. Commit to total change.
- Opportunity 12: Become the BIG ISSUE EDUCATOR. You have a social and moral responsibility to educate everyone from your employees to your shoppers about the big issues we all face.
- Opportunity 13: Become the BIG ISSUE IMPLEMENTER. Change your total product line, your packaging, your communications and your distribution to reflect the new issues. Stop greenwashing. Start doing.

- Opportunity 14: Increase your MIND SHELF PRESENCE. In-store, make sure your presence and products are directly linked to the big issues society faces.
- Opportunity 15: OWN THINK SPACE AND LEVEL.
- Opportunity 16: Innovate to the extreme by providing FAR MORE FOR MORE. Make your product the solution over making your image the solution.
- Opportunity 17: Seek BLUE OCEANS. Innovations that leapfrog your present products and take you into new fresh dynamic markets. TRUE VALUE INNOVATIONS.
- Opportunity 18: CO-CREATE WITH YOUR CUSTOMERS. Get your customers directly involved in designing your products.
- Opportunity 19: Seek ways to be invited into your consumers' lives and homes.
- Opportunity 20: CO-CREATE with your retailers. Run JOINT VALUE INNOVATION PROGRAMMES.
- Opportunity 21: Maximize your RETURN ON INVOLVEMENT. Ensure your shoppers are participants, not just spectators.
- Opportunity 22: REJUVINATE YOUR IMAGE. Take your tired old image and give it a healthy boost through new dynamic new-age communications.
- Opportunity 23: GO WEB in a big way. Consider changing all (or the majority) of your business to the internet for direct selling.
- Opportunity 24: Open a BRAND ONLY supermarket selling brands at discount. Or buy a retailer and convert.
- Opportunity 25: POLARIZE PRICE. Become low price or high price. Eliminate all mid-price brands. They don't have a shopper future.
- Opportunity 26: Design formats that meet SOCIAL NEEDS RETAILING. Identify shoppers' situational need and provide shopping experiences/retail formats that meet them. Go to them. Don't expect them to come to you.
- Opportunity 27: Rethink your relationships with your customers in terms of their CIRCUMSTANCES rather than their attributes. The TESCO way forward.
- Opportunity 28: Sell your products when it suits your shoppers, not when it suits you. SELL TO SUIT, wherever that may be and whatever it takes.
- Opportunity 29: Get LEAN AND FRESH. Move to production systems that give you fresh products in small batches rather than ancient products in large batches.

- Opportunity 30: People need to understand it's not what you buy that's important – it's what it allows you to do. SHOW WHAT YOU ALLOW.
- Opportunity 31: If your present retailing efforts are non-involving, change them. Embrace the new concept of INVOLVEMENT RETAILING.
- Opportunity 32: CATALYSE YOUR COMMUNICATIONS. Make your communications work harder at the point of action – the store. Turn your shoppers into buyers.
- Opportunity 33: Seek HIGHLY CREATIVE SOLUTIONS. Make your agencies put their creative resources against this target.
- Opportunity 34: MAKE THE COMPARISON. Spend effort, time and money showing shoppers the brand difference. Don't take it for granted. Your product advantage has turned to parity. You must restore the advantage.
- Opportunity 35: Find ways to SURPRISE the competition and the shopper, as well as yourself.
- Opportunity 36: Get SHOPPER CLOSE where you can, starting with the web.
- Opportunity 37: EXTEND and OPTIMIZE creativity in-store.
- Opportunity 38: GET LOVED. Use Saatchi & Saatchi X's Lovemark™ approach to help you be loved by shoppers even more.
- Opportunity 39: Become a BUYING GIANT. Form alliances where you can to raise your power.
- Opportunity 40: SUE THE MIMICS. Don't put up with Private Label copying for any reason. Always challenge mimicry all the way.
- Opportunity 41: Learn to genuinely CO-OPETETE. Brands need retailers and retailers need brands.
- Opportunity 42: Develop a PRIVATE LABEL FORUM – a cooperative website where you can all learn from each other
- Opportunity 43: Look for ideas everywhere.
- Opportunity 44: Adopt a multi-tier strategy. If it grows the Private Label business, it will certainly grow yours.

Retailer opportunity summary

- Opportunity 45: THINK AHEAD. ACT TODAY. Start thinking more long term instead of your usual short-term obsessiveness.

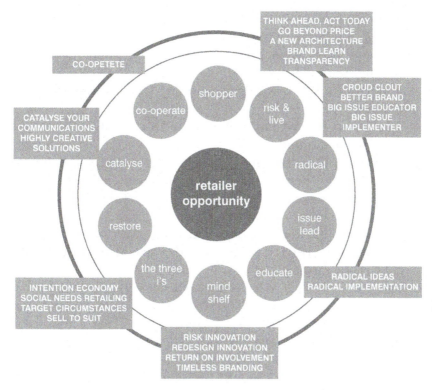

Figure 26.3 Retailer opportunity circle

- Opportunity 46: GO BEYOND PRICE. You need value way beyond price for the new future. Make sure you have it.
- Opportunity 47: Revise and improve your BRAND ARCHI-TECTURE. The present brand structure is for the past. Make sure you change to anticipate it.
- Opportunity 48: LEARN FROM BRANDS now you are one.
- Opportunity 49: Be TRANSPARENT about your Private Label success.
- Opportunity 50: Make CROUD CLOUT work for you before it works against you.
- Opportunity 51: Make your brand a BETTER BRAND. Totally socialize your brand and make it socially fit from top to bottom. Commit to total change.
- Opportunity 52: Become the BIG ISSUE EDUCATOR. You have a social and moral responsibility to educate everyone from your employees to your shoppers about the big issues we all face.

- Opportunity 53: Become the BIG ISSUE IMPLEMENTER. Change your total product line, your packaging, your communications and your distribution to reflect the new issues. Stop greenwashing. Start doing.
- Opportunity 54: Investigate your MULTI-TIER strategy and optimize it.
- Opportunity 55: Become a part of the INTENTION ECONOMY before it goes around you.
- Opportunity 56: Design formats that meet SOCIAL NEEDS RETAILING. Identify shoppers' situational needs and provide shopping experiences/retail formats that meet them. Go to them. Don't expect them to come to you.
- Opportunity 57: Rethink your relationships with your customers in terms of their CIRCUMSTANCES rather than their attributes. The TESCO way forward.
- Opportunity 58: Sell your products when it suits your shoppers, not when it suits you. SELL TO SUIT, wherever that may be and whatever it takes.
- Opportunity 59: Become a RISK INNOVATOR, the true sign of a real innovator.
- Opportunity 60: Consider REDESIGNING innovation, putting products that already exist out there in a very different way, not just copies of them.
- Opportunity 61: Create TIMELESS brands like the real brands.
- Opportunity 62: Maximize your RETURN ON INVOLVEMENT. Ensure your shoppers are participants, not just spectators.
- Opportunity 63: CATALYSE YOUR COMMUNICATIONS. Make your communications work harder at the point of action – the store. Turn your shoppers into buyers.
- Opportunity 64: Seek HIGHLY CREATIVE SOLUTIONS. Make your agencies put their creative resources against this target.
- Opportunity 65: CO-OPETITION STARTS WITH YOU. It's in your short-, medium- and long-term interests.

Clearly there are a lot of opportunities out there. We told you Private Label wasn't a threat. It's just a matter of perspective and action – a lot of action.

Postscript: Privatizing the brand

> Turbulence is life force. It is opportunity. Let's love turbulence and use it for change.
>
> Ramsay Clark

And boy, are we living in a turbulent world.

Throughout this book we have referred to privatizing the brand. Deliberately so, because Private Label is no longer a label. It's a brand. A private brand, and a very big one at that. With Wal-Mart Private Label in theory able to claim to be the biggest brand in the world, this is hardly a force that can be denied. But denied it is.

Denied by brand companies in particular, which fail to develop strategies to deal with it. It doesn't help that the advice that is available centres around increasing quality and innovation, while reducing price – things any brand should be doing every day, anyway. We're in a world where value is the only game in town. You need that value to survive against your present competitive subset, let alone the new seemingly unstoppable force of Private Label. You clearly need more to compete effectively.

Private Label is proving divisive, putting brand owners on the back foot and retailers on the offensive. Neither party seems particularly willing to discuss it openly or to collaborate on anything beyond production. Brands have taken retailers to court for copycatting and retailers have de-listed household brands from their shelves. There seems to be little room for concession.

To make matters worse, Private Label is dramatically moving up the value chain and becoming far better quality than ever. Premium Private Label is here with a vengeance and there's no point in hiding your head in the sand over it. What's more, it's a damn good product. Consumers certainly think so. And an increasingly Private Label dominated world is a very good bet.

The trust gap between Private Label and manufacturer brands is getting smaller and smaller. 'Trust', of course, is the very essence of a brand and with obsessive commitment from retailers towards customer service, convenience and increasingly community and sustainability issues, that gap must inevitably narrow, unless brands react (Figure 27.1). Retailers understand what their shoppers actually want and how they behave. As traditional brand loyalty swings increasingly over to the retailer and the role of the manufacturer brand in the category mix is beginning to change, brand owners are only just beginning to realize what retailers have known for years. Supermarket shoppers don't buy brands so much anymore. They buy solutions.

However, when it comes down to it, retailers should remember that Private Label is only a 'tool' to help them achieve their business objectives, whether that objective be profit or growth. That fact seems to have been somewhat forgotten. Eliminating the brand will not help their long-term business. All it will do is help turn it into a low-margin commodity business with little real competitor differentiation. And

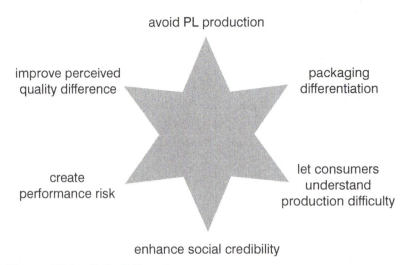

Figure 27.1 Rebuilding the trust gap

eliminating the brand is exactly what they're doing, or at least pushing the brands to a position where they have no choice except to get radical: radical in execution, radical in marketing, radical in strategy. Brands are being pushed into a position where they will have to consider radical new options, such as alliances between brand manufacturers to give them a bargaining power equal to the global retailers, or buying the retailers or at the very least taking a stake directly so that they can influence them directly. Retailers should remember that choice is good. Choice is healthy. Choice is what built them. Choice is what shoppers want. And that choice must include brand choice.

From a retailer's point of view (mostly), manufacturer brands are essentially commodities, available at their retail competitors. The retail brand is a way to avoid this commoditization and differentiate themselves from their nearest competitors. They believe that this will result in greater loyalty to their store. We think this is somewhat missing the point. The point is: what do shoppers want? We do not believe it is a brandless world. Clearly Justin King at Sainsbury's understands this point. Let us repeat it!

> Innovation should come from brands and private label. We have no agenda to push Private Label beyond what our shoppers want it to be. Knock on our door and ask us how we can help you build your brand.
>
> Justin King, CEO, Sainsbury's: IGD Trade Briefing, 7 June 2007, London

Retailers must remember that Private Label is there for essentially one thing: to give shoppers a choice of different qualities at different prices. Having too much Private Label is clearly counter to this basic premise. It limits choice, and therefore demand. Our belief is that the third and most important, most influential party in the equation is yet to be fully taken into account. The simple fact of the matter is that shoppers understand the value of Private Label better than brand owners or retailers. Shoppers realize that both brands and Private Label provide a balanced portfolio of price, quality, choice, convenience and innovation. Both are important. Both have their limits, but both are required.

Private Labels are clearly a major threat to manufacturer brands. Retailers envisage greater innovation and more premium Private Label that responds to an ever-wider range of shopper needs, from organic to healthy, locally grown to ethically responsible. Absolute commitment to authenticity, convenience and accountability is now very much top of the corporate agenda. Today, worldwide Private Label share hovers around 20 per cent. However, for sophisticated retailers there is no reason to believe that the share won't reach 40 or even 50 per cent, particularly as the inevitable globalization of mass retailers increases. A share that is value measured – a share that in volume terms could account for three out of every four shopper purchases. Even in clothing the present share of Private Label is forecast to increase from 40 to 60 per cent in the United States alone. These sorts of shifts in Private Label shares will inevitably mean revenue losses for brand owners – in the order of hundreds of billions of dollars, in the order of half of your business. Can you survive this?

Besides impressive growth rates, the very nature of the Private Labels turns them into a different type of competitor. On the one hand, they are proprietary to the distribution partners on which manufacturers depend. Therefore they cannot be dealt with in the same way as 'regular' competition. On the other hand, Private Labels typically use a very different business model (little R&D investment, little category-specific advertising, no cash expense for slotting allowances etc), which renders any benchmarking efforts against Private Labels difficult. Nonetheless, manufacturers need to better understand the key success factors of Private Labels in order to deal with their current growth patterns.

When they understand that nature, and hopefully this book helps, brand owners will start to see Private Label for what it really is: not a threat, but an opportunity – a wake-up call! This is a challenge that demands the unconventional and exceptional. Rise to that challenge, or else. Let's turn this issue on its head and seize the opportunity that it represents: opportunity for brands to reinvent themselves through dramatic innovation; opportunities for retailers to truly innovate their offerings; opportunities for manufacturers to maximize their production capacity; opportunities for agencies to reinvent communications; opportunities for all of us as shoppers to get ever better value offerings; opportunities for everyone to drive the key forces shaping today and tomorrow's society. Then we will all win–win–win.

Despite all the pressure on brands, there is still a large quality/value perception gap between Private Label and established manufacturer brands – a gap that begs opportunity. It would also seem, however, that manufacturer brands still have the upper hand when it comes to overall perceptions around quality and innovation, and the shopper still needs convincing that retailer own brands are worth paying extra for. Years of brand building may have paid off for manufacturer brands, but the landscape is changing fast, and brand image is no longer enough and is proving more difficult and expensive to maintain. The store is the new battle ground and brands that can offer not only a superior product at a good price but also a better brand experience that rewards loyalty are those that stand to gain the most.

Brand owners and retailers ultimately have to inspire loyalty beyond reason. Conventional approaches like changing pricing strategy, customizing packaging or doing a few more promotions is not going to change loyalty in the long run. Shoppers accept Private Label and they still want brands, although it's just not enough to be talked about, respected, trusted or even admired any more. You need much more. Going forward, those brands and retailers that win will be those that shoppers fall in love with. Again and again.

The best way to realize that opportunity is to realize a bigger opportunity. We started this book writing about Private Label. However, on our journey we realized that there are a number of big issues out there that need addressing almost as much as, if not more than, Private Label. Those big issues are, of course, the issues that are increasingly absorbing our society, from global warming to obesity. They need a cure. And brands and retailer can help supply that cure. We believe that most companies (brands and retailers) pander to the truth and reality of the way the world is changing. They believe that small and token gestures are enough to convince consumers they're truly responsible carers of society. By being partly responsible they are actually irresponsible. You have to become totally responsible. You have to eat the cake of healthy living, not just pick up the crumbs. And it is possible.

You have to be being serious about these changes if you want to sort yourself out from the losers. The food industry in particular needs to get serious and commit to total change. The days of line extensions or a new product flavouring variant are gone. By just producing variants food companies in particular are procrastinating against the inevitable. But often this commitment isn't evident in the marketplace. There's a lot of noise and a lot of greenwashing. The reality is that ALL FOOD SHOULD BE HEALTHY. There is no such thing in the new world as unhealthy food and healthy food. There is healthy food alone. We invented and sustained unhealthy food. The trend must be reversed.

These issues have become far more critical than the survival of a brand, or a retailer. They represent the survival of society as we know it. If they don't move here, shoppers will with their feet or governments will with legislation.

This is reality and the headlines are starting to show the reality of that fact. Unhealthy living is no longer a societal option. Healthy living is a societal prerogative. Unhealthy living is no longer a brand option. Healthy living is the only brand option. Lest you think your safe, this isn't just about food. These and associated issues are relevant in any brand category, from electronics to padlocks.

So we believe that the opportunity is there for brands and retailers to continually reinvent themselves through shopper insight, deeper brand involvement and innovation. The opportunity is there for both to continually add value. The opportunity is there for manufacturers to optimize their production capacity and for agencies to reinvent communications, branding from the self out. But most importantly of all, the opportunity is there to continually surprise and delight the shopper and far exceed his or her expectations.

Who's going to win and who's going to lose out with Private Label? The best way to predict the future is to invent it. And then manage it. Together! With your key partners. Shoppers, retailers and brand owners unite. There's a lot to be done. And the world will win, win, win. There are some things we can be very sure of. The store of today will not be the store of tomorrow. Private Label will grow and grow. The big issues that drive society are going to get bigger and bigger. Successful organizations will not and cannot be divorced from these issues. The choice is yours. Take our 10 principles and make them yours. Take some or all of our 65 opportunities and make them work.

The very first step in a winning strategy for both brand owners and retailers is in a commitment to work together with Private Label, collaborating and stretching the idea of partnership beyond pure production line capacity, innovation and profitability towards ideas that are based around the principles of 'joint value innovation'. These 10 principles help us probe into every facet of Private Label, unlock its potential and predict the impact it can have. Joint value innovation provides us with a framework for helping brand owners and retailers realize, as our research shows, that Private Label isn't a threat or a Trojan horse. It really is an opportunity. For everyone.

> We're not banking on things getting better. We're banking on us getting better.
>
> Edwin Artz, former CEO of P&G

Finally we need to leave you with maybe the ultimate opportunity. It seems to us that brand owners should consider ceasing manufacturing and return to their natural roots – brand innovation and development. In reality the retailers are increasingly outsourcing their manufacturing needs for their Private Label brands, often more cost effectively than the owners. The inevitable consequence of this is that brands should cease inefficient manufacturing and become even better product innovators and brand communicators. They should stop being conservative and become more and more radical as they free themselves from investment traps and exploit the many new issues out there. The consequence of such an action is convergence. Convergence of brands and retailers. Retailers increasingly become like brands and brands increasingly become like retailers. The result is a new branded force. A new retail force. A new converged force. And it isn't private label. It's a REBRAND, a fusion of retail and brand power. A rethink of the conventional brand. A rethink of the conventional retailer. The next stage in brand development. The next stage in Private Label development. Welcome to the REBRAND future.

Good luck... and good night.

Appendix 1: Saatchi & Saatchi X Research Questionnaire

Questions to shoppers

Do you buy Private Label?

How frequently?

Is it good quality?

Is it good quality for brands?

Is it value for money?

Do you believe there are any limitations as to what products can become Private Label?

Do you see more and more premium-type Private Label products in the future?

Is it possible to imagine a Private Label being more expensive than a brand?

Do you think Private Label is as innovative as a brand in terms of its offer to the shopper?

Do you see yourself buying more Private Label in the future?

Is it possible to imagine a store with Private Label products only?

Questions to brands

Is Private Label becoming a greater threat to your business?

Is Private Label damaging your profitability?

Do you think Private Label is better or worse quality than it used to be?

Do you think consumers think Private Label is worse or better quality than it used to be?

Why do you think shoppers buy Private Label?

Has the perception of what Private Label is changed over the years?

Do you manufacture Private Label or not?

Is your Private Label business manufacture business growing or not?

What is your main reason for manufacturing Private Label?

Are you planning to increase the level of Private Label manufacture in the future?

What strategies do you think can help you win against Private Label? Explain in more detailed please.

Do you believe there are any limitations as to what products can become Private Label?

Do you see more and more premium-type Private Label products in the future?

Is it possible to imagine a Private Label being more expensive than a brand?

Do you think Private Label is as innovative as a brand in terms of its offer to the shopper?

Do you see yourself promoting Private Label more in the future?

Is it possible to imagine a store with Private Label products only?

Questions to retailers

Is Private Label becoming more important to your business?

Is Private Label an important source of profit for you?

Is your Private Label business growing or not?

Do you think Private Label is better or worse quality than it used to be?

Do you think consumers think Private Label is worse or better quality than it used to be?

Why do you think shoppers buy Private Label?

Has the perception of what Private Label is changed over the years?

Are you planning to increase the level of Private Label in the future?

Do you believe there are any limitations as to what products can become Private Label?

Do you see more and more premium-type Private Label products in the future?

Is it possible to imagine a Private Label being more expensive than a brand?

Do you think Private Label is as innovative as a brand in terms of its offer to the shopper?
Do you see yourself promoting Private Label more in the future?
Is it possible to imagine your store with Private Label products only?

The full Saatchi & Saatchi X Private Label research report is available to purchase direct. For more information about the research and /or the Joint Value Innovation workshops to help you deal with Private Label, contact Keith Lincoln, co-author of the book *Private Label*, or Phil White, Planning Director, Saatchi & Saatchi X (klincoln.retailization@gmail.com; phil.white@saatchix.co.uk).

Appendix 2: Key references

Banks, J (2006) *Private Labels, No Longer a 'Lesser Brand' in the UK*, Jonathan Banks, Business Insight Director, ACNielsen, UK

Boston Consulting Group (2003) *Private Label Threat to Manufacturers, Opportunity for Retailers*, Boston Consulting Group Publications, Boston, MA

Chicago Tribune, May 2007, http://www.chicagotribune.com/ business/ chi-sun_greenmay27,0,4758981.story?coll=chi-bizfront-hed

Corstjens, J and Corstjens, M (2000) *Store Wars: The battle for mind space and shelf space*, JohnWiley & Sons Ltd, Chichester

Culturebox (2006) Culturebox.com

Daily Telegraph (2007) Use of organically, Stores to Shrink, 23 February

De Chertanoy, L and Macdonald, M (1998) *Creating Powerful Brands*, 2nd edition, Butterworth Heinemann, Oxford

Doyle, P (1995), Marketing in the new millennium, *European Journal of Marketing* **29**

Floor, K (2006) *Branding a Store*, Kogan Page, London

Fortune (2007) From frozen food to hot leather, *Fortune*, May

Geronimo (2005) Grocery Brand preference study

Godin, S, (1999), *Permission Marketing, Turning Strangers into Friends, and Friends into Customers*, Simon & Schuster, Inc, New York

Holmes, T E (2006) *The Advertiser*, August

Jones, D T and Womack, J P (2003) *Lean Solutions*, Simon & Schuster, Inc, New York

Kapferer, J N (1998) *Strategic Brand Management*, Kogan Page, London

Kapferer, J N (2006) DLF Conference, Stockholm

Karmaloop.com: http://www.karmaloop.com

King, S (1990) Brand building in the 90's, *Journal of Marketing Management*, **7**

Kotler P. (2001), *Reflections on Marketing*, John Wiley & Sons Inc, New York

Kumar, N and Steenkamp, J-B (2007) *Private Label Strategy*, Harvard Business School Press, Cambridge, MA

Laaksonen, H and Reynolds J (1994), Own brands and food retailing across Europe, *Journal of Brand Management*, **2** (1)

McKinsey (1995) *McKinsey Quarterly*, 4

McKinsey (2000) *McKinsey Quarterly*, 3

Nielsen (2006)

New York Times (2007) June

Ossiansson, E (2004) Brands tailored for retailers, Springwise

Pellegrini, L (1996) *Brands v Trade names: Manufacturer and retailer missions in the value system*, first draft, working paper

Springwise (2004) Retail focus: only for dads and tweens, Springwise Newsletter, 17, September/October [Online] www.springwise.com/ newsletters/SEP04/newsletter.htm (accessed 22 September 2005)

Springwise (2005a) Brand spaces, [Online] www.springwise.com/ newbusinessideas/redLounge.htm (accessed 22 September, 2005)

Springwise (2005b) Coming to a village near you, [Online] www. springwise.com/newbusinessideas/2003/08/london_fashion_bus.html (accessed 22 September, 2005)

Springwise (2005c) Mobile merchandise, [Online] www.springwise.com/ newbusinessideas/2003/08/london_fashion_bus.html (accessed 22 September, 2005)

Springwise (2005d) Really super fast pizza, April [Online] www. springwise.com/newbusinessideas/superFastPizza.htm (accessed 27 September 2005)

Springwise (2005e) Perfume meets retail theater, Springwise Newsletter, 21 April [Online] www.springwise.com/newsletter/previous_21.html (accessed 26 September, 2005)

Strasser, S (1989) *Satisfaction Guaranteed: The making of the American mass market*, Pantheon, New York

Trendwatching (2005a) Being spaces, [Online] www.trendwatching.com/ trends/2002/11/BEINGSPACES.html (accessed 22 September 2005)

Trendwatching (2005b) Pop-up retail, [Online] www.trendwatching. com/trends/POPUP_RETAIL.htm (accessed 26 September, 2005)

Trendwatching (2005c) Tryvertising, [Online] www.trendwatching.com/ trends/TRYVERTISING.htm (accessed 27 September 2005)

Trendwatching (2005d) Being spaces, [Online] www.trendwatching.com/ trends/2002/11/BEINGSPACES.html (accessed 22 September 2005)

Useem, J (2007) Simply irresistible, *Fortune*, 8 March

Wordpress.com: http://marketinggreen.wordpress.com/2007/06/06/ competing-on-green-accelerates-rate-of-change/

Index

7-Eleven 48, 190

10 principles 7, 95, 105–06, 286

Aarstiderne 164–65

Adidas 208

An Inconvenient Truth 135

Aldi 3, 17–21, 51–52, 177, 186, 207, 210, 227, 229, 262–64

American Apparel 140, 208

A&P 33

Apple 57, 73, 142, 164, 171, 178, 188, 191–95, 210

  iPhone 164, 229, 262

Arla 110, 165, 178

ASDA 21, 38, 42–44, 88, 106, 138

  George 38, 43–44

Avis 256

Barnes and Noble 22

BBDO 97

Bebo 251

Belgium 14

Ben & Jerry's 149, 210

big issue 5, 105, 110, 129, 134–35, 147, 152–153, 156, 158–160, 163, 168, 181, 205, 215, 237, 243–44, 246–47, 252–54, 258, 275–77, 279–80, 285

Blu-ray 173

Bohemian Baby 205

Boots 42–43, 219

British 19, 43, 141, 158, 164, 225

British Omlet 158

Budget 256

Carrefour 6, 18, 34, 51–52, 117, 211, 219

  Bain de Douche Extra Doux 211

Charmin 124

China 2, 64–66, 68–71, 74–79, 81, 83–84, 181–82, 251

  Chinese 13, 66, 75, 188, 251

Chippindale Foods 158

climate change 153

Coca-Cola 17, 28, 155

co-opeteting 217

co-opetition 9, 106, 216–17, 219–21, 223, 268–69, 280

copycats 127, 206, 275

CPG   2, 13–16, 18, 20–21,
   40–42, 50, 54,174
crowd clout   250–51
CrowdSpirit   252
Curry's   265

Danone   17, 151, 164, 226
   Activia   164
Days of Our Lives   142
Decathalon   22
Dell   247
Disney   258–59
DIY   63, 70–74, 191
Dixon   57, 73, 187
Dole Organic   158

Electrolux   182
Europe   14–17, 21, 23–25, 34,
   36, 38, 40–43, 49–50, 52–56,
   102, 118, 122, 133, 152,
   176–77, 206–07, 218, 230,
   250, 257, 266, 269, 291–92
Eventful   257
Evie's Organic Edibles   205

Facebook   251
Federal Express   189
Finland   20, 24, 26, 181, 219, 256
FMCG   2, 6, 16, 17, 19–20, 24,
   49, 50, 53, 63, 91, 117, 122,
   125, 155,174, 201, 208,
   263–64
France   16, 22, 24, 26, 33–34,
   55,133, 205, 211
Freedom brands   33
French   22, 33, 40, 135, 164,
   219, 252, 269

Gap   6, 242, 264
Gapa   205

General Mills   156
Germany   14–17, 21, 24, 26, 55,
   116–17, 138, 143, 165,
   179–80, 207, 219
GDA   240–41
Gore, Al   131, 135, 160, 229
Gillette   20, 37, 122, 175, 195,
   218
   brands   175
Gooh!   194
Great Britain   14, 26, 45
greenwashing   131, 147, 156,
   160, 253, 276, 280, 286

H&M   6, 21, 101, 189, 195, 242
Haribo   3
Heineken   205
Hertz   256
Homemade Baby   205
How to Succeed at Retail   101,
   151, 194
HP   247

ICA   20, 122, 178, 219
IGD   13, 63, 80, 119, 227, 273,
   283
Igglo   257
Ikea   6, 186, 264
imagineer   8, 106, 169–71, 173,
   175, 177, 179, 181–83, 264
IMRG   267
Innocent   132–33, 194
innovation   171–76
inQbox   140
intention economy   256, 269,
   280
involvement   180–82
IRMA   48
Italy   14–16, 24, 26, 43, 141,
   182

Japan 1, 15, 49–50, 135, 158, 188, 190, 229, 236
Jobs, Steve 188, 192
JWT Worldwide 228

Kaboodle 251
Karlsberg 165
  Karla 165
Karmaloop 263
King, Justin 273, 283
Kroger 18, 51–52, 258

Latin America 15, 49–50
LEGO 138, 182
Le Labo 196
Lidl 17
Loblaw 47, 103
Louis Valliant 188
Lovemarks 212–14, 265
Lunch4Kids 225

Marks & Spencer 66, 42–43
  St Michael 33
Mars 100
McDonald's 3, 226
McKinsey 28, 55, 103, 292
Mercadona 211, 219
Metro 17–18, 51–52
Metro International 175–76
Mindshelf 168
MORI 259
MyFreshEgg 158
MySpace 251

Nielsen 13, 23–24, 26–27, 37, 41, 63, 291–92
Netherlands 165, 219, 225, 256
Nestlé 17, 136, 15, 206, 218, 230, 240

Nespresso 206
Nike 142, 156, 178, 229
Nintendo 173, 178–79, 227
  Wii 173, 179, 227
Nivea 179–80
No Haggles 245
Nokia 181
Nordic 21, 55

Oliver, Jamie 225

Padbury, Geraldine 227
PC World 267
Pepsi 17, 28, 118, 155, 215
Philippines 49
Polman, Paul 177
POPAI 53–54
Premium 19, 38, 40, 42–46, 56, 58, 75–76, 91–93, 99, 100, 102–04, 109, 119, 124–25, 141, 157, 170, 180, 187, 206, 211, 221, 248–49, 282, 284, 288–90
President's Choice 47–48
Priceline 256
private wheel of opportunity 10
Proctor & Gamble (P&G) 17, 20, 97, 122, 174–75, 177, 195, 218, 263, 267, 287
  Tremor 263
product parity 68, 70
private active 12, 275–76
private brands 1, 2, 32, 40
private centric 110, 112, 275–76
privatized 2, 28

Reebok 208–09
relationship marketing 265–66

responsible brands   226,
  235–37
retailize   8, 105, 106, 115, 119,
  121, 123, 125, 127, 166, 209
return on involvement   145,
  180, 183, 263, 269–70, 275,
  277, 279, 280
RTV   200–01

Saatchi & Saatchi X   6, 7, 61, 63,
  93, 204, 212–14, 265, 278,
  289–90
Samsung   211, 262, 265
Safeway   259
Sainsbury   33, 42–44, 100, 102,
  133, 138, 154, 163–64, 219,
  227, 273, 283
Scandinavia   2, 42, 110, 173,
  262
Second Life   208–09
ShoptoCook   201–03
Singapore   140
Snapple   210
Sony   173
  PS3   173, 179
Spain   14–16, 24, 26, 165, 219
spiffing   97
Stadmission   242
Starbucks   149, 196
Stonyfield Farm   151
Superdrug   42–43
Superquinn   195, 219
surprise buys   207
Sweden   4, 14–16, 20, 24, 37, 43,
  55–56, 64, 65–66, 68–70, 72,
  74–79, 81, 83–84, 86, 93,
  122, 133, 165, 178, 200, 205,
  219, 242, 246
Switzerland   14, 16, 24, 26, 40,
  49–50, 142, 230

Tchibo   194, 207
TCM   207
Tesco   3, 4, 6, 17–18, 28, 38–39,
  41–47, 51–52, 54, 57–58,
  80–81, 88–89, 93, 101–02,
  117–18, 137–39, 154, 157,
  177, 188, 190, 197, 215, 237,
  240, 267, 269, 271, 277, 280
  brands   45, 46
Tescoland   43, 54
The Shop at Bluebird   197
ThisNext   251
three i's   8, 159, 178–80, 182–83
Timberland   157
Toyota   150, 190
Toys 'r Us   187
traffic lights system   240–41
Trader Joe's   17, 41, 102, 210
true value innovations   172,
  183, 277
trust gap   83, 88, 282

Unilever   17, 211, 226, 240
UK   2, 4, 16, 21, 24–28, 33–34,
  37–38, 41–44, 55–57, 64–66,
  70, 72, 74–81, 83–84, 86–89,
  91–93, 100, 102, 106, 109,
  113–14, 119, 122, 130,
  132–33, 136–39, 141, 154,
  157–58, 164–65, 177, 180,
  182, 190, 217, 219, 238–41,
  246–47, 251, 261, 267, 269,
  271, 290–91
United States   4, 16–17, 23, 25,
  33, 38, 40–41, 47, 52, 56,
  64–66, 73, 75, 79–80, 85–87,
  93, 102, 109, 124, 130, 140,
  142, 152, 155, 165, 178, 182,
  190, 205, 210, 225, 239, 250,
  252, 256, 258, 260, 263, 284